A COMMENTARY ON
THE ANATHEMATA
OF DAVID JONES

David J.

EG Dec 1921

A COMMENTARY ON

THE ANATHEMATA
of
DAVID JONES

by

RENÉ HAGUE

'As a student of poetry, I take delight in tracing, word by word, his delicate intricacies of expression, which stimulate curiosity while they baffle analysis, as well as in endeavouring to appreciate the broader features of his work as a whole.'
— JOHN CONINGTON, on Vergil, 1865

CHRISTOPHER SKELTON
1977

Published by
CHRISTOPHER SKELTON
Skelton's Press, Wellingborough, England
1977

ISBN 0 950 3226 1 X

Printed by Skelton's Press
Cannon Place, Wellingborough, Northamptonshire NN 8 4DJ

DILECTISSIMAE

MEAE IOANNAE

TOT PER ANNOS

SVAVIS ISTIVS

NECESSITVDINIS

PARTICIPI

CONTENTS

ILLUSTRATIONS

PREFACE

WHEN my brother and I were very small children in a convent
boarding school (our mother being far away in pre-revolution
Russia) the nuns would frequently impress upon us that because we had been 'born into the household of the faith' we
had a special responsibility: it was far more shameful for
us to steal biscuits or tell lies (the latter our only armour
against what seemed to us impertinent inquisition) than it was
for those poor children who lacked our privilege. It was a
similar sense of shame that lay behind my determination to
write this commentary. Many of my acquaintance would tell me
that while they found much to delight them in *The Anathemata*,
they were often unable to attach a distinct literal meaning
to many passages. Was I not myself, perhaps, in the same
position? and was it not my duty in particular (since fifty
years of close friendship with the poet corresponded to the gift of
which the nuns had reminded me) to make sure that I understood
his meaning at every single point — so far, at least, as I could
attain such clarity?

I very soon met two difficulties. The first was the problem
of whom I was addressing, and what knowledge, apt to help
him in his interpretation, could I attribute to him. For while
it is annoying not to be told something of which you are ignorant,
it is equally, or even more, annoying, to be told what you have
known since childhood: it is as bad as having an obvious joke
carefully explained to you. I could only take my own friends, so
often better informed than I, and my own self as a standard. I
found it impossible to be consistent, and in the end I had to
write as though simply for myself, with a friend reading over my
shoulder.

The second difficulty arose from the impossibility of defining
a literal meaning. That exists as no more than a syntactical
abstraction, which has little use unless it allows the reader to
move onward into the intricacies of allusion, allegory, spiritual
and even mystical interpretation; and here (even though a

commentator may provide a useful starting-point) every reader must do his own work, based on his own reading and thinking. Anyone who has studied the great poets closely and for many years will know how endless is that work, and how entrancing.

The work was started some years before David's death, and I had the good fortune to be able to send him a first draft of the first three sections, on which he wrote his comments, and later to elucidate many points in conversation and correspondence. In offering the result to my friends (to all, that is, who delight in this great poem) I ask them to sympathise with me in doing what I am sure they would themselves do: that is, always follow those lines of interpretation and extension of meaning which accord best with their own knowledge, sensibility and experience.

I have a number of friends to thank for their help and encouragement in my attempt to put together this commentary. First, David Jones himself, ever patient, generous and comradely; then, those closest to him in kinship, Mollie Elkin, Stella Wright and Tony Hyne, who have given me the privilege of seeing much unpublished writing and have allowed me freedom in quotation; I am indebted to David's publishers, Messrs Faber & Faber, for permission to quote from printed work; and I am most grateful to William Blissett, with his tribunes, Thomas Dilworth, Vincent Sherry and W. J. Keith (wards, all four, of the angel in skins); Helen Suggett (fellow-tracker in the glades of Auvergne); Harman Grisewood (ever since we met in the passage); Walter Shewring (for more than that one he wots of); Peter Campbell (Lancelot, he, in the south porch); my printer, and more than printer, Christopher Skelton (who must not be blamed for my wayward and perverse pen); Anthony d'Offay (adjuvant indeed); Michael Richey (who knows both straight-edge and leaden rule); my sister-in-law Petra Tegetmeier (who lent us her father's drawing of the young David); last, Omega to the poet's alpha, the lady whose name appears on an earlier page.

R. H.

I

RITE AND FORE-TIME

THE title, *The Anathemata*, is sufficiently explained in the
Preface, pp. 26–9. A phrase in *The Sleeping Lord* (p.35, 'between
the Anathema and the Common Will'), which applies to the
victim on the cross, is a reminder that in this poem we are
concerned with the greatest and most perfect of 'things set up,
lifted up, or in whatever manner made over to the gods'. The
pronunciation (about which some appear to be puzzled)
becomes clear when the word is written anathêmata, the long
Greek eta being pronounced as in *meat* or *mate*, according to
your taste and upbringing.

For the quotation from *King Lear* on the title-page, see below
on *Middle-Sea and Lear-Sea;* and for the epigraph on page 45
('It was a dark and stormy night . . ,) see the end of the commentary on this section.

Teste David cum Sibylla: the *Dies Irae*, the Sequence (a
poem sung or said immediately before the Gospel) in masses
for the dead, begins with this stanza:

'Dies irae, dies illa,
Solvet saeclum in favilla,
Teste David cum Sibylla.'

'The day of wrath, that day, shall destroy the world in ash,
as David, with the Sibyl, testifies.' The date and authorship of
the poem are disputed, but it is generally attributed to Thomas
of Celano, the thirteenth-century companion of St Francis (and
so in the *Ana.* p. 68 n.3). The opening of the poem is borrowed
from the seventh-century Hebrew prophet Zephaniah, who is
speaking of 'the great day of the Lord':

'Dies irae dies illa, dies tribulationis et angustiae, dies
calamitatis et miseriae, dies tenebrarum et caliginis, dies

49 nebulae et turbinis, dies tubae et clangoris super civitates munitas.' (Vulgate.) 'That day is a day of wrath, a day of trouble and distress, a day of wasteness and desolation, a day of darkness and gloominess, a day of clouds and thick darkness, a day of the trumpet and alarm against the fenced cities.' (A.V.)

The more closely *The Anathemata* is read, the more apparent become the Biblical inspiration, and the following of a pattern and the use of imagery found in the prophetic books: so that here we open with the doom-laden prophecy, and the whole poem is to start with the promise of, and end with the realisation of, redemption. The wrong choice represented by sin is looked on by D. from a different point of view from that adopted by the Prophets when they castigated breaches of the covenant: but D.'s distress at man's betrayal of his near-angelic poten-tialities is of the same nature as that suffered by the ancients (see for example, the opening poem in *The Sleeping Lord*, whose title – an essential part of the poem – repeats the cry of Jeremiah, 1:6; and the 'utile infiltration' we shall be meeting on the next page). 'Sin' is there the application of man's faculties to purely technical achievement, directed to profit and power, at the ex-pense of that culture which is both creation and worship.

D. (we know for a fact) took a hidden delight in sharing the name of the Psalmist: so that the witnesses are both ancient and modern poet. So much of the latter's thought is concerned with protection, the walled city (the 'civitates munitae' of the Vulgate, the 'fenced cities' of the A.V.), the queen and mother, with the memory of all the dead and their entry into Paradise, that this reference to the *Dies Irae* is most proper at the beginning of his poem, particularly when we remember the final verse, 'Pie Jesu Domine, Dona eis requiem'. 'Yes', writes D., 'it's that sway from the Majesty and power to the tender and consoling that is so moving in the *Dies Irae*: Rex tremendae majestatis.'

Compare with this the long commemoration of the dead in *The Sleeping Lord*, which is ended by the candle-bearer, p.87, who 'sings out in a high, clear and distinct voice, the respond;

Et Lux perpetua luceat eis' ('and may perpetual light shine upon   **49**
them').

The Psalmist's association with the prophecy of the 'day of
trouble and distress' is obvious enough; the Sibyl is a different
matter. In a note added to the Preface, as reprinted in *Epoch and
Artist* (p.134), D. says that 'clearly the Sibyl belongs to what,
for the Christian Church, is an extra-revelational body of
tradition'. This is true enough if it means no more than that the
notion of an ecstatic cave-dwelling prophetess or priestess can
be assimilated, as a reflection or foreshadowing, into the Chris-
t an mystery, as was so much of non-Christian myth. The Sibyl
of the *Dies Irae*, and of the middle age in general, is derived
from the Sibyl of Cumae, described by Vergil in the Third
Aeneid and the Sixth. In the former we are told how she writes
her oracular utterances on leaves which are scattered by the
wind ('Five-fronded your name, Sibyl-noted, Princess, On
buck-eye lance. Clear the cipher runs, far from Cumae, Though
hinge creak, and wind scatter manic leaf.') In the latter book, she
is Aeneas's guide to the underworld. Her importance was
greatly magnified for the middle age by Vergil's reference, in the
Fourth Eclogue, to the coming of 'the last age of the song of
Cumae', coinciding with the birth of a child, and by the fact
that the Eclogue could (if its historical setting were neglected)
be read as a prophecy of the coming of the Messiah (cf. *Ana.*
p.112 ('Iam redit Roma', and p.219, 'Iam redit Virgo' and note).
There is an anticipation of the Sibylline reference to the day
of wrath in *In Parenthesis*, pp. 120–1, 'of how it's at our very
door, as Dai Davies and the Sibyl do agree'. The various
Sibyls, and the Cumaean Sibyl in particular, are dealt with
at some length in Jackson Knight's *Vergil: Epic and Anthropology*. Of him D. writes, 'His particular *numen* or sprite is
something of an Ariadne, who pays out more than one length of
thread'. Whether we can retain the clew in the labyrinth of man's
collective unconscious is, maybe, another matter. D.'s attachment to the Sibyl will be understood by a reader of Jackson
Knight, *op. cit.* pp. 166ff. Sibyl *and* cave are irresistible.

49   Augustine has a good deal to say about the Sibyl (or rather the pseudo-Sibyl) and her association with the Christian fish-symbol, which we shall be meeting later (*De Civ. Dei*, xviii. 23). And Varro's reference to her, towards the end of the second century B.C., as he introduces his instructions on running a farm, will amuse the reader. D.'s Sibyl, to judge from the company she keeps in *Mabinog's Liturgy* (*Ana.* pp. 190–1) was far removed from the aged priestess of the Aeneid.

I. Rite and Fore-time. Fore-time: this includes not only the historical pre-Christian, but all the ages of the world as far back as the mind can reach. The meaning of 'rite' in this context, and its association with fore-time, is illustrated by the following from Maurice de la Taille:

'*Latria*, eucharist, impetration (adoration, thanksgiving, petition) go side by side and hand in hand in this first approach towards God. But because man is not a pure spirit, he feels a need to translate this interior gift of himself into an outward rite which symbolises it. For this reason he presents to God the homage of some material gift, the whole reason and purpose of which is to represent and attest the inmost consecration of his soul . . . This brings us to St Augustine's definition, which is traditional in the Church: "The ritual sacrifice is the visible sign of the invisible sacrifice – *invisibilis sacrificii sacramentum visibile*".' (*The Mystery of Faith, an outline*, London, 1930, pp. 5–6.)

Maurice de la Taille was the first person whose name came from D.'s pen when he acknowledged his debt to a long list of 'living or recently living authors' – uncomfortably shouldered by Spengler, of whom more, perhaps, later. Since the very scheme upon which *The Anathemata* is built is derived from de la Taille's presentation of the Last Supper and Calvary, it may be well to have, in the French Jesuit's own words, a brief statement of what, as early as 1920 or 1921, bit so deeply into our poet's mind. (The date is taken from a letter dated many years later, and agrees with the note on p.36 of *The Sleeping Lord*.)

'I hold that Christ our Lord, on the night of the Last Supper, **49**
by consecrating the bread into his Body delivered up to death
for us, and the wine into his Blood shed for many unto remis-
sion of sins, visibly, ritually, liturgically offered up to God his
Death and Passion, whereby he was to be immolated at the hands
of the Jews, a Victim for the ransom of the world. Thus, in that
sacred mystery of our faith which is the redemption of mankind
by the sacrifice of the Body and Blood of our Saviour, I distinguish a twofold immolation. One perfectly real, even bloody;
another, previous to that, in the Supper, not real, but representa-
tive – symbolical – sacramental – mystical (all these words in the
present case express but one thought), not bloody, but unbloody. I hold that the unbloody immolation, which represented
the bloody one to come, was the act by which Christ pledged
himself to death in the sight of his Father and of men; thus
making over to God the Lamb to be slain, and by the very fact
offering in the ritual sense of the word, not internally only, but
outwardly, not by a mere purpose or promise to give, but by the
actual giving and delivering up of the gift, not in mere figure, but
most really and formally, the Victim that was henceforth sacred
to God, and as such due to its ultimate fate. I consider then that
Christ offered as High Priest according to the order and likeness
of Melchisedech, and yet in that very same capacity offered
nothing but the sacrifice of redemption, the sacrifice of his
Passion and Death; but he offered it in the Eucharist of the
Supper night. I do not therefore admit that there were two
distinct and complete sacrifices offered by Christ, one in the
Cenacle, the other on Calvary. There was a sacrifice at the Last
Supper, but it was the sacrifice of redemption; and there was a
sacrifice on the Cross, but it was the self-same sacrifice,
continued and completed. The Supper and the Cross made up
one complete sacrifice, properly so called, not invisible but
visible, not metaphorical like the death of martyrs either under
the Old or New Covenant, but in the strictest sense of the word,
even as the sacrifices of the Law, which it came to abolish.
We have then first a Priest and his sacerdotal action, a liturgy,

49   a sacred rite; we have at the same time a Victim, offered by the Priest in that liturgical rite which he performs; and next we have the slaying of the Victim, the true and real immolation, which, as to its physical element, is the work not of the Priest, but of the executioners: although it is freely accepted and gone through by the Victim, who happens to be the Priest, never ceasing for a moment to ratify and carry out in a visible and tangible manner the obligation which he has incurred by his solemn oblation, thus subscribing to that sacramental donation of his own self and of his own life by every drop of his own Blood unto death. After which God takes unto himself the gift, removing it from its former earthly sphere to the realm of heavenly light and bliss, of that glory which transfers it into the proper condition and state of a thing divine, of a thing assumed by God, owned by him and resting in his hand as the first-fruits of creation, and in his bosom as the Lamb, dear for his own sake and endeared by his cruel passion. For our Melchisedech has entered the heavens with his first-fruits changed into the Flesh and Blood of the Lamb, but the Lamb glorified, of the Lamb that was slain and liveth, of the Lamb once dedicated to God and accepted by God for ever and ever, and for ever remaining what his sacrifice has made him, the *Lamb of God*. Thus were the mysteries of the unleavened bread, of the paschal lamb, and of the sheaf of first-fruits to be brought before Jehovah "the next day after the Sabbath", those three blended into one in that one sacrifice of the Lord, which, as we are told by the earliest Fathers, ran from the Supper night and its Eucharistic feast to the morrow that dawned on the empty Sepulchre.' (*The Mystery of Faith and Human Opinion contrasted and defined*, London, 1930, 231–3.)

De la Taille's argument forms the background of another book which had a deep and lasting influence on D. – Martin D'Arcy's *The Mass and the Redemption* (1926): 'to some degree', says Fr D'Arcy, 'an English synopsis of *Mysterium Fidei*, though I have given it a different setting'. D. not only adopted the explanation of the relation of Last Supper, Calvary and Mass offered by the French and the English Jesuit, but also recogni-

sed in the latter his own view of the divine contriving as artefacture, handiwork, from which emerges the only true delight,
the splendour of form.

Père de la Taille's views were bitterly contested by some
theologians and ardently defended by others. Why was D. so
moved by this apparently technical argument? Because de la
Taille insisted on the efficacy of the significant act contained in
the Last Supper, where the sign (the breaking of the bread,
the drinking of the wine) made inevitable, in a sense created,
what took place on Calvary. The poet was thus enabled to
relate that supreme sign to what is done by the artist, when
a gesture, of hand, of the faculty that orders words ('I have
tried', he wrote, 'to make a shape in words') brings into being a
reality that goes beyond the mark on the paper or the sound
vibrating in the air. It is this, that, for him, lends weight to the
notion of sign, the effective, not (in Maritain's phrase) the
hieroglyphic sign: the sacramental. Nevertheless there may have
been some confusion even in D.'s mind between the sign that
'shows forth' (that stands for some other thing) and the sign that
'effects'.

We may complement this with a book which bridges the
stream between theology and poetry, Hugo Rahner's *Greek
Myths and Christian Mystery*. It is not included in the list which
D. gives in his Preface, for the English translation was not
published until 1963 and even the German original (1957) was
later than *The Anathemata*, but it was certainly read soon after
its appearance in English.

Remembering that the poet will be recalling not only the
immolation on Golgotha but also the unbloody sacrifice of the
consecrated bread and wine; remembering, too, his insistence
on the particularity of place and time in the institution of that
sacrament, we may preface the whole poem, and this section in
particular, with the following from Hugo Rahner:

'The nature of this Christian mystery' (i.e. of the cross)
'can be discerned above all else in the decisive saving event
which is the death of God upon the cross. In that death from

49 Paul's day onwards the ancient Christian saw *the* mystery of all creation. For, though we must never seek to detract from its harsh and uncompromising historicity, it is a mystery precisely in this: that *being both retroactive and predetermining, it embraces everything that has happened or will happen in the world.*' The clause we have italicised expresses the theme with which *The Anathemata* both opens and closes.

It is the revelation of this mystery which D. would call (incorrectly, to my mind, but acceptably if qualified as a personal use) the Christian myth. And it is here, again, that as witnesses to the revelation 'at the appointed time' it is appropriate to refer to the Psalmist (as typical of the Biblical witness), the Sibyl (in a retroactive sharing of the witness) and the poet D. himself (as a witness 'at the turn of a civilisation').

'Myth' is a word that D. uses frequently, and seldom in a normal sense: so that ambiguity and even confusion can arise when others interpret normally what was used idiosyncratically. What he meant by myth is plain in the following from a letter: he has been speaking of the vagueness with which the word 'mystic' is used, and continues:

'. . . not indeed quite so bad as the word myth, for that is about the limit in the loss of meaning. The S.O.D., the only Dict. I have here, starts off in defining myth as (i) "a purely fictitious narrative", a bloody lie in fact'.

In a note about the Sibyl, referred to above (*Epoch and Artist*, p.134) he says the same, a little less forcibly, and repeats his plea for a return to what he takes to be the real meaning of the word. His 'loss of meaning' between the Greek *mythos* and our *myth* is, in fact, a begging of the question. He can say that there is this loss only by attributing to the Greek word a meaning it never bore, which he wishes to attach to the English word. The whole series of meanings that belongs to *mythos* centres on the mere word, the story, the fiction.

We use myth, it is true, in a more precise sense than that which it bears in such sentences as 'He said he'd won the D.C.M., but it was a pure myth'; but in that case we adhere to a more

exact definition – that, for example, given by H. J. Rose in the **49**
Oxford Classical Dictionary, which seems serviceable:

'This' [the myth proper] 'may be defined as a pre-scientific
and imaginative attempt to explain some phenomenon, real or
supposed, which excites the curiosity of the myth-maker, or
perhaps more accurately as an effort to reach a feeling of satisfaction in place of uneasy bewilderment concerning such phenomena.'

Compared with this, the 'bloody lie' is, of course, a debase-
ment, but the definition quoted embraces only a part of what D.
has in mind. Imagination, explanation, mental satisfaction: these
are included in D.'s myth. The third we recognise in his acceptance of the phrase used by his friend Saunders Lewis about the
Mass 'making sense of everything'; the second, when he praises
a legend or traditional story for being 'straight, exact, rational and
true'. And the first element in that definition, the imagination,
touches the most important element in D.'s myth, the working
of the human spirit upon the material provided by the universe –
in doing which it draws upon or is guided by imponderables that
lie deep in the individual or collective unconscious or sub-
conscious – working in such a way as to produce that which is
rightly called *made*, an artefact and not a mere fiction: or, if
you so prefer it, a fiction which is an artefact.

It is this insistence on the artefacture of the myth (for the
work of man's art has a higher being than the being of the concrete upon which it works) that gives the word the commanding
force D. attaches to it: so that for him myth is truth expressed
in artefacture, the truth of the former consisting in the being
of the latter. And it is here that his use coincides with the Christian use of 'mystery', so that what, in pre-Christian times, was
'mere' myth becomes, when Christianised, the revelation of
mystery. This theme is worked out in detail by Hugo Rahner.

David's own suspicion of the word 'myth', even when used
by himself, is shown by his frequent use of 'mythos' or 'mythus',
by his acceptance even of the Victorian 'mythe' (with the long
vowel) as a possible alternative, and, most strikingly, by the

49 phrase that occurs more than once in his essays and notes, 'the Christian myth or mystery'.

It is here, too, that we see that Spengler is not, perhaps, too uncomfortable as a neighbour for de la Taille: for it was in Spengler that D. saw reflected – this, I believe, is a more correct way of putting it than to say that from Spengler he drew – his view of the place in history of man's 'mytho-poetic power' and of its flowering in the 'spring-time' of cultures: see, in particular, pp. 399 ff. of the first volume of the 1932 London edition of *The Decline of the West*.

There can be little doubt but that, when D. uses the apparent oxymoron 'genuine myth', he means something very close to 'poetry'. Speaking of 'the myth of Arthur' (*Epoch and Artist*, p.243) he describes it as doing or making precisely what he tries to do or make in his own work: 'To conserve, to develop, to bring together, to make significant for the present what the past holds, without dilution or any deleting, but rather by understanding and transubstantiating the material, this is the function of genuine myth, neither pedantic nor popularising, not indifferent to scholarship, not antiquarian, but saying always: "Of these thou has given me I have lost none".' And it is because he sees myth as artistic creation that he can speak of it (*Ana.* 124 n.3) as 'proposing for our acceptance a truth more real than the historic facts alone discover', and (167 n.2) of 'mythological requirements' that have to be satisfied, in the same way as he will say of his own work that certain words, or words arranged in a certain order, had to be used because they were artistically necessary. We might, indeed say that the test of the 'genuineness' of myth depends on the answer to the question (in the poet's own words (*Ana.* p.129) 'Is Lady Verity to Poesy now wed?' So long as we bear this in mind, we may well accept D.'s vocabulary: caution is needed when, in Christianity, 'myth' and historical fact coincide, and the 'truth' of the former may undermine the truth of the latter.

D.'s view of the progress from fact, through legend, to the fulness of 'myth' is illustrated with great clarity by a passage

from an unpublished MS. Here the poet speaks through the **49**
mouth of a Roman legionary who has served on Hadrian's Wall
at a time when Roman Britain is already under severe pressure
from; he foresees the impending collapse, and wonders whether
'a mortal man of our tradition of arms but of outstanding genius
. . . some *dux* or *comes*, by chance accident of the Artorian gens
but a family long rooted in Britain, should not save this island
for maybe half a century, and most certainly be thought of as the
celestial Arcturus, and by a complex twist of etymology be
known as *arctos*, the Bear, in the dialect of the Keltoi: and
centuries after that, by men of a culture wholly other again, we
may come full circle and have a cooked-up *quondam lux, luxque
futura* . . . A futile effort, you'll say, seeing that by then our own
imperium will be not declined but fallen. That's rather the point:
from the inevitable failure the splendour of the extra-utile will
shine out. I'd guess it might be some centuries from the time of
his effort before the weave of marvel gathered round his name.
So that the extra-utile will lend him fame and mysterium other
than what his actual achievement as *dux bellorum* may have been.'
'The splendour of the extra-utile', with its reminiscence of
splendor formae, its rejection of the finality of the useful, and its
acknowledgment of mystery, summarises that poetic argument;
it shows, too, how, in rejecting the normal use of the words, D.
fails to distinguish between myth and legend.

Finally, it should be pointed out that D. himself, by his use of
myth and *mythus* in connection with the Mosaic and Christian
tradition, blurs the essential distinction (to which he was fully
alive) between pagan myth and Christian *revelation*.

The opening paragraph: D. frequently, particularly when
beginning a passage, uses 'he' or 'his', 'him' etc., to indicate that,
while he has an individual in mind, that individual is to be
regarded as typical. Only two of the eight sections of *The
Anathemata* do not begin in this way, 'Middle-Sea and Lear-
Sea' and 'Mabinog's Liturgy' – and the first of these is quick to
introduce a named person as 'him'.

The 'him' whom we discern in line 1 is (however far back

49 we are looking into pre-history) a priest – or, if that is putting it too strongly, he is at least sacerdotal in his intention; he is performing a ritual act, and thereby 'making this thing other'. The repetition of the verb 'discern' at the very end of the poem (p.243, 'discern the Child', 'discern a lord's body') shows that here, too, it carries more than the meaning of 'distinguish', for it contains (see comment on the later passage) the Pauline sense of 'recognise the true nature of'. We could paraphrase the poet's words in this paragraph by saying that so soon as man makes that which is significant, which is a sign of something other and greater, we can already see that his act is of the same nature as the transubstantiation effected in the Mass by a re-presentation of what was done at the Last Supper.

D. is always a little wary of the word 'priest', maybe because of its derivation from 'presbyter' – 'elder' – which does not suggest the associations he requires. He prefers *sacerdos* (for its emphasis on the sacred, devoted, dedicated) or *pontifex* (where the original connection, obscure though it may be, with bridge-building and so with the transition from one order to another, is most acceptable), or such periphrases as 'the man in the planeta' (i.e. chasuble) or (what we shall soon meet) 'the cult-man'. This last is specially favoured because of the link between the initial meaning of *colere*, to till (the land – to serve Demeter – see note to p.230, 'dear and grave Demeter') and the derived meanings of to cherish, to reverence and, in a religious sense, to worship.

Because this, at which we are looking back, is a fore-shadowing, 'his' syntax is 'groping'; in other words he is feeling his way towards what will be said with certainty by the supreme man-priest, Christ, and later by the Christian who re-enacts Christ's sacramental act. There is a certain ambiguity here, but the double meaning does not detract from the clarity: 'his groping syntax' can be read as an anticipation, too (*his* groping syntax), of the 'groping syntax' of the celebrant of the Roman Mass. If you read the prayer referred to in the note, you will see that the careful wording seems to be gradually feeling its way to a for-mula that will be unmistakably clear and precise: and here we

should note that when D. was writing the Tridentine rite, to **49**
which he was deeply attached, had not been surrendered to the
men of fact.

Either way of reading the words allows the introduction of
'Adscriptam, ratam, rationabilem'. The translation given is not
very satisfactory, for God is not being asked to 'ascribe to' the
offering (even if the word could so be used) but to make it
'ascribed', i.e. enrolled as his own, made his own. The prayer
from which D. is quoting runs: 'Quam oblationem tu, Deus, in
omnibus, quaesumus, bene + dictam, adscri + ptam, ra +
tam, acceptabilemque facere digneris: ut nobis Cor + pus et
San + guis fiat dilectissimi Filii tui Domini nostri Jesu Christi.'
(The crosses are inserted where the priest is directed to make the
sign, because the careful formality of the gestures was also in
D.'s mind when he wrote of 'groping'.) 'We pray thee, God, to
make this offering wholly blessed, to make it a thing consecrated
to thyself (*adscriptam*) and approved, worthy of the human spirit
and of thy acceptance, that so it may become for us the body and
blood of thy most dear son, Jesus Christ our Lord.' 'Worthy of
the human spirit' is taken from the translation of Fr J. O'Connell
and Dr H. P. R. Finberg, published in 1949; it may seem a
cumbersome paraphrase of *rationabilem*, but "reasonable" does
not, without further explanation, suggest the notion of *recta
ratio*: the *recta ratio factibilium* which governs the artefact –
and here the poet is introducing rite as artefacture. Cf. *In
Parenthesis*, p.154, 'But he made them a little lower than the
angels and their inventions are according to right reason'.

D. comments on this in a letter: '. . . dont much like Dr.
Finberg and Fr O'Connell's "worthy of the human spirit"
for *rationabilem*, but as you say "reasonable" just by itself does
not evoke all that is required. Curiously enough when the boys
were trying to vernacularize the Latin text, I was told that
rationabilem did not equate with what was intended by the
Greek-Hebraic, Aramaic, in which it would have had a meaning
more like righteous or holy – I forget now but I know there was
an argument about it. Bur rather up the same street of the dif-

49 ference between the Catholic use of "justice" when Protestants would say "righteousness".

'The truth is that you cant [note in margin: not at least without re-casting the whole passage in such a way as to evoke what is evoked by the Latin words and what might be managed with regard to some of the words in one vernacular would fail in another. After all, English is not the only vernacular, not by a long chalk] "translate" bene + dictam, adscri + ptam, ra + tam, rationabilem acceptabilemque facere digneris . . . and those three crux-signs together with the words make one superb whole. And after all the petition in the *Quam oblationem tu* prayer could not be made acceptable by God the Father Almighty, had what was offered lacked in any way, *ratam*, *rationabilem*, for 'right reason' and 'rationality' is required of anthropos – whether he is considered under the command of *Prudentia* or abiding by the judgments of *Ars* – whether it be *praxis* or *poiesis*.

'. . . that chap, Fr. N., who said Irenaeus [note in margin: that's why I speak in praise of him (Irenaeus) in *The Sleeping Lord*, p.83, and how he had been the disciple of Polycarp, who had been taught by St John himself] was much more what I preferred than Augustine – *my God! how right he is, how bloody right* – and then goes on to speak of the 'groping syntax" that he himself feels as he makes those three crux-signs in the *Te Igitur*, haec + dona haec + munera haec + sancta sacrificia illibata, "it is as though you were feeling your way to an exact formulation" – God bless him! [note in margin: If we had more priests of the Order of Melchisedec who (as obviously Fr. N. does) understood that liturgy is pure poiesis we should not have tolerated the awful havoc inflicted on us by these blasted apostles of change and yet more change, no doubt with the most pious pastoral intentions.]'

With this *adscriptam* passage, cf. *In Parenthesis*, p.162, Cain's unacceptable offering (Genesis 4), 'neither approved nor ratified nor made acceptable'.

by pre-application and for them: the applicability of the

as though I had read the front to Anna Livia to Joan & yourself
whereas it was of course you who had read it to Joan & myself
became with an imitative feeling for the Irish words you read it
almost straight off & I was astonished. That was in fact
my first 'feel' of that incomparable genius James Joyce
later I got the record he spoke made for the Orthological
Institute ~~~~~~~ at Cambridge — long ~~~~~~
defunct. That record was stolen with other stuff
for a home I stayed in for a while in London.

Then after the war Arthur Wheen (dona ei requiem)
got me another copy when the Cambridge Institute
sold up.

This passage refers to above and the reading is
accurate if the reader understands it in a context
of my letter but as it stands it sounds as
though I was the reader whereas it was yourself dear
René.

To Noel
That chap who said Irenaeus was ~~much more~~
what I prefer, than Augustine — my God how
right he is, ~~~~~~ then goes on ~~~~ to speak of the 'groping
syntax' what he ... as he makes those
three crux signs in the Te igitur.

haec ✝ dona haec ✝ munera . haec ✝ sancta
sacrificia illibata : ... it is as though you were
feeling your way to an exact formulation."
got them ... I've always loved
those words & the careful making of those
signs, coming so early in the Te igitur.
Meichtery in that fragment of Badami Ass
~~Ducky Austin~~ ~~~~~ Austin was called by
~~the Scotti~~ And as before he was named by
the Scotti Ducky Austin so afterwards
he was called Austin the Dodger.

But for all the rest there was no help
on that open plain.   End of fragment for Bk of Badami
Ass
... catch characteristics of that great
African ... as he starting.

[left margin notes:]

That's why I shank to proved him in 'The Sleeping Lord'

p. 83
... had been the director of
Polycarp who ...

If there was more
priests of the
Order of Melchi...
... Noel dear)
... understood that
... in pure
Polaris ...
... would not have
... it stands the
... and of those
... implicit on its
... of these things
... apostles of
... change ...
... rule change ...
... own ... with the more
... pious personal intention.
P.111

sacrament, and its efficacious power, is anticipated, even though   **49**
the immolation on Calvary has not yet been effected: hence
Christ's 'harrying' or 'harrowing' of Hell, so popular a theme in
the middle age, when he 'descended into Hell' to release the
just – a theme often introduced by D. also; see, for one of many
examples, *Ana.* p.224 and note. 'Is not the term (pre-application)
ordinarily used by Catholic theologians, the technical term is
"pre-applied grace"?' (D.). With this we may include 'efficacious sign', an allusion to the definition of a sacrament as an
efficacious, or effective, sign of a sanctifying reality.

under modes and patterns: the particularity and diversity
of rite, custom, cult, each with its special value, constantly recurs.
Cf. in particular 'The Tutelar of the Place', which is a prayer to
her that 'loves place, time, demarcation, hearth, kin, enclosure,
site, differentiated cult . . .'

the holy and venerable hands: the prayer referred to in
D.'s note runs thus: 'Simili modo, postquam coenatum est (he
takes up the chalice in both hands) accipiens et hunc praeclarum
calicem in sanctas et venerabiles manus suas: item (he bows his
head) tibi gratias agens, (holding the chalice in his left hand, he
makes the sign – i.e. of the Cross – over it with his right hand)
bene + dixit, deditque discipulis suis, dicens, Accipite, et
bibite ex eo omnes'. 'In the same way, when supper was done,
taking up this noble Cup too [see *The Sleeping Lord*, p.110 and
n., for the weight which *praeclarus calix* bears for D.] and giving
thanks he blessed ┆ it and gave it to his disciples, saying, Take,
and let all of you drink from it.'

In D.'s use of the words, we may note that the hands of
the priest, and even of 'he' in fore-time, are identified with the
hands of Christ; secondly, that he has incorporated the *significant* act of taking up and lifting; and thirdly, that he insists on
the *efficacy* of this sign.

These, at the sagging end: here there is no ambiguity.
Mass is being celebrated in our own day, for we are at the
'sagging end' and have lost the vigour of the 'young-time',
the 'sap-years'. Cf. *Ana.* pp. 92–3, 'and West-wood springs new'.

49 We are 'these', standing in the 'apsidal houses' – house, because, like the Latin *aedes*, the first meaning of 'habitation' is extended to cover the dwelling of a God. 'Apsidal' is of interest for the apse is first used in connection with Roman houses and public buildings, which were so built and laid out, with provision for a presiding magistrate, altar, etc., that from the fourth century onwards the pagan basilica could easily be adapted to the needs of the Christian ecclesia. (See also a book much valued by D. and often useful in the interpretation of his work – Gregory Dix's *The Shape of the Liturgy*, pp. 26–7.) Correspondingly, the pre-Roman churches in the legendary 'drowned' Lyonesse, between Land's End and the Scillies (*Ana*. p.101) are 'unapsed eglwysau', like St Declan's tiny oratory at Ardmore, Co. Waterford, which is pre-Patrician. Cf. also 'every rounded apse-end' (*Ana*. p.162), the 'lighted apses' of p.227, and 'apse' as a verb (p.140). The only good thing 'those goddam Norman panzer-gangs' brought us, says D. in a letter, was the apse. We 'intend life', both because of the intention behind the act of consecration, and because from that act we intend to draw life.

'Apsidal houses' is a peculiarly happy phrase here, because in the next paragraph we have 'column, entablature' (classical) introduced with 'spire and triforium' (gothic).

The contrast between the 'sterile ornaments . . . pasteboard baldachins' and the 'living floriations' of what was built in a true culture, suggests that D. may well have had in mind an old favourite of his, Browning's *Bishop Blougram's* Apology:

'It's different, preaching in basilicas,
And doing duty in some masterpiece
Like this of Brother Pugin's, bless his heart!
I doubt if they're half-baked, those chalk rosettes,
Ciphers and stucco-twiddlings everywhere.'

('sure enough' – D. – and the Browning allusion is confirmed again by a phrase in the ms. of *The Book of Balaam's Ass*, 'or like when Northumbrian brides make the stucco-twiddlings seem to ring . . .')

The source of the image used in this paragraph lies in a **49** passage of Tacitus (Annals 2.16), where the historian is describing the wooded country in which Germanicus defeated the German Arminius. That this is so is clear from a later and unmistakable use of the same passage, in 'The Dream of Private Clitus' (*The Sleeping Lord*, p.16). 'Long corridors of arches stretched all ways. Smooth, straight boles those trees had, and no low growth between each as it were like a pavement.' We recognise Tacitus' 'pone tergum insurgebat silva, editis in altum ramis et pura humo inter arborum truncos' even more clearly in an earlier draft, where 'pura humo' appears as 'The ground-space clear'. 'The Dream' continues, 'And it was as if the rounded arches of our basilicas were suddenly to bestir themselves and the genius of each column to exert itself and reach across toward the numen of the column opposite'. The dreamer applies to the trees the metaphor which the poet here reverses and applies to the 'cramped repeats' of Gothic and Classical revival.

the failing numina: 'numen' being used in the sense of the divine power or spirit associated with a particular site: they are failing because of the petrifying ('ossific') effect of modern materials and building methods ('Dieu' says Gustave Martelet in his *Résurrection, Eucharistie et genèse de l'homme*, p.30, 'ne s'est fait ni acier ni nylon,) – the soulless repetition of what had been 'leaping arches' produces death.

In the first paragraph of p.50, the nature of the corruption that has set in is explained in a typical military metaphor: it is the 'utile infiltration', making its way into the whole of our culture, the substitution of doing for making, technic for artefacture. For 'utile', a key word, see 'Art and Sacrament' *passim*, in *Epoch and Artist*, and the shorter 'The Utile'. 'I restrict it [the word 'utile'] to man's functional contrivances and to the contrivances of animals and the processes of nature'. D. was writing before the drastic changes in liturgy, when the utile was no more than an infiltration, and a rearguard action could still be fought·

Here there comes into play an important distinction, for

49 which D. was ever ready to acknowledge his debt to Spengler. Thus, he writes in March 1973, 'I think Spengler's distinction between a "culture" and a "civilisation", for all its complexities in any given case, is a much neglected notion; in a sense it corresponds to or has affinity with the business of what we used to call "The Break" [see Preface, pp. 15–16]. In a "culture" the "utile" and the "extra-utile" are, to this degree or that, married, inter-meddled, the maiden called "sign" or "sacrament" is not by any means wholly "forlorn" (to revert to the rhyme about the cow and the crumpled horn). In a "civilization" the tendency is for the deep things of a true culture-phase to lose their signification, and while the outward forms may to some extent be observed or even, for imperialistic aims, deliberately "revived", yet the "utile" is in fact all that matters. Technics may, as you say, be "built-in" to the mammal called "man" . . . but owing to certain slowly developed thought-processes an obsession with the technological causes man to be Man-the-Technocrat; then it becomes next to impossible for him to see any sense in the sign-world. He can and does still require "entertainment" of every conceivable sort. It is a psychological necessity. ("Cultural activities".) . . . But it is extremely difficult for men to even begin to see that the wholly extra-utile act of sending by *Interflora* a bunch of special flowers on some special day to his beloved is *neither more nor less* of the realm of sign and sacrament than is the careful keeping of some given rite proper to some particular day . . .'

Christopher Dawson's estimate of Spengler in *Progress and Religion* makes it clear that the notion which D. developed so profitably is extracted from a background that is fundamentally abhorrent to the poet. A shorter and much more severe judgment of Spengler will be found in W. F. Albright's *From the Stone Age to Christianity* (1940), pp. 56–7, with references to more detailed criticisms. Professor Albright notes the 'tremendous influence Spengler has exercised on racist thought, with his intuitive racial and national mysticism and his fatalism, as well as his glorification of "Aryan" racial achievements'.

With this distinction between culture and civilisation – itself allied to the distinction between 'myth' and fact – in my mind, my eye was arrested by a paragraph in Albert Speer's Spandau diaries: '. . . the products of industry are not susceptible to monumentalization. In order to achieve real impressiveness . . . a monument has to have a mythic quality. Technology is always opposed to mythology.'

rear-guard details: a similar metaphor is used on pp. 189–90   50 of the birth of our western culture (as opposed to its Near-Eastern origins): the Epiphany, 'Our van / where *we* come in: / not our advanced details now, but us and all our baggage'. We find the 'advanced details' in Abraham, *Ana.* p.58, and Melchisedec, p.230, where see comment.

heedless of incongruity: incongruity between the traditional clothing, gesture and language of the liturgy, and the unsacramental world in which they survive. D. elaborates 'incongruity' in a MS. fragment: 'It creates that contradictory tug in the mind which we experience when we see a Bishop in the sacerdotal garments of a genuine and unbroken religious and cultural tradition speaking into the microphone as he blesses some engine of our technological age. The contradictory tug is not of a moral nature; it is because of the incongruity of two cultures at total variance as to inner feeling and so of outward forms. It has been said that art (like nature) hates a vacuum: similarly art demands the congruous. Integration is its own desire – it builds the city whose parts are united as one': the Psalmist's 'civitas cujus participatio ejus in idipsum' we shall meet later in the poem.

utile infiltrations: 'utile' (see above and the discussion of the word in *Epoch and Artist*, pp. 180–1) is used with an emphasis that varies. Here it is used with some scorn, of what is concerned merely with fulfilling a practical purpose ('why not a plastic chalice ?'); on other, rarer, occasions there is the nobler sense of 'well adapted to, well made for, a particular function', e.g. the 'utile shovels fashioned of clavicle bones' used in a palaeolithic burial (*The Sleeping Lord*, p.71), the 'utile spares for the mobile columns' (*Ana.* p.90); there is the sense, too, of

50 'profitable', as in the 'utile seams' of the Welsh coal-fields (*ibid*. p.72).

creeps vestibule: the verb being made transitive (i.e. invades by creeping), a common device with this poet.

Here we meet the three symbols, the tree-stem, the stone, and the stream, which will reappear on p.56 as (in Troy) 'the stone / the fonted water / the fronded wood': the three elementary symbols, raised to their highest value in Christianity, of wood (the cross, the mast, the ship), the stone (of the altar) and the water (of life and Baptism).

the closed lattices . . . each door: this contains a memory of a little song, often sung by a painter whose friendship with D. reached back into the twenties: 'Close the door, they're coming through the window; close the window, they're coming through the door; close the door . . . my God, they're coming through the floor!' ('I still think it bloody funny and very true' – D., fifty years later). With this cf. *In Parenthesis*, p.180, 'and Jesus Christ, they're coming through the floor.'

Paragraph 3 (**The cult-man . . .**) is sufficiently annotated by D., but we may note the doom-laden 'more precariously than he knows', particularly when we remember that since D. wrote the 'rear-guard details' have been savagely mauled: so that many things written here about the liturgy should be in the past tense, and D. was forced into an apparent antiquarianism that was completely foreign to him. **Pellam's land:** the Grail story in Malory is Books XIII–XVII, King Pellam or Pelles appearing most in the last. D.'s reading in this field, apart from Malory himself, and the oddly involved Peredur (Percival) story in the *Mabinogion*, started in or about 1920 with Jessie Weston's *From Ritual to Romance*: about the time of Eliot's *Waste Land* (1922) – but those dates may be a little early.

The cult man . . . the pontifex: see above on p.49.

the twin-urbes: better, the 'twin-urbs' ('It was perhaps a mistake to use the plural *urbes*, for I never, if possible, use *urbs* for anywhere but *Urbs Roma*.' D. And: 'I think I wrote *urbes* because it sounded better on the ear', 10.9.74.) The duality of the

urbs is an extension of 'things new and old', combined with a **50**
reminder that the city in which old 'rite' is merged in new was
the city of Romulus. The reference in 'new and old' is to
Matthew 13.52 ('every scribe which is instructed unto the kingdom of heaven is like unto an householder, which bringeth forth
out of his treasure things new and old'). Such being the context,
and Matthew's point being that 'the Jewish teacher who becomes
a disciple of Christ has at his disposal all the wealth of the Old
Testament as well as the perfection of the New' (Jerusalem
Bible), there is a temptation to interpret 'twin-*urbes*' as the two
cities of Jerusalem and Rome – 'emphatically not' says D. (see
above) sacrificing sense to sound. We may embroider the interpretation a little more and take Matthew's scribe to be the poet,
who (as so often) brings out, in more senses than one, both new
and old. In both cases the pre-Messianic foreshadows the
Christian. The 'matrices' are the sources, of legend, myth,
culture, of everything that blinks us, particularly in the West,
with our beginnings. Troy (p. 57) is 'matrix of West-oppida', and
'matrix' is used both of Eve and Venus.'

the ancilia: the *ancile* (the singular of the plural *ancilia*) was a
small oval shield that fell from heaven during the reign of
Numa, king of Rome in the first century of the city (the eighth
century B.C.). Since the safety of the city was regarded as being
bound up with the safety of this shield, Numa had eleven exact
copies made, so that the loss or theft of the original could not be
determined. The craftsman's name was Mamurius, which has
suggested a connection with Mamers, Mavors, Mars, and the
ancilia were in the care of the Salii, priests of Mars. D. introduces them here, because of his regard for Mars as originally an
agricultural God (cf. *Ana* pp. 86–7, 176 and notes), with the
consequent cult-culture link. The Palladium (of 'palladic foreshadowings') was also sent down from heaven; an image of
Pallas Athene, which guaranteed the safety of the city of Ilium.
Diomede and Odysseus stole it (see Vergil in the Second Aeneid),
and thereby enraged the goddess, even though their theft made
the taking of the city possible. The 'kept memorials' refers also to

50 the relics of saints enclosed in the stone of the altar (cf. *The Kensington Mass*, 'sanctorum tuorum, quorum reliquiae HIC SUNT', and earlier, 'He asks the adjuvance of / these athletes of God / tokens of whom are cisted / immediately beneath / and central to / the Stone of Oblation'); the 'fertile ashes': the ashes, of straw and of an unborn calf burned on the feast of Tellus, the Earth Mother, which were scattered as an act of purification and fertilisation, on the feast of Pales, the pastoral goddess (21 April).

The notion that our own age is the 'December of our culture', under the dominance of 'the Ram' – by which we understand the forces of levelling-down, of technical supremacy, of 'central economies' – is developed again in 'The Tutelar of the Place' (*The Sleeping Lord*, pp. 59–64), with the same imagery, and often the same wording: for example (p.64) 'the ancilia, the palladia, the kept memorials'.

The last paragraph, describing the formal gestures of the celebrant, is carried further in detail, and complemented, in *The Kensington Mass*, a draft of which has been published (London, 1975) with reproductions of part of the ms. 'the salted cake': cf. *Ana.* p.201, and the, to D., particularly moving account of the burning by Dido of the *mola salsa*, Aeneid, IV 517–18, 'Ipsa mola manibusque piis altaria iuxta, Unum exuta pedem vinclis . . .', 'The queen herself with [salted] cake, hallowed of hand beside the stone, one foot bare from sandal-tie . . .'. 'gens . . . gentes': this, again, the preaching of the gospel to the 'gentiles' is elaborated in *The Kensington Mass*, from a starting-point in Peter's Galilaean origin and Isaiah's reference (9.1) to *Galilaea gentium*.

Note 4 on this page: there is a reference to this poem in a letter dated 16 June 1966: 'Older Protestants from the Reformers of the 16th cent. to the last century did, generally speaking, take over a great deal of the Church's structure, observances etc. intact – the Canon of Scripture taken very literally, hence the Incarnation was of as much importance to them as it was to the Catholic religion. They rejected the Mass on various grounds but

retained the Commemorative rite of Holy Communion. Without questioning their sincerity – and just considering the matter
in itself, the penetration of the timeless into time at some long
past historic date is more easy than accepting an analogous event
in the historic-present. I mean in the words of the 14th cent. carol
"the flour spreng in heye Bedlem, That is both bryht and schen"
is "more easy" of acceptance, because more remote in time
apart from being in the written Scriptures than is a later verse
in that carol or poem, "The thredde braunche is good and swote,
It sprang to hevene crop and rote, Therein to dwellyn and ben our
bote: Every day it schewit in prystes hond". Yet the "difficulties"
of giving credence to the birth in the reign of Caesar Augustus
(itself no less a *signum* and what is signified) [are no less] than
the "difficulties" of giving credence to that sign which is also
signified, shown, "every day" in "priest's hand".'
    Again: 'Yes, it used to worry me as a child or in my teens that
in the Protestant milieu chaps appeared to have no difficulty
in accepting the Birth Narrative and the thirty years or so of
God Incarnate, then Salvation through the Cross, the Resurrection and Ascension, and yet found the same Incarnate God,
as held by Catholics to be under the species of Bread and Wine
(Dogma datur Xtianis Quod in carnem transit panis et vinum
in sanguinem) a monstrous perversion & anyway impossible to
believe, whereas I found it, regardless of its truth or untruth
far more "easy" to believe than the idea of "he by whom all
things are that are" should live for thirty years or so as an
ordinary human being in 1st cent. Palestine.'
    railed tumulus: the reference to 'altar-rails' by which the 51
mound is Christianised is on the way to being an anachronism;
but see comment on 'white bangors', *Ana.* p.201.
    he sings high and he sings low: 'he' is still the priest of to-
day, but we are very soon to have one of D.'s carefully contrived
transitions from one time and place, or one theme, to another.
'high . . . low': 'No, that is not derived from the *Raggle-taggle
gypsies,* but from various other sources, rubrics, for instance,
in *voce secreto* [this is developed in *The Kensington Mass*] and

51 the rubric directing him to raise his voice somewhat at [note in margin: old John O'Connor used to speak about that – "Very good rubric that – we bloody sinners need that prayer"] *Nobis quoque peccatoribus* and elsewhere, such as *intelligibili voce dicit* at the *Agnus Dei* and the *et dicit intelligibili voce vel cantat* before he says *per omnia saecula saeculorum*. Amen and continues *Oremus praeceptis salutaribus moniti* etc. immediately before the *Pater Noster*. I use the same words in I.P. when the Queen of the Woods is calling for those for whom she has her varied flower awards, Hansel and Goronwy and that swine Lillywhite and Dai Greatcoat. Cant find a copy of I.P. in this chaos of stuff, but the "Queen of the Woods" – "she calls high and she calls low" or something of that sort'. (D.)

In *In Parenthesis*, p.186, it is: 'Dai Great-coat, she cant find him anywhere – she calls both high and low, she had a very special one for him.' In this 'both high and low' takes on a peculiar force, both from its double meaning ('high and low' being used of the voice, and also referring to the fact that the Queen of the Woods – cf. the preceding page – has 'cut bright boughs of various flowering' and 'speaks to them according to precedence') and from the pathos of her search for Dai of the great boast. D. draws attention in a note to this identification.

High and low provides the opportunity for the transition referred to above, for 'low voice' leads into 'high room', and the scene moves to the Upper Room of the Last Supper.

as one who speaks: 'as', not merely suggesting an analogy between what 'this man' of our own day is doing and what was done at the Last Supper, but with emphasis, asserting that the former act is a representation of the latter. The white line between 'and one, gone out' and 'There's conspiracy here' indicates, by the break, that we have moved from to-day back to the time of the institution. There is close kinship linking the words used here with those in which what is re-presented on the altar is described on Ana. pp. 241–2; and ms. drafts show how closely the two passages were brought together in the port's mind. Thus, on the same sheet we read a version of 'as one who

speaks . . . gone out' which is immediately followed by a version 51
of what later appeared on pp. 241–2. This lends further weight
to the word 'conspiracy'(on which see below), for it becomes clear
that there is also 'conspiracy' (in the sense of unity of mind and
heart) between 'now' and 'then'.

To this passage we should attach another, most relevant,
passage from 'The Book of Balaam's Ass' (in *The Sleeping Lord*,
pp. 107–9). There, the wounded and dying cry out to all that
is most sacred to them, and their cry (for which the poet uses
the word *epiklesis*, which is applied to the prayer *Quam oblationem* noted above) culminates in an appeal to the great priest
who, two thousand years before this scene in *The Anathemata*,
'foretokened that Oblation', Melchisedec: 'Twenty centuries of
waste land back / this summus sacerdos and Rex Salem / [a
terrible irony in that title, 'King of Peace', in that context]
had foreshewn, under the same signa of Ceres fractured, of /
Liber made confluent with / this, thy creature of water [i.e.
both nature, expressed through the deities of corn and wine,
and nature-by-man-handled] / yn y Caregl Rhagorol' (where
the 'notion of the *praeclarus Calix* might to some degree be
conveyed to us by considering what we feel when we speak of
the Grail'). 'Balaam's Ass' was written before *The Anathemata*,
so that we have here one more example of the continuing homogeneity of D.'s work, and the power that one part has to develop,
illuminate and illustrate another.

and one, gone out: i.e. Judas. By ending with this phrase,
followed by a gap, D. emphasises the same point as does Fr.
D'Arcy (*The Mass and the Redemption*, pp. 50–1), the change
from the joy with which Christ hastened to the upper room to
the 'awful sense of responsibility', followed by the cry, in the
Garden, 'as of a Victim dedicated, no longer free to choose, but
bound by an oblation self-made to death . . . And this change all
four Gospels attest, for they fix on one incident – that of the
betrayal, the departure of Judas – as the beginning of the Passion
they are about to narrate'. The 'high room' is the 'Salem
cenacle' of *Ana.* p.241.

51 **conspiracy** artfully combines *conspiratio*, conspiration, breathing together, concord (in a sense in which Teilhard is fond of using it), which may be applied to those gathered, all of one mind, to celebrate the Pasch, with the conspiracy or plot of Judas. (The O.E.D. quotes Sidney in the former sense, *Arcadia*, 3. 282D, 'So is the conspiracy of her several graces, held best together to make one perfect figure of beauty', and Emerson, *Ode to Beauty*, 'All that's good and great with thee Works in close conspiracy'.) The former meaning covers (with 'where a few are') the *turba duodena*, the band of twelve, in Aquinas's hymn *Pange lingua*, which is referred to at the very end of *The Anathemata* in 'What did he (Christ) do other / recumbent at the garnished supper?' In this 'recumbent' echoes Aquinas's words in the same hymn, *recumbens cum fratribus*, reclining with his brothers. This again, the starting from and ending with the Mass, illustrates what D. meant when in a letter to Saunders Lewis (printed in the 1974 D.J. issue of *Agenda*) he wrote: 'When I say somewhere in Preface [p.32, par.1] that one can think of a lot of things in the brief moment it takes the celebrant of the Mass to move the missal from the Epistle to the Gospel side of the *mensa domini*, I literally meant that. The action of the Mass was meant to be the central theme of the work, for as you once said to me, "The Mass makes sense of everything".' – Not only, we might add, the action, but also the effect of the Mass as extending to every individual and to the whole cosmos. For all the divergence of D.'s and Teilhard's views on modern civilisation, Teilhard keeps inserting himself into consideration of *The Anathemata*. 'From the beginning', writes Teilhard, for example, 'of the Messianic preparation [i.e. D.'s Fore-time in general and the Covenant with Abraham in particular], passing through the historic manifestation of Christ and the growth and development of his Church, a single event has been maturing in the world, realised, in each individual, by the Eucharist.'

birthday and anniversary: the former, because it is the first institution of the 'Cup of the New Testament', and the latter, because it is the annual celebration of the Passover of the Old. D.'s note on the next page explains the calendar references (see also *The Kensington Mass* and comment, and *The Sleeping Lord*, p.109 n.). While there is 'continuity' between the old dispensation and the new, this scene in the upper room marks a new 'beginning'.

appointed: a Biblical word of great weight, emphasising this stage in the pre-ordained plan of redemption and 'adoption'. Among other New Testament passages, D. must have had particularly in mind Galatians 4.2.

note 2: we might add that when the Malory MS. gives 'on Estir Day', did not 'Estir Day' mean the Jewish Passover, a sense obsolete since. 1611, according to the O.E.D., which quotes from the Authorised Version, 'He [Herod] apprehended him . . . intending after Easter to bring him forth to the people', Acts 12.4; Caxton's variant was no mistake but, for D.'s purpose, a much more powerful translation of Malory's source. When the French *Queste del Saint Graal* says (ed. Pauphilet, p.270), 'Ce est . . . l'escuele [dish] ou Jhesucriz menja l'aignel le jor de Pasques o ses deciples', it is the Thursday that is meant. The 'sheer' of Sherthursdaye' contains the notion of fineness, brightness, purity, that survives in some of its modern uses. David Blamires (p.188) notes the Norwegian *Skjaertorsdag*.

the vernal turn: (see note 1), the first full moon after the 52 spring equinox – though 'turn' would seem more appropriate to the solstice: 'she', the moon, and 'he', the sun.

Aquarius: D. uses the same oblique method of identifying time and place (the zodiac's Aries suggesting the use of Aquarius for the 'man carrying a pitcher of water'), and of emphasising the solemnity of the occasion, in 'The Fatigue' (*S.L.*, p.28), where the first hint of the vast significance of this 'fatigue' is contained in '. . . a movement, out beyond the Water Gate' through which the water would be brought.

nave: this not only connects the upper room with the church, but, because of the derivation of 'nave' from *navis*, ship (cf. Old French *nef*, ship, and modern French *nef*, nave of church),

52   it also paves the way to the introduction on the next page of the metaphor of the sea-voyager which will run through the rest of the poem. The ship is an early Christian symbol for the Church, often accompanied by the fish or anchor (of hope), and sometimes with oars and (as here) steersman – there are many examples, in inscriptions from the Roman catacombs, on engraved gems, carvings on tombs etc. The three allied symbols of ship, mast and cross, go back into the most distant of man's cultural origins, and particularly in relation to man's life regarded as a journey to a haven. It was their use in Homer, in particular, which endeared itself to the early Christians. They eagerly adopted the symbolism of Odysseus bound to the mast that so he might escape the dangers of the sirens. This subject is beautifully treated by Hugo Rahner (*op. cit.*), who illustrates a fourth-century sarcophagus on which Odysseus is shown so bound, the yard above his head forming a cross, with the rowers bent to their oars. D., like many other poets – Horace and Propertius are obvious examples – had the landsman's terror of the raging sea, and was filled with wonder by the fragility of the timber that carried the seaman, and its simultaneous strength and security. This theme will be elaborated throughout *The Anathemata*, building up to a first climax in 'Keel, Ram, Stauros' (Odysseus, we should remember, was saved on another occasion by clinging to the keelson of his boat), which is a vast hymn to the timber of salvation; and to a further climax in the last section, where the haven is reached and the cross is seen as the axis upon which the cosmos turns. *Stat crux dum volvitur orbis*, as D. quotes when discussing one of many 'wonder-voyages', the Antarctic adventure of Coleridge's Ancient Mariner.

Here comes the gap to be filled between D. and Teilhard, for the latter sees man's continued evolution (in the right use of his vastly developed technical skill and power) as culminating in the final 'appointed time' that will bring the complete Christification of the cosmos; the former, who shares the same eschatological views, sees a sharp break between our civilisational trend and man's normal progress as man-the-maker. How this is to be repaired he does not know, but his faith is unshaken that 'we were homo faber, homo sapiens before Lascaux and we shall be homo faber, homo sapiens after the last atomic bomb has fallen': *dies illa*.

the board-cloth: not only in the literal sense of the cloth for this table, but with an eye on the 'three-fold, fine abbed fair cloths / of Eblana [Dublin] flax / that must pall / the mensa Domini' – the altar-cloth of *The Kensington Mass* (Agenda edition, p.9); and cf. below, *Ana.* p.196.

the ritual light: for the 'lighting and blessing of a lamp for the evening meal' and its place 'in jewish domestic piety', and its survival in Christian worship as the *Lucernarium*, see Gregory Dix, *The Shape of the Liturgy*, p.87. There must also have been present in the poet's mind the single candle which, in the Dominican rite is lit – which, indeed, he himself had often lit – at the Offertory – though this stands, it is true, at the Epistle side of the altar – and the central, 'sanctuary' lamp, which hangs over the altar.

in the high cave: the upper room, with a backward look at the 'cave' of Bethlehem, the 'Liknites' cave of bread' of p.232.

for guest to be the hostia: i.e. to be victim; but there is more than the visual word-play of *hostia* and host, in that the 'hostia' (the victim) *is* the host who receives his guests, that 'host' has passed into common usage for the consecrated victim, and finally that for *hospes* (meaning both guest and host) there is the parallel form *hospita*, in which there is again an echo of *hostia*, victim.

The scene continues in the upper room, the metaphor of the 53 ship being re-introduced first by the 'thwart-boards', i.e. the seats, benches or couches for the twelve and for Christ himself.

the swordsman . . . feel afloat: Peter, the swordsman who slashed the servant of the High Priest in the Garden, is appropriately the steersman too (this is elaborated in the *K.M.*). 'at the rightboard': on the starboard side, where the steering-oar was controlled. 'To make him feel afloat': D. (rejecting any sugges-

53 tion of a reference to Christ's walking on the water and Peter's fear of sinking, in Matthew 14): 'No, I actually meant that Peter would feel more at home if he could think of the seats at the supper board as the 'thwart-boards'' of a ship. I always think of Peter as first and foremost a sailor and ship's master [cf. particularly, of Peter, in the *K.M.*, 'his hands wide-fisted / hands and whole frame built to / haul & reef & steer / His steer-tree more than most / could manage']. So the ref. has *nothing* to do with the Matthew xiv text. I say "One for the swordsman, *at the right-board, after* to make him feel afloat" because it would be on the "steer-board" quarter that the chap who handled the heavy "steer-oar" in one of our western type of ship. (In Roman galleys no less than in the "long ships" of those bloody god-damned Vikings the helm control was on the starboard quarter and you will recall that Nelson was pacing the quarter-deck when he fell and in medieval ships it was in the *After Castle* that the important "great lords in harness" had their place, and that navigator our dear Michael R. (no less than Peter the Apostle) checked her bearings at "right-board after". These continuities are about the only thing that bring me a measure of delight. I recall my pleasure (when staying with Helen Sutherland [at Rock in Northumberland]) I saw boats with eye-shaped decorations on each side of their bows, and from earliest times the forward extremity of painted or carved "eyes" outboard and with narrowing timbers outboard made a sacred place where the goddess or cult-figure had her chapel – where the focsle is.' [Cf. p.97, and Aeneas's libation *stans procul in prora*: here, as so often, there is a corresponding Biblical image, Wisdom 14.1, 'Again, another designing to sail, and beginning to make his voyage through the raging waves, calleth upon a piece of wood more frail than the wood that carrieth him', i.e. upon the carved image of a tutelary deity, the making of which has been descri-bed in the preceding chapter 13.] ' "But, from the drenched focsle, / the stifled murmur is what each heart's wry gloss reads: / Rock ahead and shoal to lee / less than half a Goidel's league" – that's where our Taplow would have been for sure –

It is always the riff-raff who know only endless labour, inter- **53**
meddled with ropes and lashes, that sing from brined throats
the shanties "Maiden, help y'r own!" It was a very oblique
sense of connection between "brined throats" in the focsle with
the goddess in her shrine in bows of vessels of prehistoric date.
Always for countless epochs of time, it has always been the same
distinction – Control, Admiralty, command, Caesar's panoply,
put it how you will, always abaft the beam, and the crew always
at or toward the forward part of the vessel.' (On this see R. H.
Dana's *Two Years Before the Mast*, the date of which (1840)
is in many ways perfect for the spirit and detail of the later section 'Redriff': a book well known to D. by repute but, by an
odd chance, never in his hands until just before his death.)

William Taplow: the central character or fictitious author of
The Private Opinions of a British Bluejacket, 'edited' by Hamish
Maclaren, first published in 1929, a book that gave endless
amusement to D. and many of his friends. More of William
Taplow passed into D.'s work than is at first apparent: 'ditty-
box' comes from Taplow, as does 'Knashing', and as late as
1974 D. is using his name as he might Tom Bowline, Ned
Mizzen or Ben Backstay.

The ship metaphor is continued with 'shipshape . . . trim . . .
dressed (i.e. 'dressed over all', as a ship ceremonially) . . .
Bristol fashion'. With 'Who d'you think is Master of her'
folk-song is introduced, bringing this poet's special combination
of humble, colloquial, work-a-day, with the greatest solemnity.
From *Shallow Brown*: 'A Yankee ship came down the river.
Shallow-ow, Shallow Brown . . . and who d'you think was master
of her . . . but a Yankee mate and a lime-juice skipper'. The lime-
juice skipper re-appears with even greater boldness in the 'vine-
juice skipper' of p.182.

The Christ-voyage, or man-voyage with Christ as Master of
the ship – which is the voyage of redemption – runs throughout
the poem, paralleled by and imaged in the particular, separate,
voyages described (two in 'Middle-sea and Lear-sea', a third
in 'Angle-land', and a fourth, short, return voyage in 'Keel,

53 Ram, Stauros'. Later, the poet will speak of Mary as the 'cause'
(p.128 and n. 5) of the voyage introduced here. 'Her fiat is our
fortune, sir: like Helen's face / 'twas that [i.e. Mary's *fiat mihi*, be
it done to me according to thy word] as launched the ship'.

In a letter of 10 September 1974, D., after carefully distin-
guishing the several voyages, says that he has seen references to
'a "mystic ship" that appears to have the Aegean for its point of
departure, to call at the port of Athens, and then makes for the
Scillies, as the ancients considered those islands to be the place
for tin, and then ventured up the whole length of the Channel,
round the Kentish coast and up the East Coast of England.
Whereas each of the three was intended to be seen in purely
factual terms.' [Writing quickly, D. uses a phrase that exag-
gerates the factual basis of the narratives.] 'That is why I am so
glad you pointed out clearly that a space of centuries separates
'Middle-sea and Lear-sea' from 'Angle-land', for unless the
distinction is clear to the reader, well, it is incomprehensible and
"mystic" indeed. All are in one way or another involved in the
coming from the Middle-sea and the lands either along its shores
or at some remove such as Mesopotamia & Upper Egypt & the
Euxine, "was his dam in far Colchis abed" & "did an Argo's
Grogram sire him" (p.96), but "Old Grog" gave me a slight
pace towards Nelson & his tars which I wanted to bring in much
later, & to what I wanted to ask Mike R. as to where the Captain
stood in relation to the 2nd mate at the wheel – the answer to
some question may not be given until much later – that's the
bugger of my perverse way of writing – as for example "He's
drained it again, & again they brim it" Brim what? not answered
until the end of section VI Keel, Ram, Stauros (p.182). Of
course in what I think is called an *ontological* sense there is
only *one* voyage. I mean as the Church says (or used to!) that
what is oblated in the sacrament of the altar is the same as
what was, under the *signum* of real, substantial, mortal flesh of
the flesh of Mair, puella et mater yn y preseb [*in praesaepio*,
in the stable] and the same as he who oblated himself at the
Supper . . . ontologically all this and these actions where argosy

is predicted of *one* voyage and *one* vine-juice skipper.'

When speaking of such voyagings, D. generally takes as the pattern the story of Jason and the Argonauts rather than that of Odysseus; and this may well be not only because of the symbol of the Golden Fleece as the treasure to be obtained, but also because it is the story of an ordered company sailing in a specially favoured vessel, and not that of the salvation of a single man. Thus *Argo* commends herself to the poet both as a symbol of the corporate body of the Church and as a companion to the vessels that took part in the Celtic wonder-voyages, including Arthur's *Prydwen*, of which he writes at the beginning of his *Introduction to the Rime of The Ancient Mariner*.

indelibly marked by locale and incidence: in other words, what is happening in the upper room is done according to the liturgical custom and rule of the Jewish Passover, an expression, in this time and place, of what was pre-ordained even before the created world: so, too, on p.49, the earliest 'ritual' men proceed 'under modes and patterns altogether theirs'.

on this hill: on the hill of Jerusalem, or rather the twin-spurred ridge on which the city stands: the burial place of the first Adam, and the place where the new Adam is to die.

at a time's turn: the final paragraph of this page emphasises the historicity of the event; but a great deal may be read into this particular phrase. It is a borrowing from Spengler (see *The Decline of the West*, 1932, edn, vol. 2, p.33), or rather an adaptation of his use of the word *epoch*, that moment when something new is born. Hence the title of D.'s collection of essays, *Epoch and Artist*, where 'epoch' means not 'period' or 'age' but 'critical or turning point'; hence, too, the peculiar significance of a sentence in the poem which opens *The Sleeping Lord*, 'For it is easy to miss him / at the turn of a civilisation'.

The general meaning of the long parenthesis which begins 55 at the head of p.55 is explained in the notes to that page, with much of the detail. The transition to the new theme is again made with an overlapping joint, provided in this instance by the introduction of 'this hill' – high room, hill, this hill, this *un-*

55 *abiding* rock (of Jerusalem). In the letter quoted above we read
an indication of this method of progression, where D. says that
'Old Grog gave me a step towards Nelson'.

The notion of the great cosmic cycle, the 'Great Year' of
Plato, was adopted by the Stoics from the sixth-century B.C.
Heraclitus, to whom they attributed (probably without warrant)
the doctrine of a final conflagration; and this again was taken up
by Christians, so that here again we meet the *in-favilla* day of the
Sibyl (cf. p.68), with which the poem opens. It is now used to
introduce the theme of the many millions of years of climatic
and geological change from which our earth, and man, emerged.
For the complexities of the Great Year and the teaching of
Heraclitus, see Professor Burnet's *Early Greek Philosophy*,
pp. 156ff. Here D. (as so often) notes his debt to Christopher
Dawson; readers of the opening chapters of *The Age of the Gods*
will recognise how Dawson provided the concrete historical
framework on which 'Rite and Fore-time' is constructed, just
as de la Taille provided the theological and spiritual – indeed,
the mystical – foundation of the whole poem.

This parenthetical passage may be taken as an insistence on
the impermanence of the created world – even those hillsites,
those places of refuge which are sacred – which adds to the
actuality of the choice of one person, in one time and place
(in spite of that impermanence) as finally the supreme mother
and guardian; of one child born; of one specific hill as the
supreme site. D. is constantly stressing the imposition of the
permanent upon the impermanent, of the timeless upon time.
Hence the phrase from Ecclesiasticus which is included in the
inscription facing the title-page of *Epoch and Artist*: they (the
artificers) 'give solidity to the created world'. In other words (if
we may allow ourselves a little licence in our interpretation)
every artefact is that much added to real being, and so the
supreme artefact, represented in the Mass, 'makes sense of',
as in the quotation earlier, gives reality to, 'everything'.

as low as Parnassus: does not, I think, mean more than that
even Parnassus, the home of the Muses, is 'down'. Parnassus is

mentioned, too, because in the Greek Deluge story it was to 55
Deucalion what Ararat ('Ark-hill', below) was to Noah.

it's Ossa on Pelion now: 'About Ossa on Pelion, I fear I
merely used the names analogously intending, as you say, a
"reversal". I thought I'd heard chaps use the tag "Pelion on
Ossa", I might have said "it's hollow Elis on Olympia now"
or "Omega is first and Alpha last", or what you will. I wrote
"it's Ossa on Pelion now" without a thought except that I
thought it served in the context of that page of reversals.' (D.)

Both the Idas: the two mountains, one in the Troas, and
the other in Crete, the former being associated with the worship
of Cybele, the Asiatic Great Mother, and the latter with Rhea,
the daughter of Ouranos and Gaia, and so the mother of all the
gods: though the two mountains and the two persons become
confused. The Trojan Ida was the scene of Aphrodite's union
with Anchises, and of the judgment of Paris (cf. p.194, 'Had
she been to Ida mountains / to whose lap would have fallen y'r
golden ball'); and this allows the introduction, almost immediately, of the 'Trojan dregs' which legend deposited in
Wales. 'Both the Idas' accordingly encloses much of the poem's
imagery. With the Idas, again, are associated the 'Dactyli'
('Fingers') born from Rhea's fingers when giving birth to
Zeus (to simplify a most intricate mixture of stories), and these
beings were the first artificers, working both in metals and in the
sounds of music.

West horse-hills: see (though this is but a tentative suggestion) the reproduction of the copper-engraving 'Ponies on hill-
slope' in *Word and Image IV*, or 'Hill pastures, Capel-y-ffin'
a watercolour drawing of the same date (1926) in the 'Penguin
Modern Painters' booklet – to mention but two of such 'horse-
hill' pictures. There are a couple more in the 1974 D.J. *Agenda*.

Volcae remnants: another version of (see note 3 and 8)
'dregs of the Trojans'. The Volcae appear in Livy (Bk 21), when
they try to prevent Hanibal from crossing the Rhone.

Moel of the Mothers: with D.'s note 4 cf. p.233 n.

efficacious asylums . . . cavern for: the noun 'cavern'

55   serving, again, as a verb. D's preoccupation with the 'Sleeping
Lord' (see note 6) culminates in the poem of that title; 'efficacious'
is used, as always, in the sense in which it is applied to a sacrament, that is, as implying supernatural help. 'asylum', no
doubt from Vergil, Aeneid 8.342 (where Aeneas is being
shewn the site of what will be Rome): Hinc lucum ingentem,
quem Romulus acer asylum Rettulit, et gelida monstrat sub
rupe Lupercal' – the sense is not clear – 'Then he shows
Aeneas a huge wood, where Romulus, sharp of sword, sharp of
wit, set up again a refuge' (for desperate men); 'he shows him,
too, the Lupercal lying under its cold rock'. There is a corresponding reference in Livy (1.8). The Lupercal was a cave
sacred to the pastoral god Faunus (Lupercus, as though 'wolf-
god'), the scene of the festival of the Lupercalia – when Mark
Antony offered the diadem to Caesar.

    ogofau: see, in addition to D.'s note, a passage on these
caves in Alwyn and Brinley Rees, *Celtic Heritage* (1961) pp.
303 ff, and *The Sleeping Lord*, p.20, 'Porth Annwfyn . . . did
plainly signify: Gate of Elysium'.

    Children of Troy: with n. 8, see also *The Sleeping Lord*, p.95,
where the Norman sentry looking towards Hay Bluff (the eastern
end of the northern escarpment of the Black Mountains: an
easy walk from Capel-y-ffin) wonders whether 'what's on the
west wind / . . . may signify that in the broken / tir y blaenau
[the title of one of the watercolours referred to above] / these
broken dregs of Troea / yet again muster'; and Powicke's
The Thirteenth Century, p.383: 'A fragmentary history, which
was compiled about 1282, possibly by a clerk in Archbishop
Pecham's circle, describes the Welsh as a Trojan débris swept
into the wooded savagery of Cambria under the guidance of the
devil'; and D. may have had in mind Vergil's 'Troas, reliquias
Danaum atque immitis Achilli' (Aen. 1.30).

    Nine-strata'd Hissarlik: (the nine super-imposed cities
of Troy, excavated at the modern Hissarlik) introduces a passage
on p. 57, which Christianised, encloses the very core of D.'s
mythe. Here, as he says on p.57, he finds the matrix of the West.

Although the legend of the Trojan origin of Rome and of our western culture persisted in the middle age, no poet has so stressed it as D.; nor, indeed, could he have done so before the first excavations of Schliemann. D. goes much further than any other writer, in particular (as we shall see later) when he draws parallels – acceptable if only through their artistry – between Hector and Christ, and Helen and Mary.

a but forty-metre height: the smallness of scale in comparison with the vastness of significance is emphasised throughout this passage; this corresponds to the contrast between the fragility of the timber and the raging seas it masters, and between the humility of the cross and its triumph. Leaf's Iliad has a pleasant note, quoting from Schliemann's *Ilios*, on the adjective *ênemoessan* (windy, 'windy Troy') which makes vivid a reader's picture of D.'s 'archetype of sung-heights'; 'Our wooden huts (at Hissarlik) which had been put up at the foot of the hill, well below the level of the old city, looked straight down upon the plain from a height of at least 60 feet, and the winds blew about us with such force that we often felt as if our whole settlement might be hurled down the precipice'.

Crux-mound at the node: to describe Troy as 'hill of the **56** cross' is to attribute to it, retroactively, the virtue of the hill of Calvary. There may well be a connection between node and cross; for the node is one of the two points at which the path of a planet, or of the moon, crosses the ecliptic (the sun's apparent path through the stars). The ecliptic was seen as forming a great letter chi, or cross, with the celestial equator, so that the earth was overshadowed by a huge cross.

gammadion'd castle: the *crux* and the *gammadion* go one with the other, the Christian symbol with the most ancient of Eastern symbols of beneficence (passed on to us by the Byzantines). The *gammadion* is the swastika (Sanskrit swasti, good fortune) – 'gammadion' because it is formed from the Greek letter gamma, shaped like a Roman capital L, four of these put together forming the hooked cross or *Hakenkreuz* (an ominous anticipation of the theme which is to recur in David's poetry of

56 the levelling-down of the individual and particular in favour of centralisation, technology, universal dominion, Caesarism). The original practical reason for building a gammadioned castle, i.e. one whose gate or gates can be approached only while the attacker is exposed to counter-attack from the projection of the gamma, is discussed at length in Jackson Knight's *Cumaean Gates* (in *Vergil: Epic and Anthropology*, 1967, pp. 188ff.), with illustrations, where he goes on to discuss the magical or supernatural developments of the labyrinthine idea.

the megaron and note: the 'agelastos petra' (associated with Demeter) appears in D.'s pictured 'Aphrodite in Aulis'; the long spear of the soldier in the foreground points almost directly to it, and the 'modelled cult-object' is just to the left of the spear-head. This picture is described at some length in David Blamires's *David Jones*, pp.67–9, where this passage in *The Anathemata* is referred to. It is reproduced in *Word and Image IV*. The Aphrodite is of the same type as the Aphrodite of Ana. p. 57, 'florid she breached'. The title of the picture is a little worrying, for the substitution of Aphrodite for Iphigeneia seems a little high-handed.

'My intention', writes D., 'in changing Iphigeneia to Aphrodite in the title was to include *all* female cult-figures, as I have written somewhere the figure is all goddesses rolled into one – wounded of necessity as are all things worthy of our worship – she's mother-figure and *virgo inter virgines* – the pierced woman and mother & all her foretypes. She is "Elen the bracelet-giver" of I.P. also, & also the many-wounded Mair, Rhiannon of the *Mabinogion, Ceidwades Wen, mundi Domina*, "not a puff of wind without her" in L. of P. section. p.128. In *The Ana.*, the Lady of the Pool refers to Our Lady as comprehending in herself all the potent pre-Xtian cult-figures and their sufferings:

> She's as she of Aulis, master:
> not a puff of wind without her!
> her fiat is our fortune, sir: like Helen's face
> t'was that as launched the ship.

. . . I quote the line only as having *a bearing* on my reason for **56**
changing Iphigeneia to Aphrodite in the title of that watercolour.
I remember being rather pleased with "not a puff of wind without her". Odd how one likes certain chance lines and suppose it
is because one feels most of one's attempts may be outers or
some not on the bloody target at all.'

According to Apollodorus, writing probably in the first century of our era, (so Frazer, in the Loeb edition, with his translation and notes), it was on the Laughless Rock that Demeter
sat, when she came to Eleusis during her search for ravished
Persephone; but see below, comment on *Ana.* p.230, 'our
chrism'd Triptolemus', and *Ana.* pp. 58, 102, 104.

The adjective *agelastos* and the nature and position of the
rock are discussed also in N. J. Richardson's edition of the
Homeric Hymn to Demeter (Oxford, 1974), pp. 219–21.

megaron is the normal Homeric word for the great hall of
a princely dwelling. *Margaron, margarites*, is our Margaret,
pearl; so that to D., with his affection for the Middle English
poem *Pearl*, Helen is rightly 'a precios pyece in perles pyght'
or the pearl itself.

echelon'd Skaian: the Skaian Gate of Troy, 'echelon'd',
i.e. with the walls or entrances staggered, as in 'gammadion'd'.
Hector leans his shield (Iliad 22.97) *pyrgôi epi prouchonti*,
against the projecting wall – 'shimmer of bronze glared from the
walled embrasure where Hector stood'.

Hector the Wall is etymologically justified, Hector meaning
he who holds fast (so *hektores* is applied to anchors), and Hector's
part in the Iliad is to be the bulwark of Troy – *oios gar eryeto
Ilion Hektor*, for Hector alone was Troy's warden.

Helen the Moon: for the identification of Helen with the
moon (Elene, Selene) see Jackson Knight's *Vergil's Troy*
(*Vergil, epic and anthropology*, pp. 88–91), a passage which raises
interesting speculations about Vergil's treatment of Helen and
Homer's. The difference between the hated traitress of the
Second and Sixth Aeneid, and the god-blinded unhappy victim
of the Iliad, between, too, both those Helens and the cult-figure

of the moon-, tree-, and light-goddess, illustrates the difference between legend and myth, in D.'s sense of the latter.

57   **traversed Hissarlik . . . revetted:** the adjectives continue the earlier 'gammadion'd' reference. 'Revetted', like 'echelon'd' earlier, is an *I.P.* word, used of trenches and fire-bays. 'anguish-heights': the force of 'anguish' is made clear by *Ana.* p.233 n.1 and the context to which that note applies; we would not be going too far if we were to say that its use here is a bold linking of Troy and the hill of Calvary, even of Hector and Christ.

matrix we have met before, on p.50. **Oppida** (towns), used, appropriately of walled towns such as Troy, rising up from a plain. 'For me, *oppida* evokes the powerful constructions of which Caesar talks about in the *Gallic War*, Vercingetorix etc. and also that *huge* defence work at Maiden Castle – after the Claudian invasion. How the P.B.I. of the Roman army took that one shows how "the Legion" were equal to any task.' (D.)

West-saga sums up the position of Troy as source and symbol of all Western poetry, organisation, technical and artistic development: and the use of 'technic' is a reminder of the desolation (see the opening poem of the *S.L.*) which will inevitably come with technological supremacy.

We should not leave this Ilian passage without noting two Vergilian parallels. The first is the obvious reference, annotated by D., to the bay-tree, the altar and the water, in the courtyard of Priam's palace; as D. points out, Vergil makes this into a Roman atrium, which was roofed. Professor R. G. Austin, in his commentary on Book 2, reminds us of the famous tree in the parish church of Ross-on-Wye, which projects through the roof. Transferred to a Roman setting, the tree was under the impluvium, the opening in the roof and the stone basin beneath it. The altar was the altar of Zeus Herkeios (of the fenced enclosure – like D.'s favourite 'wattles'), where again we meet the root of Hector. Here, too, we cannot but think of Capel-y-ffin (stone, water, tree) and D.'s much-quoted words (in *Word and Image IV*, for example), 'It was at this propitious time [1924–6] that circumstances occasioned my living in Nant Honddu, there

to feel the impact of the strong hill-rhythms and the bright
counter-rhythms of the afonydd dyffroed [the water brooks]
which make so much of Wales such a "plurabelle".'

'That bay-tree', he says again, 'recalls in me the Welsh captain
in Richard II, "the bay-trees in our country are all wither'd And
meteors fright the fixed stars of heaven" [Act 2.4.8].' There is,
in fact, a connection through another Vergilian passage,
Aeneid 7.59ff: the magical bay-tree in the inner court of King
Latinus. D., in his modesty, said that his friends exaggerated
his knowledge of the classics; but what he knew of them he knew
by making it completely his own, and he was quick as a stoat to
seize the appropriateness, for his purpose, of any word, phrase
or idea. In this passage Vergil says that 'Ipse ferebatur Phoebo
sacrasse Latinus, Laurentisque ab ea nomen posuisse colonis' –
it was said, had himself dedicated the laurel to Phoebus, and
from that tree had given his settlers the name Laurentes. The
line from Priam's tree to Latinus's, from Troy to Italy, and so to
Wales, is precisely the line D. would pick up from the Welsh
bay-trees of the captain in Richard II.

The second parallel is between the pathos of this 'little
Hissarlik' episode and the Vergilian pathos of Aeneas's visit
to Evander in the Eighth Aeneid. In need of allies, Aeneas has
been told to seek help from Evander, who had come from Arcadia
many years earlier and settled in Italy. (Readers of Trollope
will remember 'quod minime reris, Graia pandetur ab urbe').
Evander's little city was built on the site of what was later to be
great Rome and, poor though it was, it had been helped by, and
had entertained, Hercules himself. Welcoming Aeneas, Evander
uses words which have the same emotional force as D.'s
invocation of this 'least of acclivities', and moved Dryden to
grand words of praise. 'For my part, I am lost in the admiration
of it (8.364–5): I contemn the world when I think of it, and
myself when I translate it'. Vergil insists on the poverty and
richness of Evander, as D. does on the smallness, grandeur and
dearness of Troy. The Vergilian lines are:

'Aude, hospes, contemnere opes, et te quoque dignum

57   Finge deo, rebusque veni non asper egenis'
which Dryden translates (not too happily, as he feared)
   'Dare to be poor; accept our homely food,
   Which feasted him, and emulate a god.'

It is, to my mind, odd that when D. took over as part of his material the story of the connection between Troy, Aeneas's descendant Brutus, and Albion, culminating and ending – or ending that stage – in the hero-of-failure Arthur, he did not make more of Aeneas himself: for the parallel between Arthur's mission and that of Aeneas, between the latter's foundation of the West as part of a divine plan and the former's rescue of the plan, between the nobility of the two figures as presented in literature – these seem matters to which D. could not possibly be blind. Sad to say, however, there are few to champion Aeneas, for all his very special position in the Iliad and his rock-like *pietas* in the Aeneid.

With line 5 of p.57, we are reminded that all these 'help-heights' are *down*: down because the poet is looking forward to a new ice-ages. By one of the usual neatly 'scarfed' transitions, we are introduced to the elaboration of the theme stated at the head of p.55 (Great Summer . . . Great Winter), the aeons of vast climatic changes.

sheet-darkt Hellespont: (and cf. on the next page, 'storm-dark sea') – the Homeric spirit is maintained by the choice of 'sheet-darkt', for the Hellespont here is not the narrows but Homer's broad (platys) Hellespont, over which Argives and Trojans looked from the windy plain of battle, and the expanse is dark with the sheet-ice. Moreover, the form of the adjective is Homeric, of the same shape as Homer's *oinops*, applied to the sea and often translated 'wine-dark'; so that under cover of this echo, the poet can introduce the darkness of the sheet-ice for the broad, flat, open sea, and the pack-ice for the Cyclades, themselves a pack of islands. We now see the force of the 'Great Winter', earlier, and the allegory (see note 1, p.58) of a complete freeze-up of culture.

And where, from the potent flotsam: the birth of Aphro-

dite from the sea – so Cyprus, where the goddess came ashore, 57
and her most famous shrine at Paphos, will be covered with ice,
and the whales will blow as in the Arctic and Antarctic. In
'potent' we have both the Christian *Virgo potens* and, possibly, a
suggestion that the flotsam is potent from having received the
virility of Uranus when he was castrated by Cronos. 'Florid'
keeps close to the simple, original meaning of *florida* (close,
indeed, to *Flora Dea* in sound) as flowery, beautiful, without the
over-exuberance we sometimes attach to the word, as we do in
'flowery speech'. In connection with this passage, D. would
express his amused delight in what Dickens's Scrooge said to
the ghost of his former partner, 'Don't be flowery, Jacob'.

florid she breached: all are familiar with 'There she blows!
There she breaches!' – but a pleasant Vergilian shade can be
spread over 'florid' from pp. 87–9 of Warde Fowler's *Virgil's
Gathering of the Clans*, 1916. W.F. refers to Henry on the
subject of the word *florentes* (*et florentes aere catervas*, and the
bronze-flowering squadrons) in Vergil's description in the
seventh Aeneid, of Camilla's entry. Henry notes that '*florere* is
anthein' and both words preserve the secondary sense of scent
and the freshness of the flower-garden. 'I would add', says
Warde Fowler, 'that while words like "fulgentes" or "splenden-
tes" give the effect produced without a hint of what produces it,
"florentes" suggests life and beauty, young life and fresh beauty,
as the organic cause'. To me, a delightful attachment to D.'s
'florid'.

glaciation cones her (i.e. Aphrodite's) *own Thebes*: under
the meaning 'covers with a cone of ice' lies an allusion to the
cone as a representation of Aphrodite. (I had just been looking
at an illustration of a Cyprian coin of Caracalla, emperor 211–17,
which shows a large cone standing in the centre of a stylised
temple.) On these aniconic (not in human likeness) representa-
tions of deities, see T. B. L. Webster's *From Mycenae to Homer*
(1964), pp. 41–2. Aphrodite was certainly shown as armed, and
was the goddess of seafarers and fishermen. Her title Aphrodite
Panoplios (armed) sharpens the point of 'potent' above.

57 **loess drifts Leo-gate:** the fine wind-driven loam drifts over the famous Lion Gate at Mycenae.

With **montes . . . et omnes colles** there is an open move into the Christian tradition (Vulgate: e.g. Psalm 148, Laudate Dominum montes et omnes colles – which comes, appropriately, immediately after *ignis, grando, nix, glacies, spiritus procellarum, quae faciunt verbum ejus,* fire and hail; snow, and vapour; stormy wind fulfilling his word.

hautes eagle-heights has a Pyrenean-epic ring that we cannot determine more closely, except that D. (as he says in a letter 11 August 1974) wanted the two sounds *hautes* and *heights,* did *not* want any suggestion of Alps or Switzerland, and thought of the Pyrenean heights he saw when staying at Salies de Béarn and near Lourdes: and one reader at least, who walked with three close friends of D. through the pass of Roncesvalles, must think of the eagles swooping over the ground where Roland stood with Oliver and Turpin. 'Halt sunt li pui, et li val tenebrus', the hills are high and the valleys are full of darkness.

Lambourn Down: often regarded as the site of the battle of 'Mount Badon', where, about the year 500, the Romano-Britons under Arthur may have defeated the Saxons and won a respite for Christianity: brilliantly re-drawn by Masefield in his *Badon Parchment.* Bredon Hill, between Tewkesbury, is topped by an iron-age fort (Banbury Castle) where there appears to have been a massacre of the Belgae.

as solitary tump, so massif: 'tump', according to the O.E.D. is a western or west midland word, not Welsh. D. took the word, for a great mass of hill, from 'The Tump' which closes the head of the Honddu valley, above Capel-y-ffin; it appears in water-colours of the twenties (e.g. 'Tir y Blaenau', reproduced in the 1974 D.J. *Agenda*); and cf. 'The Tutelar of the Place', in *S.L.,* p.59; 'From this tump she [Tellus] answers Jac o' the Tump only if he call Great-Jill-of-the-tump-that-bare-me'. 'massif' as in 'Massif Central' (Teilhard's home, incidentally; and he, too, was moved by the notion of the sacred 'help-height' and saw Tellus herself as a great altar.)

und icy counter-drag: 'that was an attempt to reinforce
the allusion to the Germanic association of the adjacent words
"stress" and "drag", "Sturm und Drang" and p.58 "storm-darkt
sea" . . . I wanted to hold the reader up slightly on that word.
I wanted a word that had a more positive sound than "and" as
usually pronounced in English' (D.). He comments here, not
remembering that he himself wrote the sentence just quoted,
'Good, for quite informed chaps have sometimes said why the
lapse into German *und*, not seeing that "icy counter-drag" recalled old Jerry's *Sturm und Drang*.' There is a softened version
of this later, *Ana.* p.197, of Helen the Moon, 'because of her the
stress and drag' (of the tides).

Lord! what a morning: cf. the negro spiritual which starts, **58**
'Oh, Lord, what a morning . . .'

The consummation in ice described in this parenthesis
(pp. 55–8) is the complement of the Stoics' *ekpyrôsis* (the day
which *solvet saeclum in favilla*), the periodic general conflagration. But as the *Dies Irae* holds out hope ('mihi quoque spem
dedisti') so here, too, there is hope in the allegory of a new
continental (Oberland, uplands) emergence. See note 1, which
further emphasises the impermanence of material havens;
for the note makes it clear that the poet looks both back to
and forward to the time when the heights are down. When the
parentheses close at 'new-founded Oberland', we return to the
time and place of the Last Supper.

unabiding Omphalos: the other most important of the
many 'navel-stones' marking the centre of the earth's surface was
at Delphi: hence the association with 'laughless rock', akin to the
'calling rock' at Delphi (see comment on *Ana.* p.230).

the lord-out-of-Ur: Abraham's journey from Ur of the
Chaldees (Genesis 11–12) is, for the poet, where our West
comes in, the 'advanced details' of *Ana.* p.190. The date to
which we have now returned in the poem is determined as the
year of the Crucifixion (say A.D. 27) by the two thousand years
since the migration of the first of patriarchs. The corresponding
date of **twenty millennia** since the 'first examples of visual **59**

59 art' (p.59 n.1) introduces the next theme, the evolution of man the maker, in both the technical and poetic senses of the word. It was in 1929 that D. first read in Christopher Dawson's *Progress and Religion:* 'If man is essentially a tool-using animal, the tool is from the beginning that of the artist, no less than that of the labourer'. Dawson's judgment of Spengler makes it clear how wide is the gulf that separates D., in spite of his magpie-like borrowings, from the loquacious German. 'Since the first barley-mow', at the foot of p.58, is attached to the opening lines of p.59, for it is a reminder of *colere, cultus*, agriculture and artefacture, artefacture and sacrament, with which the poem opened, and with which this section (as the whole poem) will end: (*Ana.* p.82) 'How else . . . should his barlies grow / who said / I am your Bread.'

Hausname: we might say, as with the Latin *gens*, 'clan-name' (cf. p.113, where the word is applied to a Saxon invader). 'Nomen' and '*fecit*-mark' are borrowed from the lettering stamped on Romano-Gaulish or British pottery, such as 'Satto fecit', 'Ripanus fecit', etc., the potter's *nomen* being followed by 'fecit' (made).

whose man-hands god-handled: as clear an affirmation as one could wish of the reflection in human artefacture of the divine creation.

This page is well annotated by D., but there is some complexity in the reference to the blue Danube (with the Strauss and 'gay Vindobona' – Vienna – allusion in the next paragraph). The Danube (Donau) is feminine: the two ancient names for the river, Ister and Danubius, are both masculine, so that 'Romanitas' may be said to have 'manned' *her* stream. 'Manned', however, may bear the sense (as in 'manning a ship') of providing with a sailing complement; 'lateen'd', again, may be taken as 'expressed in Latin' or as 'subjected to the lateen sail', for the *voile latine* is characteristic of the Mediterranean. 'It was a bit of luck that one could make the lateen sail evoke the Latin lingua & hands that manned the Roman craft, that and the change in gender in the grammatical sense. I remember labouring with this bit & how to cover these very differing matters within as compact as possible the form of the poiesis.' (D.)

the ramshackle last phases: 'ramshackle' was used in a Jingo speech by Lloyd George, of the Austro-Hungarian Empire: 'we'll tear down their ramshackle Empire'. The adjective remained with D., who never wasted anything: in a note, written much later, about the so-called 'prospectors' who were thought to be responsible for the diffusion of megaliths, he says, 'The word "prospector" seems to have a poetic appropriateness with regard to the dissemination of that culture, for some form of commercialism seems to have been bound up with it, and, like the "prospectors" of more ramshackle and more recent 'cultures', this solemn burial-culture was semi-global in extent, and tended to be maritime'. As the 'ramshackle last phases' are 'the sagging end of the chapter's close' of p.49, so 'the young-time' is the 'sap-years' of the early middle age.

the Years of the City: D. takes the date of the foundation of Rome as 753 B.C.

her we declare? Who else? (with the magnificent note); **60** an anticipation of the *How else* argument, later, pp. 75ff. However far back we go in the history of man master-of-plastic, we find the same, or some shadow of the same, supreme feminine whom we now worship. In the paragraph 'And see how they run' (starting from the three blind mice of the nursery rhyme) reference is made to the practical purpose of cave-drawings, the ensuring of success by graphic representation. (The use of the word 'wedded' may remind us that as early as the 'vaults of Lascaux' there is a union of the two complementary, and yet potentially conflicting, factors of the useful and the gratuitous.). For 'within, in an unbloody manner' cf. *Epoch and Artist*, p.169: 'It is said of the eucharistic signs that they are a showing forth of something "in an unbloody manner". That particular instance from the domain of theological definition might, *mutatis mutandis*, be used to help us to understand better something of the function, in general, of Ars as a shower-forth.' The analogy is expressed even more plainly at the head of this page in 'under

60 the species of worked lime-rock' ('under the species of bread
and wine'). To this we may attatch Peter Levi's words in
Westminster Cathedral at the solemn requiem on 13 December
1974: 'He [the priest] does in another form what the painters in
the cave at Lascaux already did for their fellows, only now
substantially'. He then quoted this passage from p.60 and asked,
'Is it very remote to illuminate the early emergence of man on
this planet from what we understand of the Mass ?'

O the Academies!: there is a wry looking-forward to Helle-
nism (cf. *Ana.* p.94, where fifth-century Greek sculpture has
'grandeurs enough and to snare: West-academic'), and the notion
that in some sense or other 'all that is valuable derives from an
Hellenistic norm', the 'academic' notion as opposed to the notion that there are endless metamorphoses of equally valuable
art-forms dictated by differentiation of locality and tradition.
The exclamation calls for lengthy comment, best provided in
D.'s review of Berenson's *Aesthetics and History* (*Epoch and
Artist*, pp. 267–77); pages 274–5 apply particularly to this
passage and to pp. 90–95.

D. writes: '. . . but my outcry 'O the Academies' was, so to
say, automatic when I considered the art of these men of the
Aurignacian culture & hunters on the tundra and the depiction
in the inmost caves of the animals hunted, the artists being
rather as mass-priests in the sense of making artefactions that
would literally aid by their work the strenuous and dangerous
work of the hunters far on the ringing tundra. For if they failed
there would be no life-giving food to sustain the tribe; in short,
the work on the tundra and the work within the limestone
caverns were essential to the life of that culture, whereas the
"Academies", broadly speaking, [were] hardly a necessity [to]
folk, but cultivated an art patronised by a "civilisation" [D. uses
the word, following Spengler, in contrast with 'culture'] at a
certain phase of its development, an Art which, at its best,
could be of much beauty . . . Your feeling that the words "O
God! O the Academies!" had some echo of Maritain or something French might well be based on some forgotten thing.

But, for me, writing this I suppose in 1947 or 1948 in Mr Carlile's house on Harrow Hill, they came as a natural exclamation, but that does not rule out a forgotten connection within the mind of the 1920's or '30's when Maritain was more in our minds.' (The connection is with Maritain's treatment of artist and artisan, and the elevation (with the Academies) into fine arts of what had in antiquity and the Schools been regarded as servile arts; see *Art et Scolastique*, pp. 70, 272–5 (pp. 62, 137–40 of John O'Connor's translation, read by D.).

A somewhat different light, parallel rather than conflicting, is thrown on these palaeolithic artefacts by Professor E. O. James in the first chapter of his *Sacrament and Sacrifice*, a book which adds greatly to a reader's understanding of the place occupied in D.'s thought by the significant act. In particular (pp. 21–22) Professor James sees as a conclusive argument against such things being regarded primarily as works of art precisely what D. would regard as equally conclusive in a contrary sense, 'their having been created in the most inaccessible and distant chambers, nooks and crannies of tortuous caverns.'

Running on from the 'marvel-day' of p.60, p.61 introduces a **61** figure or event dear to Teilhard, Prometheus and the use of fire in the 'Easter of Technics' (the note explains the reference to Holy Saturday and Easter).

the first New Fire wormed: 'wormed', for the first little creeping glow of red, followed by the curl of flame and wisp of smoke in the charcoal. We read in an unpublished MS., 'long long before, long anterior and before again, before the early whirling sticks caught the worm of fire'.

In this discovery we have the first appearance of the 'utile': another example of our universal dialectic, for the very invention (fire and the working of metals) that made culture possible inevitably started the technical progress that was to annihilate it.

From here until p.66, when the geography becomes more precisely defined, we run through the development of man, side by side with the geological development of the earth. And in these pages man is considered as a creature progressing towards

61 'sacramental' man: and he is questioned, the poet wondering how far the first evidence of artefacture is evidence of rite and culture. This is, again, the 'groping syntax' with which the poem opens; nor do I think that it is going too far to say that the progression is towards the supreme artifex, the incarnate Christ, and his supreme artefact. There is little obscurity here (in the sense of recondite allusions) but great intricacy; the chronology (necessarily approximate) and the cycles of change (e.g. 'the boreal oscillations' at the head of p.62) need to be followed with care.

    cupped the ritual stones: 'The name "cup-marks" has been given to the small circular artificial pittings found in some megaliths – they are presumably of ritual intention'. (MS. note by D.).

    for the faithful departed: concern for the dead, marked by even the vestige of a ritual act, is taken by D. as specific to mankind. (See *Epoch and Artist*, pp. 155–7, a long paragraph on the theme that it is 'on account of the anthropic sign-making that we first suspect that anthropos has some part in a without-endness'.) Ritual, as opposed to functional or what D. would call 'utile'. 'Poor Angharad or Sally or Jill', he writes in *Use and Sign* of one whose Johnny has decided *not* to give her a bunch of blue ribbons to tie up her bonny brown hair, for on the way he has been converted to the strictly utile. 'She were better affianced to a baboon, for even these primates have, according to certain observers, an elementary perception of otherness in that they are said to ceremonially mourn their dead.' 'For the faithful departed' (*pro omnibus fidelibus Christianis vivis atque defunctis*) takes that primordial concern to its supreme expression in the Roman Mass.

    What, from this one's cranial data: with this paragraph cf. *Ana.* p.65, 'By the uteral marks . . . viatic meats'. The 'ritual' is emphasised by the wording: 'journey-food' (*viaticum*: and the Eucharist is the soul's viaticum); '*pietas*' (dutiful observance), a word that cannot be used without a memory of Aeneas and the sacred images he saved from Troy; 'gloss', 'rubric' and 'use' (as we speak of 'the use of Sarum').

Heidelberg gaffer: gaffer, as being the oldest of the types of 'man' that are mentioned. 'Piltdown': the controversial Piltdown skull (1912). 'The girl from Lime Street' refers to the 'London skull' found in 1925 when the foundations of the Lloyds building were excavated, between Leadenhall Street and Lime Street. 'The eight Carmel fathers' (eight or twelve?) were found in 1931–2 in caves at the foot of Mount Carmel in Palestine. The unsaid third term, 'spiritual relationship', has a certain weight here, even though barely suggested as the accompaniment to 'consanguinity' and 'affinity'.

From **cranial data** to the end of the first paragraph of p.63, the question is asked, 'At what stage can we say that man is now created as man?'

palmy arbours began again to pine: it is quite possible 62 that this play on Kipling's 'Beneath whose awful Hand we hold Dominion over palm and pine' may be connected with the fact that when D. was in Palestine in 1934, it was a British mandated territory: though the words, as used here, refer to the 'pining' of palm trees which are unable to survive as the ice again spreads. In such pieces as 'The Tribune's Visitation', and even more clearly in much unpublished MSS., it is clear that D., without ever saying so in any well-defined way, saw a parallel between Roman and British colonial administration, and was not blind to the *pietas* of the best administrators, even though he detested the commercial megalopolis they served.

groping disciplina: (the latter word in the sense of method of instruction or learning) – another echo of the 'groping syntax' of p.49. 'proto-routes': of culture-diffusion; 'lithic foci': the hearths of stone-age man.

Cronos: there was confusion in antiquity between Cronos, youngest son of Uranus and Gaia, and Chronos, time: of which D. regularly takes advantage.

see how his lemmings run: the animals are forced by the glaciation to move southwards, and again, when Arctic conditions disappear, to move northwards. The lemmings are chosen for the repetition of the 'see how they run' of p.60 because of their blind and seld-destructive migrations. 'from south of the sixties, from into the forties': the sixtieth parallel runs through Leningrad, Oslo and the southern tip of the Shetlands; the fortieth, through Ankara, just south of Taranto and Madrid; i.e. enclosing what D. calls 'our dear West'.

the five men of Jutland: cf. *The Bog People*, by P. V. Glob (1969, original Danish, 1965), though this is embroidering D's reference. 'Can't remember, but a jacket and a pair of trousers preserved in the peat, late pre-historic. There is a photograph in Robin Hodgkin's two-vol. Hist. of Anglo-Saxon England & as some of the barbarian invaders came from Jutland it was of interest to see the clothes of chaps in Jutland.' (D.)

A further hint of rite is given by the use of 'cope' in 'the bear-coped Gilyak' (a Siberian people).

the world's a stage: a metaphor to be continued on p.63 with 'the mimes', 'green room', 'flats' etc.; 'the Master of Harlequinade' (p.63) neatly picking up the 'transformed scenes' (of the pantomine) from here. W.J.K. points out the modern source of the old metaphor: 'When did creatures recognisably human first begin to play their part against this geological background? . . . But with the scene set for the Ice Age man steps well onto the stage and begins the play in which we ourselves are acting.' (Jacquetta and Christopher Hawkes, *Prehistoric Britain*, 1948, p.8: cf. references in the Preface, pp. 36–7 and 79n.)

The first paragraph, which puts the question directly, should have been read by Teilhard. That the Creator, 'himself not made', should be likened to the Master of Harlequinade, a purely gratuitous drama, is peculiarly happy.

63   **the draughty flats:** in both the geographical and theatrical sense (and both are draughty). There is a similar combination in 'the ageless cherubs': both the old cartographers' conventional representation of the winds blowing from the four corners, and the traditional theatrical ornamentation.

antlered mummers: as the cherubs 'agelessly' brought the **63**
warm south winds, so we revert to an endlessly long period of
cold; the Christmas mummers glow in the frost – mummers, as
in Hardy's *Return of the Native*; antlered, like the horned Herne
the Hunter (who will re-appear on *Ana.* p.113 as the *Wilde
Jäger*), associated with that season. Why the Greek *hêmera* for
'day'? Partly because the trisyllable ending is stronger, and
partly because the very English 'mummers' is embraced by the
Latin *Januarius* and Greek *hêmera*.

Vorzeit: the notion of the 'harlequinade' is carried on into
the 'fore-time' masque, through the 'Funeral Games' (above),
into the 'cosmic introit' (the introit is, appropriately, the true
beginning of the Mass and the first part to be *sung*) and so to the
final, fully Christian metaphor of the antiphon and response of
the Divine Office: all these being applied to the cycles of climatic
change. So the Dog (Sirius, the dog-star of summer, whose heliacal rising coincides with the hottest days in our west) calls on
fire to bless the Lord ('*Benedicite ignis*') and is answered by the
Bear, the cold circumpolar constellation, with a similar sum-
mons to the cold (*frigus*) – this from the *Benedicite*, the song of
the three young men in the furnace (Daniel 3.52–90, Vulg.).

As so often, the metaphor is not stressed without first being
introduced incidentally: stage, transformation scene, pantomine,
properties, set, mimes, dance, music, chant.

Col canto: with the *canto fermo* or plainsong. 'Schola' ('all
the boreal schola') is used of the *schola cantorum*, a school of
music attached to a great church, and so a choir. The metaphor
from the modes of plainsong is clear (cf. *Ana.* p.143 and n., and
the current edn. of Grove's Dictionary of Music): the tonic or
key-note, which determines the mode, the dominant or recita-
tive note, the fifth, the final or cadence. These correspond to the
'vast sway' from one meteorological extreme to another, the week
of the 'hebdomodarius' being extended to endless aeons.
'Unmeasured' is an exact word for the unbarred music of plainsong and early polyphony, where movement is freer and parts
are rhythmically more independent than in later music.

Cantor Notus and Favonius . . . numina: the south and west winds, seen as supernatural beings; 'south-aisled' continues the metaphor of the choir. This line is uncommonly reminiscent of *The Rime of the Ancient Mariner* and D.'s *Introduction* to it. Coleridge's 'lonesome spirit from the South Pole' becomes D.'s 'numen'.

64   Page 64 and n. should be read in the light of the 'General Note to Section 1', p.82.

con flora calida . . . fauna fria: the ingenious inter-twining of capital and lower-case initials continues the antiphonal pattern, and emphasises the names of the two goddesses and the things they stand for. There is a neat chiasmus (diagonal arrangement, or criss-cross, as in the letter chi): line 1 (*con flora calida*) goes with line 4 (*con fauna fria*), and line 2 (*mit warmer Fauna*) with line 3 (*mit kalter Flora*), and at the same time line 1 goes with line 3, and line 2 with line 4.

D. writes: 'the reason (for the Spanish and German) is accidental except that I like the sound of contrasted forms for cold and hot & it so happened that a book about glacial and geological changes, in I think T.'s house, has a note from a German scholar translated into Spanish, and also because Tiger Dawson [i.e. Christopher Dawson: another friend, after meeting Dawson for the first time and being overwhelmed by his learning, exclaimed 'What a tiger!'; cf. *Ana.* p.137, where the hoarded phrase finds a very different use] had told me (I *think* it's mentioned in his *Age of the Gods*) that the earliest known buildings with cupola'd roofs were in southern Spain at an incredibly early period either in the late Palaeolithic or early Neolithic epochs – then the technique was forgotten for many centuries . . . so you see, while it was due to a number of accidents that I used these terms, they happened to be just what I wanted as materia poetica, the swaying to and fro over huge periods of time of the various "ice ages", the wide areas of tundra followed by a bit of a warm up and then a great ice offensive; "who is able to abide his frost?" You guessed rightly that Jerry was lurking somewhere in my use of the words, but in a very roundabout way.'

Dawson's *The Age of the Gods* was published, and read by **64**
D., in 1928. It was from this that he drew his general picture of
the spread of human culture and much of the detail that appears
in his writing: the cupola tombs in Spain, for example (Dawson,
p.214) and (pp. 215–16) the 'prospectors', ('the Sumer director', 'the company-promoter from the Persian Gulf') who are
behind the trading voyages described in this voyage and are a
foreshadowing of the 'prospectors of more ramshackle and more
recent cultures', when the vast difference in scale of activity has
brought a devastating change in quality. Nearly thirty years
(which included the writing of *In Parenthesis*) lay between this
reading and the final version of *The Anathemata*, but during all
that time the main idea, and some of the phraseology, had been
nursed in the poet's mind.

The literal meaning is a little obscured by the page-turn
from 63 to 64: when the warm winds (Notus and Favonius)
are blowing, it is with the warm flowers and warm beasts. When
the Bear answers, 'Bless the Lord, cold', the fur-wrapped choir
in stalls of ice (crystallos) on the gospel side (gospel, because that
is the north side) sings with cold flora, cold beasts.

where Thames falls into Rhine: i.e. before the separation
of Britain as an island. The spinning and weaving of wool
reaches far back into the history of primitive man, and when it is
profitable, in this great cold, to make a 'corner' in woolly
skins ('ulotrichious hides') sewn (vegetable) fibre is superfluous.

Tellus: Teilhard had the same feeling as D. for Tellus Mater,
the Italian Earth Mother in whom Demeter re-appears. He
speaks of man as evolving towards 'Tellurian' man.

elect and plucked-out: here there is the Biblical insistence
on the Creator's free choice (cf. the early reference to Abraham
and the Covenant, p.58). D. goes on to consider how far back in
time the choice extends, and concludes that not one will be lost
of all 'whose works follow them'.

ideate begetting is also a Teilhardian concept, T. being
at pains to establish that ideological, or psychic, evolution, by
memory, collective awareness, education, is a true continuation

64 of biological evolution. 'I see how it is that reviewers of my stuff (especially U.S. ones) note my Teilhardian connections. That's o.k., but this stuff *The Anathemata* was written in 1947 or so. So a decade before I had heard of Teilhard. [The English translation of *The Phenomenon of Man* was published in 1959, four years after it appeared in French.] Not that it matters, but may as well get the dating more or less right. Whatever was Teilhardian in my stuff was accidental – I dont mean that I disapprove of that very, very great mind. But my approach was that of a chap, an artist perhaps, who was and is very attracted to the endless "stratification" in geology or other matter. "Wonder what *underlies* that yarn or that behaviour etc. etc.".' (D.)

The point is not any direct connection with T., but simply that both writers have the same overpowering concern for the cosmos as a rational unity (*rationabilis*). T. is constantly saying that any attitude to cosmic development which is not 'worthy of the human spirit', not acceptable psychologically as well as rationally, is suicidal. And T., like D., brings into one all the female cult-figures; he would have recognised the force of D.'s 'not a puff of wind without her': and this in spite of his blindness to what is meant by poiesis and in spite of his unbounded admiration for man's technological achievements. T., like D., could say, 'I have said to the perfected steel, be my sister', but, unlike D., he stood happily by his offer and did not find 'the glazed work unrefined and the terrible crystal a stage-paste'. Cf. T.'s shocking essay, 'The spiritual repercussions of the atom bomb'.

had they the suffrage: 'suffrage' in the original (English) sense of 'liturgical petition': by what rote, i.e. in virtue of what custom, were such men in a position to make a ritual invocation which we may compare to that with which the poem opens, 'adscriptam, ratam, rationabilem . . .'? It may well be that the notion of being 'enlisted' or 'inscribed' which is present in 'adscriptam' allows the further suggestion of 'suffrage' as 'vote or choice', with a corresponding link between 'rote' and 'rota', roll or roster.

D. is investigating what he calls in *Epoch and Artist*, p.90,   **64**
'the kind of creature man is at his deepest foundations – at
his determining foundations – the foundations of his nature as
the animal-who-is-man-the-artist,' For the 'intransitivity and
gratuitousness in man's art that is the sign of man's unique-
ness' as opposed to the 'ingenuity of certain beast-made works'
in which the making is wholly functional, see *Epoch and Artist*,
pp. 149–50 and p.88. This was a subject that D. could never
leave alone: he first formulated his ideas on the arts and the
nature of man as fundamentally the artist, in Thomistic terms,
and found it difficult to accommodate a vocabulary derived
from an age that ignored the modern distinction between the
fine and the useful arts to an age in which that distinction is
generally the first to be made.

It should not be forgotten, however, that D.'s 'gratuitous'
is an accompaniment to, or in addition to, that quality which is
manifest in the 'right ordering of things to be made': in an
almost over-simplified way this is seen in the phrase at the foot of
this page, 'the uteral marks that make the covering stone an
artefact', i.e. the womb-like cup-marks show that the covering
stone is both 'use' and 'sign'. The devotion of the workman to
the *bonum operis*, the good of the work, which we see when the
craft of the shipwright is glorified in the 'Redriff' section, argues
a similar awareness of something other than, and transcending,
the good of the worker, the *bonum operantis*; and the satisfying
of that 'other' is an equally gratuitous act.

Since D. has been using the metaphor of Gregorian chant,
and we have stumbled once more on the conflict of the functional
and the gratuitous, this may be an appropriate moment to borrow (with her permission) what N. K. Sandars borrowed from
Imogen Holst, who herself is quoting from A. Z. Idelsohn's
Jewish Music. This will now come to the reader at fourth hand,
but it is a valuable sign-post showing the direction in which the
reconciliation of the two may be found. Thus:

'Gregorian reciting-tones were made for use, not for ornament. As with street cries, their memorable patterns have

grown from the practical need for making the human voice
audible at a distance . . . the laziest way of transforming speech
into song is to chant each word on the same note . . . [but this]
is far more exhausting in the end, for it lacks the give-and-take-
of a two-note chant, where the relaxation of the cadence stores
up new energy for continuing'. (See N. K. Sandars. *Poems of
Heaven and Hell from Ancient Mesopotamia.* 1971, p.18.)

65 **all whose works follow them:** D. makes it plain in the note
that he adapts *opera* to mean artefacts, so that the being who
produces such *opera* (which follow him both in that he is their
cause and that they survive him), or anything in which the germ
of such artefacts may be discerned – that being is man, and so is
chosen and is not to be lost. The same idea returns on *Ana.* p.78.
'he would lose none': for D. it sets the seal upon humanity that
one can say *dona ei requiem.* The poignancy of the words here,
repeated on the next page, lies in their context, for they were
spoken by Christ immediately before he was arrested in the
Garden (John 18.9). A slightly different application of the
phrase 'would lose none' is to be found in *E. and A.*, p.243.
There it is used of 'genuine myth' – for which oxymoron some
would prefer 'poetry' – as conserver of the significant.

There is a re-handling of the same theme in *The Sleeping
Lord*, pp.71, 73, 'Donated the life signa: / the crocked viatic
meal / the flint-worked ivory agalma', . . . 'These delicate
agalma' (where D. would have preferred, and should have used,
the plural *agalmata*). The later poem may be read as an enlargement of this passage in the *Ana.*, as *The Kensington Mass* is of
the opening. Cf. also 'the penile ivory' here and the 'gleam-
white rodded ivory' (which explains the unusual 'penile') of the
S.L. Viatic is used both of primitive man's ingenuous provision
for the dead, and for the Christian's spiritual 'journey-food'.

66 **Himself at the cave-mouth:** see William Blissett's essay,
incorporating that phrase in its title, for the 'recurrent, omni-
present cave in the work of D.J.'. (*University of Toronto
Quarterly* 36 (3), 1967.)

There is a designed ambiguity in the first half of the page.

First, there is the identification of the last of the cave-dwellers **66**
as truly a sheep of the fold; and beneath this lies the suggestion,
contained in the phrase 'Himself at the cave-mouth', of the
Resurrection of Christ: the completion of the Incarnation, and
man's warrant for a corresponding incorporation in divinity.
While this is not contained in the literal meaning of the words,
a poet for whom the symbol of the cave is so manifestly full of
significance, could not have introduced the cave here, particularly with the capitalised 'Himself', and following upon an
allusion to the arrest in the Garden, without anticipating the
images that would be added by the reader. With 'father-figures'
cf. the 'Carmel fathers' of *Ana.* p.61. The metaphor of the
shepherd in Christ's words cannot have been so often used by
D. without his remembering that the Homeric hero, too, was the
poimên laôn, the shepherd of the people.

the diriment stroke: the adjective, hardly used except in
the expression 'diriment impediment' (to matrimony), meaning
severing, breaking-off, nullifying, cannot be used here without
an eye to the 'dolorous stroke' of the Grail legend, in Malory,
for example (Book 17, ch. 3). There is no exactness in the parallel
– suggested partly by D.'s affection for the Latin form of a
word – but (as with cave-mouth) there is an elusive association
with sacrifice and the identification with the whole people of one
person who suffers; here the last of the cave-dwellers falls, on
behalf of his kindred, to the gigantic beast.

D. may well have had in mind the use of the verb *dirimere*
in connection with fighting, by Caesar, Livy and Vergil: in
particular Aeneid xii. 79, *nostro dirimamus sanguine bellum*,
let us two settle this war with our own blood. It is Turnus who
speaks there, and, at the end of the poem, it is indeed a diriment
stroke (in D.'s sense) that he receives at the hands of Aeneas.

In the second paragraph, the poet turns from the evolution
of man to that of the earth he inhabits. We look forward to the
disappearance of the ice and the effect of glacial action, and
attention is concentrated on what will be the British isles, and
their geo-physical development. The use of geological terms is

careful, and it is a happy chance that the Ordovician Period (some four hundred million years ago) was named after the Ordovices, the name which Tacitus gives to the British who inhabited the part of Wales which includes Snowdon (which will appear on the next page.) 'old Paternus' and n.2: see below, *Ana.* p.71, with note, and comment.

67   **holy Deva . . . devious exit:** this word-play, with the addition of John Dee, recurs ingeniously on pp. 69 and 137 (where D.'s note calls for some qualification). Enclosed in the verbal elegancies of this first paragraph, Parthenos (Virgin), with its capital initial, retains the link with Troy and Greece, through the virgin goddess, Pallas Athene. Woodhouse and Bush in their *Variorum Commentary* on Milton annotate Lycidas v.55 as follows (Vol. II part 2, New York 1972): 'The Dee . . . was supposed to possess magic powers of divination. Camden (*Britain*, 1610, p.602) says that "Divinitie" was ascribed to the river because "now and then it changed the chanell, and thereby foreshewed a sure token of victory to the inhabitants upon it [i.e. the English and the Welsh] according as it inclined more to this side or to that . . .". Drayton (*Poly-Olbion*, 10, 186–218) recounts substantially the same superstition regarding Dee's "ominous flood"; he applies the phrase "Wizard River" to the Weaver, the rival to the Dee in "prophetick skill" (II.71, 77).'

   gestatorial couch of Camber: for Camber, see *Ana.* p.54, n. 8. Here again we have the Sleeping Lord, Snowdonia being seen as his couch, 'gestatorial': originally merely a *sella gestatoria*, or sedan chair, but borrowing a grander sense from the papal *sedia gestatoria*.

   pre-Cambrian oreos-heavers: the adjective in two senses, before Camber, and before the Cambrian period (preceding the Ordovician). To the general sense of 'heavers' (heaving up the mass of mountain) we may add the particular geological sense of 'heave', the horizontal displacement produced by a fault; cf. 'hade' etc., *Ana.* p.74., so that 'heavers' also means 'producers of heaves'. Strictly speaking, 'oreos' is incorrect, but permissible as being more euphonic than 'oros-heavers' and by analogy with 'oreogenesis', 'oread' etc.

the Combroges' epode: i.e., an epode being a grave poem', to lament the wasting-away of the Welsh people. The Combroges appear in a later unpublished MS., akin to the 'Sleeping Lord', (with which this passage, again, of the *Ana.* has kinship) as 'the innate men of the equal kindreds and the men of equal privilege'; a note expands what we have here in note 2, as follows: 'Prof. Lloyd has illuminated one use of the vexed word "Cymry" in suggesting that it may well have meant "the co-proprietors" before it was used to describe a race or was employed in its now usually accepted sense of "comrades", These free men were termed the "innate gentlemen".'

the mundus, which *sounds* like 'mound', is the pit for sacrificial offerings, found in the pile-built villages of the Terramara culture in Bronze Age Italy, and similarly at Rome, where it was looked upon as an entrance to the lower world. Here it is explanatory of hypogeum (subterranean burial-chamber). For the Terramara, see *Ana.* p.81 and n. 1.

dragons . . . Pendragon: D. connects the dragon of Wales **68** (a red dragon: hence 'bleached' for this buried Pendragon, or chief dragon) with the *draco* which the Romans borrowed from the Parthians to be the standard for the cohort. 'This was the image of a large dragon fixed upon a lance, with gaping jaws of silver, and with the rest of its body formed of coloured silk. When the wind blew down the open jaws, the body was inflated' (like the wind-sock on an airfield). (Seyffert, under *signum*). Another useful little brick in D.'s Romano-British edifice.

Annotating a 'dragon' passage in an unpublished MS., D. adds, 'It has been suggested that the name of the flag came to be applied to the officer or chief who employed it: hence "Pendragon" as a rank-name.' The passage runs as follows:

'At the disembarkation point, the green-gilled details fall in, as best they may on the shivering markers, with a bawling *optio* barking 'em into some sort of shape; and at the usual command

68 the sea-doused signifer, spitting out the briny, doubles to his
column station and ports the section's *draco*, and she droops like
a wet Monday wash on an old mare's prop – but now for a cup
full of wind she flaps a bit, but now the bright jaws drink,
   and now
she bellies fine to the breeze of Guenedota [Gwynedd, N.W.
Wales], and they see for the first time their destined totem.
   So, mate, their very signa we fetch for them . . .'
   Cf. also *Ana*. p.154 and n. 3. Graham Webster writes of these
dragon standards (p.136) and illustrates one from Trajan's
column – but it was Sarmatia, not Parthia.

   unconforming bed: (misprinted *uncomforming*, unless you
accept the, to me, unpalatable suggestion that 'com' is used to
give a Joyce-like conflation with 'uncomfortable') in the geolo-
gist's sense of the adjective, 'having two sets of rocks of different ages, usually dipping in different directions and at different angles'.

   is by the muses kept: as though Snowdon were the Welsh
Parnassus – which, indeed, it is here. The phrase must surely
have a reminiscence of another poet, which unhappily eludes me.
With this we may also read Milton, *Lycidas*, vv. 51–5, 'For
neither were ye [the nymphs] playing on the steep, Where your
old bards, the famous Druids, lie, Nor on the shaggy top of
Mona high, Nor yet where Deva spreads her wizard stream'.
I suspect that 'kept' is, by design, used in more than one sense –
tended and preserved, inhabited by (as a person would say,
in better days, 'Where does he keep ?', i.e. where are his rooms ?)
and in the sense in which we say 'She keeps her bed'; for the
muses suffer and will not emerge.

   the thick rotundities: 'And thou, all-shaking thunder,
Strike flat the thick rotundity o' the world., *King Lear*, Act 3,
sc. 2, the scene from which D. drew the epigraph on the title-
page, 'This prophecie Merlin shall make; for I live before his
time', and the storm passage on *Ana*. p.97.

   the bent flanks of space: a unique reference, in D.'s printed
work, to relativity theory. D. must have read Eddington's

Space, Time and Gravitation, which was published in 1922. 'I **68**
may have read a bit of Eddington's book – but about that time
the relativity thing was much in the air.' (D.) Gill certainly read,
and spoke of, Eddington, whom he had met in Cambridge. That
relativity was in D.'s mind is confirmed by the following from
the as yet unpublished MS. of *The Book of Balaam's Ass,*
dating from the late 30's or early 40's, in which are included
versions of what were printed later in *The Sleeping Lord* as
'A, a, a, Domine Deus' and 'From the Book of Balaam's Ass':
'. . . when a living sail turns the headland close in, to change the
shape of the small sea, sets free the constricting esplanade and
bends the rigid sea-rail to a native curvature (for space itself,
they say, leans, is kindly, with ourselves, who make wide devia-
tions to meet ourselves.)'

The adjectives *native* and *kindly* are important here, particularly if 'kindly' is taken to mean not only 'of a kindly disposition'
but also 'acting according to its kind' and 'of one kind or kin
with ourselves': and this could lead into an over-lengthy
disquisition, on Teilhard's view of the homogeneity of the
universe, so similar to D.'s, and his avoidance of the Scylla of
materialism and the Charybdis of pantheism; the progression
of the cosmos towards personalisation (T. takes the roots of this
right back to cosmic space); the foundation of metaphysics in
physics; these are all aspects of D.'s 'I have not lost of them any
single one'. Here Sir Edmund Whittaker's *Space and Spirit,*
which deals with St Thomas Aquinas's 'Five Ways', considering them in the light of developing theories of the cosmos, is
apposite. It was first published in 1946, a date that may not
be too late for D. to have used it in one of the drafts of *Balaam's
Ass,* the plan behind which is not apparent from the extract
printed in *The Sleeping Lord.* Speaking of the function of curvature in the theory of General Relativity, Whittaker writes, in
words which could well be reflected in the MS. referred to:

'In Einstein's conception, space is no longer the stage on which
the drama of physics is performed: it is itself one of the per-
formers; for gravitation, which is a physical property, is entirely

68 controlled by curvature, which is a geometrical property of space.

'In Einstein's theory of gravitation, the Newtonian concept of force is completely done away with: a free particle moves in a path determined solely by the curvature properties of space. The changes of position of the particle, in their turn, bring about changes in the curvature of space, so that the particle and space together may be regarded as a single system, whose evolution is determined by the law that the total curvature of space-time is to be the minimum; as we may say, *gravitation represents a continual effort of the universe to straighten itself out*: a statement so completely teleological that it would certainly have delighted the hearts of the schoolmen.'

the whitest of the Wanderers: of the planets, Venus. 'in-favilla day' (with the hyphen moved), the final debacle of the next paragraph, and a reminder of D.'s eschatology. 'the penultimate debacle', the last ice-age.

Arcturus deploys ... chills: as though the glaciation were directed by the circumpolar constellation Arcturus, the watcher of the Bear. Arcturus or Arctophylax, a frequent symbol in D. for the cold north, was the name the ancients gave to the constellation we now call Boötes, the plowman. We use 'Arcturus' for the brightest star in that constellation. *Putsch* is used with the same sort of association as that which attaches to 'storm-groups', used on p.90 of the Dorian invasion, to 'liquidated' on p.51, 'panzer'd lover' on p.105, 'Norman panzer-gangs' in *Epoch and Artist*, p.99, 'our ever accelerating utility-putsch' in 'Use and Sign', p.7.

dim-eyed Clio: the muse of history, for we are just emerging from pre-history into history (in the 'proto-historic transmogrification of the land-face'). On page 86 Clio will be the 'ageing midwife' who 'found her (Rhea Silvia or Ilia) nine calends gone / huge in labour', i.e. about to record the birth of Romulus and Remus.

69 **albescent:** both 'whitening' (of the ice) and 'beginning to be or to form Albion'.

Here and in the following pages, the whole of the British and **69**
Irish land-masses are emerging in the form we know. D. worked
with, and the reader needs, geological maps, as in the series of
British Regional Geology published by H.M.S.O. The exact
meaning of some phrases at the head of this page may not be
immediately apparent. 'Across the watersphere over the atmosphere, preventing the crystal formations etc.': the note to which
D. refers makes it clear that it is the pressure which 'prevents
the formation,' i.e. keeps the ice on the move. The cold, and the
pressure produced by the cold, works 'across the watersphere'
and in the upper air, 'above the atmosphere'. So, in a different
context (*Ana.* p.95) the influence of the sun is active 'across the
atmosphere, on the watersphere'. Similarly, we read in an unpublished MS. a development of the same idea, applied this time
to animal life: 'Ichthus of the three liaisons, who mirrors in his
saucer-eye the feathered things and the things of fur when he
breaks the rippled filament of the water-sphere to drink the
atmosphere.'

trauma and thauma, both: shock and marvel, to be understood in the light of *frangit per medium*, the shock of the breaking
and the mystery accomplished (in the Mass) at the moment of the
breaking of the host; the shock of the breaking away of the ice
and the emergence of the land-masses. This lends some colour
to the suggestion that there is, in 'land-masses', a play on 'mass'
and 'the Mass'. To my mind, the pun is too poor to be anything
but accidental. Cronos, it is true, brings fertility and healing to
the land-masses by breaking the ice: as the three-personed
Creator, in the unpublished passage quoted above, brings life
by opening the watersphere to the atmosphere. The priest's
breaking of the host, however, brings life not the Mass or 'the
masses' but to the faithful.

The rubric 'frangit per medium' was full of extended meaning for the poet, breaking, wounding, the giving of life by
sacrifice. It recurs on p.227 ('where it's very still / the fracture /
sound / when . . . he parts . . .') which strengthens the analogy
offered on this page, and again in the MS. already quoted on

69 page 62: A Roman legionary is telling how his company was held up by a great elm tree which 'had tangled in its fall a fair flexing fraxinus and snapt it right at the middle bole, as though some still small voice, unheard for the crowing of wind and weather, had from outside time quietly commanded, *frangit per medium*. The sound of that rending is with me yet: the gods alone know why, for often enough I have heard the curious cleavage-cry of breaking living timber'.

Eden is the river and valley in Cumberland and Westmorland. The river runs through Carlisle. Hence 'becked fells', with the north-country words for streams and moors. D. used to stay near Troutbeck.

Sabrina is the Roman name for the Severn: and D.'s Sabrina is the nymph in *Comus*. For 'Sibylline' cf. *Ana.* p.67.

70 *She* in the first line is still Severn. *Stour* may be confusing to one who knows only the Kent, Dorset or Essex and Suffolk rivers of that name. The following (from *Chamber's Encyclopaedia*) makes all this passage more clear:

'In the Shropshire plain the Severn and Vyrnwy (tributary to the Severn) once flowed northward to join the Dee, but during the later phases of the ice age when this route was blocked the combined river turned eastward by Shrewsbury along the southern margin of the plain and overflowed the rim just south of the Wrekin. This overflow channel now forms the striking gorge from Buildwas to Ironbridge. The waters of the Severn thus found their way into a tributary of the Worcestershire Stour and followed its course southward by Bridgnorth to Stourport.'

parthenogenic waters is explained in note 1 to p.67. 'marl', a deposit of clay and calcium carbonate, the noun being used here, as so often, as a verb: so, too, 'glen'.

Before, trans-Solway: D.'s note explains the shifting of deposits across the Solway Firth, from 'Caledonia into Cambria' through 'Cumbria'.

Manannan: the Irish form of the sea-god is used, because it is across the Irish sea that the 'debris-freighted floes' are carried, and Manannan was associated with the Isle of Man (see *Ana.* p.107 and n. 2).

winter calends . . . calends of Maia: the two divisions of 71 the year, corresponding to, if not coinciding with, the two solstices.

For a less mythologised view of **Cunedda**, see, in addition to D.'s note, Collingwood and Myres, pp. 289–90 (*conditor noster*, our founder, may perhaps move a reader to sympathy with Huck Finn's comment on *The Pilgrim's Progress*: 'I read considerable in it now and then. The statements was interesting, but tough') – Writing of Stilicho's re-organisation of the defences of Britain at the end of the fourth century, they say: 'The story of Cunedda must indicate that, just before the close of the century, the Roman government applied this well-worn device to the Scotic problem: enlisting a tribe from the north and planting it with the status of *foederati* in the west, there to act as a local militia under its own king, and replace the unruly Irish, who had hitherto been allowed to possess the land. If the date given [in Nennius's *Historia Brittonum*] is correct, and it is at least circumstantial – 146 years before the reign of Mailcun – the transplantation of Cunedda was part of Stilicho's work.'

For the Roman roads, and what D. can make of them, see *Epoch and Artist*, pp. 189–95, a shining example of his fusion of argument and poetry. Here a digression must be pardoned, for a glance at that essay disclosed a remarkable parallel between what is written there as mere statement, and what appears later (in one of the MSS. already referred to) as designed poetic composition. The two passages run as follows (that from *Epoch and Artist* first); the MS. passage was written some fifteen years later.

'The blackthorn is out and the thrush sings but though she is in April there are no English here. Beneath the starry, white-budded black bough of the windy tree he [a Roman centurion] sits on a pile of white rubble eyeing a work in progress. His rain-proof cloak is of fine-wove British goat-hair fabric in Silchester-dyed cockle-red; an export market product. He was lucky to come by a length of the stuff at all. But no one could say it wasn't reg'mental as to cut.'

The second extract, it should be remembered, is no more than a draft for a poem:

'. . . if her husband, his [again a centurion, a *primipilus*] Commander, if he must wear Caesar's paludament as signum for his authority, here *yn yr ynys hon* [in this our island], then it shall be of the finest weave Britain can provide, and radiant with the madder-dye the receipt of which was known only to the great ones years since before Cunobelin . . . and if we raid the deepest *coed*-ways and sylvae of Britain for the finest cat-pelts to interline more warm the shoulder-pieces while retaining the required military cut, it shall be done, much as I love the quick-limbed denizens of flaming fury . . .'

The **Otadini** or Votadini (the Goddodin of *In Parenthesis*) inhabited the country between the Firth of Forth and Hadrian's Wall. Hence 'Forth into Conwy, Clyde into Clwyd' (the latter being the river in Denbighshire), a movement from Scotland into Wales. Rhys believed that it was from the country of the Otadini that Cunedda came. Venedotia, Snowdonia: Demetia, south-west Wales, Irish-occupied.

Combroges (see p.67 n. 2) **bore us:** as Eliot's 'Highbury bore me' (293), where he refers to Dante's 'Siena mi fe', disfecemi Maremma', itself based on Vergil's epitaph, 'Mantua me genuit, Calabri rapuere, tenet nunc / Parthenope: cecini pascua, rura, duces'.

72   The debt of Britain to Rome could not be expressed with greater concentration. 'Tottering': for it was the eve of Rome's being forced to abandon Britain; 'experienced' in more than one sense; and, most important of all, 'crux-signed', Christianised.

The second paragraph of p.72 refers to the formation of the South Wales coal-fields. 'Seat-earth' is another word for 'underclay', the soil underneath a coal-bed in which carboniferous swamp-forests (hence 'slow estuarine alchemies') have been rooted. 'Utile' is used for once, possibly, in the sense of 'profitable', although there may be a suggestion of the dependence on coal of industrialism, with its degradation of the workman, who is robbed of the responsibility without which he cannot go beyond the 'utile'.

Aldasa is Ailsa Craig, in the Firth of Clyde; Goat Height is Arran; Clota, Clyde.

from either Dalriada: (D.'s Dumbarton friend may retain the pronunciation Daldriada, if we may retain the Irish Dal Riada) 'There is abundant evidence to show that at this time – the fourth and early fifth centuries – there was great activity in the Highland zone and especially an expansive energy in Ireland. From Ulster about this time warriors of the Dal Riata sept began their conquests in the land of the Picts, which were to bring the culture and language of Ireland to Scotland.' (Maire and Liam de Paor, *Early Christian Ireland*, 1960, p.68.)

The origin and development (under the inspiration of Columba) of the Scottish (i.e. Irish) kingdom of Dalriada (Argyll), later to grow into the kingdom of Scotland, is discussed more fully, but without prolixity, by Norah Chadwick, in Myles Dillon and Norah Chadwick, *The Celtic Realms*, 1967, chapter 4. Dalriada, north of the Forth-Clyde Antonine Wall, should be distinguished from Strathclyde, south of the Clyde to the Solway Firth.

The gouging-out of the Irish Sea and St George's Channel 73 is described in modern military terms: *mare*, *strategi*, and *axis*, bring together the idea of force as seen in Roman and Hellenistic times, and in the days of the Second World War ('the axis powers'). As the sea moves south (the latitude decreasing from 55N at the Mull of Kintyre to a little less than 52 at St Bride's Bay) so it widens. One degree beyond the latter takes us out into the Atlantic (where Brendan sails). It is not like D. to use the incorrect spelling 'weigh' for 'way' (line 4), and he may have had in mind the 'weight' of pressure.

Careful use has been made in this part of the poem of Bernard Smith and T. Neville George's admirably illustrated *North Wales* in H.M.S.O.'s *British Regional Geology*, to which D. refers both in his Preface and his notes. (First pub-

73 lished in 1935; the current, revised, edition, dates from 1961).

the New Light . . . infulsit: as in the inscription facing p.77, from the Christmas Preface: 'Quia per incarnati Verbi mysterium, nova mentis nostrae oculis lux tuae claritatis infulsit: ut dum visibiliter Deum cognoscimus, per hunc in invisibilium amorem rapiamur' – 'For through the mystery of the Word made flesh the new light of thy brightness has shone upon the eyes of our mind, so that as we see God in visible form, we are through him caught up into love of things invisible.' Here is summed-up the theme of 'Rite and Fore-time', that this New Light shone upon all from all time.

The words are a 'preface' to the Canon of the Mass, when the tiny wafer will be consecrated; and the contrast between the pathetic fragility of the visible sign (by which *visibiliter Deum cognoscimus*) and the massive power of the mystery has long been emphasised. Hugo Rahner writes in this connection: 'It is always the simple primitive human things that are used as symbols: ears of grain, a blossoming tree, washing, the life-giving union of the sexes, light, darkness, sun and moon, and there is in their very simplicity a quality of the self-explanatory and self-sufficient which actually makes them more, and not less, apt vehicles for expressing the inexpressible (arrhêton), the unspeakable (aneklalêton) nature of that which their use in the mystery is seeking to convey. Now this fundamental character is repeated in the mystery of the cross, though at a different level, and though divine action has made the actual content of the mystery into something entirely new – the human death, the blood, the wound, the primitively simple shape of the crossed pieces of wood all these are small things . . . in which the mystery hides itself, so that through the slight thing which is the visible symbol we behold the glory that embraces the world'. (*Greek Myths and Christian Mystery*, p.48.) All this – and the splendour of the form that shines through the humblest artefact – lies behind D.'s 'New Light infulsit'.

athwart: to be pronounced, I would wager, athort. The light shone upon (*in*fulsit) and across, or through, the fore-times. The prepositions hold an echo, too, of another prayer from the Canon, *Per ipsum, et cum ipso, et in ipso:* 'through him, and *with* him, and *in* him . . .)

Page 74 calls for a dictionary rather than a commentary. **74** Calypso is used to typify the enchantress who muddles the geological layers. D.'s **Calypso** is Jackson Knight's (see a number of references in *Vergil: Epic and Anthropology*), and has, too, something of the nature of a sibyl, shuffling the 'marked pack' as the Sibyl allowed the wind to shuffle the marked leaves. J.K. would blur the distinction between Calypso and Circe, and D. would be ready to follow him in so doing; yet it was Calypso who helped Odysseus to build his boat. 'unconformities', again in the geological sense, as on *Ana*. p.68.

five life-layers: T.D. points out the careful reflection of the tables printed in W. W. Watts, *Geology for Beginners* (1929), pp. 219 and 288, pages noted on the fly-leaf of D.'s copy of the book.

Tyrannosaurus . . . herbivores: i.e. the lion must lie down with the lamb; cf. Isaiah 11.6: 'The wolf also shall dwell with the lamb, and the leopard shall lie down with the kid; and the calf and the young lion and the fatling together; and a little child shall lead them'. The poet's truth is warranted by his prophecy of the Messiah. 'Tyrannosaurus' is used with 'herbivores' because that huge beast was the largest of the carnivores.

hade 'is a miner's term, also used by geologists. It means a deviation from the vertical. A *normal* fault in geological strata is said to "hade to the down-throw", an "abnormal fault" vice-versa.' (D. in a letter.) The corresponding inclination to the horizontal is the 'dip'. The 'down-throw' is the vertical displacement of the fractured strata; in the 'upcast' (upthrow) the displacement is upward. 'Fault' is used of any fracture in the rock which causes displacement. These displacements are marked by symbols on geological maps. Here, and in 'The Sleeping Lord', the reader will be well served by such a map. 'Pseudomorphs' and 'metamorphs' are both used by geologists of changes in rocks. The former, occurring here, is a happy

74   reminder of 'However Calypso has shuffled . . .' above; being applied to a mineral 'whose external form is not one usually assumed by its particular species', it shows how the poet has assimilated Calypso to Circe. Spengler, I fear, cannot have been entirely absent from D.'s mind when he wrote 'pseudomorph' for S. has much to say about 'Historic Pseudomorphoses', some of it most unpalatable to less wildly imaginative readers. See Chapter 7 of the second volume of *The Decline of the West*.

he brights his ichthyic sign: the Christian symbol of the fish, ichthys, the letters of which form (in Greek) the initials of Iesous Christos Theou Yios Soter, Jesus Christ Son of God Saviour (see comment below, on 'fish-eye', *Ana.* p.125). The phrase is essential to this recapitulation of human and terrestrial development. It is an expansion of the shining of the 'new light' and attaches it strictly to the Christian mystery. From the very earliest beginnings of life ('the palaeozoe'), that symbol shines out: it is brighter still in the 'middle zone' where the 'uterine forms' point to man. The phrase is echoed or anticipated, or both, in 'A, a, a, Domine Deus', which opens *The Sleeping Lord* (and is dated c. 1938 and 1966), where the poet seeks in vain for some 'beginnings of his creature' in the 'glassy towers' of techno-plutocracy. In that poem, he says that he had hoped to 'see the Living God projected from the Machine': here, in *The Anathemata*, it is the Living God whom he sees in the rudiments of human making.

That same light, indicative of the divine presence, is **brighter yet** in the **continuings**, i.e. in the later history of evolution. And those continuings praise in the sense of the *Benedicite* (Ana. p.63) and in as much as every artefact is an act of worship.

We meet the same language in *Epoch and Artist*, p.104 n. 2: speaking of 'a severe, disinterested, unalloyed "functional-art" (as the best examples of which D. takes weapons, 'the superb instruments of death') he says, 'the living God, the life-giver, is not, after all, projected from the machine'. His prose seldom remains within the boundaries of purely logical or explanatory progression, for the use of words and images has always the curiously (in the sense of 'curious workmanship') contrived splendour of his poetry. The note quoted is an attempt to reconcile the functional and the gratuitous: no more than an attempt, for while D. admits that 'Beauty of a certain order undeniably belongs to these forms, the beauty of a mathematical formula "made flesh",' yet he sees that 'the tendency is for creativeness to become dehumanized . . . the will toward shape to become almost indistinguishable from a mere will toward power'. 'Dehumanization' (a notion shared with Gill) is here the key: and it comes with scale. Later in the same book (p. 194) when he is speaking of the less industrialised functional work involved in the making of the Roman roads, that 'doing' is described as 'a making', 'a *praxis* which is also a *poiesis*', for 'the Rectilineal Plan *has* its poesy'.

On this page (74) we work back from the Mesozoic Era (Cretaceous and Triassic some 120–150 million years ago) to the palaeozoic (in the last paragraph), and then forward again to the mesozoic ('middle-zone') and the Tertiary Era ('the mammal'd Pliocene', the Pliocene or latest period of that era, some million years ago). And we may note that there is a special appropriateness in the attachment of 'his ichthyic sign' to 'the palaeo-zoe'; for the Devonian Period (in the middle of the Palaeozoic Era) is known as 'the age of the fishes'. With equal care, the poet notes that it was in the Pliocene that the mammals reached their peak.

Thus, from the crudest beginnings down to the elegance of **the amorous Silvy,** man, as such, is under the illumination of the supreme sign. In this lies the force of the 'How else' argument, which opens here. It is continued to its logical conclusion on the next page (75): we ourselves could not exist ('How else we ?') if the trail did not run true down the whole line, nor could the incarnate Christ himself have been man ('or he, himself ?')

He-with-us: Immanuel, Isaiah 7.14; 8.8; Matthew 1.23. 75 'Immanuel', says Matthew, 'which means God-with-us'.

because he did not abhor the uterus: the singing of those tremendous words from the Te Deum, with the majestic emphasis of the Solesmes chant, should be in the reader's, as they are in the poet's, mind: 'Tu ad liberandum suscepturus hominem, non horruisti Virginis uterum', 'that you might take on manhood, to set man free, you did not shrink from, disdain, abhor, the womb of the Virgin'. D.'s 'abhor', as he expects the reader to understand, depends upon and derives a force it would not normally have, from the Latin *horruisti*. 'uberal forms': only this poet's obliquity of approach could give fresh tenderness to the comparison of rounded hill-forms with the girl's – in this case, moreover, Mary's – breast. 'of all hills the most august' has a complexity of meaning: that of all hills the breast-like are the most august, and that these breasts are the most august of hill-forms.

How else her iconography: how can we represent Mary if the line of descent does not run true from the 'Willldendorf Venus' to Christian Rome and Byzantium? And so, too, with '*his* liturgy' and the man whom we 'already and first of all discern' at the opening of the poem. In asking this of the clerks of Rome, Oxford and Cambridge, D. uses a favourite device in the alternation or reversal of pattern; so here the legend on the sign of the Clarendon Press is given in English ('that have the Lord for your light', 'Dominus illuminatio mea', from Ps. 26) while the Cambridge University Press legend ('from this light and the sacred draughts') is left in Latin. 'Rhydychen' should be followed by a comma, and 'light' in the penultimate line by a colon (letter to D.M.C.)

77   At the head of the next page, 77, the evolution of earth and man is continued ('Pleistocene and Recent') to homo sapiens. The argument here is that primitive man, and woman, is as much entitled to the state of 'blessed' ('beata', 'beati') as post-Messiah man' 'Aureole' (halo), beata, 'cause', 'beati', make this clear. 'Cause' is used in the sense of 'cause of beatification' (or canonisation) at the Roman court. Hence 'data' (the evidence), which is known only to him, i.e. to God himself.

The **egregius** (although he bears a Roman title) is the man referred to in note 1, with which cf. *The Sleeping Lord*, p.71.

The derivation of the word (*ex* + *grex*, herd, flock) is fortunate, 77
for it allows the transition to the metaphor of the shepherd
and his flock. We have met this already, with the remembering
of all human kind, on p.65; here it is continued in more detail,
some of which calls for the explanation given in the notes on p.76.

Strayed from among the nine and ninety: the *egregius*
(see the second paragraph of note 1) is regarded as the one lost
out of the hundred (Luke 15.4–6), echoing *non perdidi ex eis
quemquam* of p.66. 'Aurignacian', as typical of Upper Palaeolithic.

by his Proserpine to himself: the part played by
Proserpine is explained in note 2. It may be over-refining to
try to read into 'secret' shearing more than that there is no witness to it, whereas modern man is openly and publicly marked
as 'made over tó himself' (to the Creator). Even so, we may say
that the word 'secret' is used because the root meaning of the
verb from which it is derived (*secerno*) is to distinguish or discern, and so to sever or separate, to 'make over' in a special way.
We may remember that Iris was sent specially (Aeneid 4.693ff)
to cut a golden lock from Dido's head, for Dido's death at her
own hand was untimely, and 'nondum illi flavum Proserpina
vertice crinem Abstulerat', Proserpina had not yet cut the
golden lock from her head. 'In a sacrifice the hair of a victim was
first removed and offered as a first-fruit; and when men die at the
appointed time, Proserpina herself cuts off a lock of hair
. . . but she could not do this for the untimely dead.' (Professor
Austin on 4.698.) 'At the appointed time' supports D.'s bold
relation to Proserpina to 'that death which is "shown forth"
and "recalled" in' the eucharist' – of all deaths the most 'appointed'.

to himself: while it is the 'egregius' who is made over to
himself' D.'s note makes it clear that he had also in mind 'that
particular death' of Christ, in which he sacrificed 'himself to
himself': cf. *Ana.* p.225, and 'himself to himself / on the Windy
Tree', with note, in 'The Fatigue' (*The Sleeping Lord*, pp.
32–3).

against the white wattles: Jacob, in Genesis 30, 'took him rods of green poplar, and of the hazel and chestnut tree, and pilled white strakes in them, and made the white appear', that so he might have more speckled sheep to count as his own. This was not, in fact, in the poet's mind, but he was, fortunately, as ready in accepting interpretations of his own work as he was in interpreting that of others. 'I was actually thinking more of how the Welsh hill-farmers at the sheep-dipping count them against the white wattles' (D.); hence the time, late in June. Wattles are often appearing in D.'s work, both pictorially and verbally: the Virgin, for example, is enclosed in a wattled fence in the 'Welsh Annunciation', reproduced in the 1974 *Agenda*; for their prominence in the poetry see the comment on 'white bangors', *Ana.* p.201.

The **Ordinale** is the book of the rite of ordination: hence 'numeri'. The metaphor is rather loose, but is justified, presumably, by the further notion of order and sequence in the *ordo* which lies behind *ordinale*. And it is ten to one that D. had in mind Propertius II.28.55–6 (which he used in an inscriptional poem) 'et quaecumque erat in numero Romana puella, occidit', particularly in view of 'occidit' – and every lovely Roman girl whom we may rank with these, every one has fallen, too. 'Numerus', again, has a military meaning, and this would commend the word, because of the suggestion of 'enlistment'.

78   **For whom . . . at centum:** not at ninety-nine, but at one hundred, so that all are included – and with an eye to the division between the *centum* and *satem* languages, according to their word for hundred; the Celtic languages belonging to the former group.

that no man may number: the antecedent of 'that' is 'flock' in the preceding line; there should be a comma after 'number', for the ingeniously obtuse could take 'but whose' to mean 'except those whose'.

Searching: who is searching? 'He' is searching, i.e. the shepherd, for traces of the one lost in the middens in which archaeologists delight. 'Magdalenian', later palaeolithic, with 78 relics of bone needles (cf. the preceding page, 'who of duck's bone had made her needle-case'). The biological term 'protomorphs' is transferred to the first beginnings of 'form', seen in the broken ('fragmented') pottery.

multifariam multisque modis: the complete sentence from which the words are drawn is appropriate to the thesis: 'Multifariam multisque modis olim Deus loquens patribus in prophetis, novissime diebus istis locutus est nobis in Filio, quem constituit heredem universorum, per quem fecit et saecula.' 'In old days, God spoke to our fathers in many ways and by many means, through the prophets; now at last in these times he has spoken to us, with a Son to speak for him, whom he has appointed to inherit all things, just as it was through him that he created this world of time.' (Knox's version of the opening of Hebrews.) Another translator emphasises *novissime diebus istis* even more: 'in our time, the last time' – on the ground, shared by our poet, that the 'inheritance in question is messianic and eschatological' (Jerusalem Bible). Cf. *Hora novissima, tempora pessima* in Peter Levi's 'In memory of David Jones'. In the next verse of Hebrews we have *splendor gloriae*, too, used of Christ in a different sense from 'the splendour of forms yet to come', but hardly a mere coincidence. 'Splendor formae' is a Thomistic phrase. 'A certain shining quality is according to all the ancients the essential character of beauty – claritas est de ratione pulchritudinis – lux pulchrificat, quia sine luce omnia sunt turpia – but it is a sunburst of intelligibility. *Splendor veri*, said the Platonists; *splendor ordinis*, said St Augustine; *splendor formae*, said St Thomas.' (Maritain, *Art et Scolastique*, pp. 37–8.)

Louis Bonnerot, now enjoying the final splendour, quotes this passage ('fragmented protomorphs . . .') to show that for D. 'the underlying shaping force, of which archaeology is the outward visible manifestation, is the "eucharist", as enshrined from the remote beginnings in the anathemata, the sacred and artistic rites.'

79   In other words, the same mystery is to be found in the 'rudi-
mentary bowl', 'the coward's dish' and the 'calix'. The dish from
which no coward could take food is referred to in *Epoch and
Artist*, p.237, and see Rees, *Celtic Heritage*, p.313. It is used
with great effect in *In Parenthesis*, p.52, where the night-sentry
wonders, 'Does he [i.e. Jerry] stir his Cup – he blesses no coward's
stir over there.'

calix . . . re-calling: the italicised *the* and the hyphen emphasise that supreme re-calling or re-presentation or re-enactment contained in Christ's words, 'Haec quotiescumque feceri-
tis, in mei memoriam facietis': the anamnesis, a key word and
notion to which D. so often returns (see numerous references in
Epoch and Artist, and in Gregory Dix's *The Shape of the Liturgy*,
to which D. was greatly indebted for his understanding of the
word.)

The same argument applies to humbler things and beings which
are part of human culture, such as the dog ('The dog is a faithful,
intelligent friend, But his hide is covered with hair').

Argos: Odysseus's faithful dog, who lived just long enough to
recognise his master with gesture of tail and ears, and then died
'in the twentieth year' since Odysseus had sailed for Troy
(*Odyssey* 17.290–327). So, too, we have John Peel's hounds,
Ranter and Ringwood, Bellman and True (cf. *The Kensington
Mass*, of hunters, 'in their coats of grey', the colour of John
Peel's coat); Spot, the conventional terrier-name; Cerberus,
who guarded the gate of Hades.

D.'s acquaintance with dogs was not exclusively literary,
as the following from a letter written in 1974 illustrates so
entertainingly as to justify the digression: 'I did not know
that confounded terrier [a large Irish terrier, called Michael]
howled when Joan tried to play on her harp. I apologise on behalf of the family, to her. The only thing I do clearly remember
about that dog – well, two things – one nise, the other nasty
(to use Taplow lingo) I was, in I suppose 1919, in bed with a
damned severe bout of influenza in my little room where I did
a lot of engraving and water colour drawings and was running a

pretty high temperature & had not been about for a week or more,   **79**
when one evening to my astonishment that dog decided, I
suppose, to investigate, anyway he pushed the door open &
found me in bed & came over and licked my hands & wagged his
tail and departed, with a look of contentment on his face. My
mother told me he had been nosing about the house for some
days as though he knew something was wrong & had eventually
discovered my whereabouts. 'Cripes' I thought 'kiss me 'Ardy'.
The other incident was *decidedly other*. It was some years later,
& I came back from London [to Brockley] rather late, probably
having spent the evening with you when you were with old
Coldwell or maybe at Tom's or Harman's in Chelsea. My parents
were out at some church affair when I came into the house &
that confounded dog had made himself comfortable on some
cushions on the sofa in the front room – I switched on the light
and told the dog to go down to his basket in the kitchen or
scullery or wherever it was that he ordinarily slept. However,
instead of doing as I bid him, he raised his head and bared his
ancient teeth & snarled in a fashion that I did not *at all* like.
Being by nature easily afraid [that is quite untrue] and having a
particular fear of dogs large or small, I thought well, this wont
do at all: coward or no, I must somehow put in practice the
'primacy of action', or that dog will *never* again do as he's told,
and moreover he *may* use those bared teeth on me now, which I
did not at all fancy – so after a further order that was met by a
further snarl, I gave the creature a whack, not hard, but with an
ash walking stick, across his muzzle – the effect was very prompt
& very satisfactory, for he came down from the sofa and went
straight to his sleeping-basket, and there was no further trouble
from him as far as I was concerned, anyway. But I afterwards
never felt *quite* at ease with him – I think I feared he might
choose his time to counter-attack!'

   poiesis, ex nihilo: although man as maker imitates divine
creation, he cannot create, as we say of the Creator, *ex nihilo*,
out of nothing.

   that quested the hog: the subject of another, later, enlargement, 'The Hunt', which is printed in *The Sleeping Lord*, and which can be heard, read by the poet, on a Argo record. (See note 1 on the next page, 80.) What D. says about 'The Hunt' on a note which accompanies the record, is applicable here – particularly since he introduces the 'procedure from the known to the unknown'.

'In *The Hunt* I tried to evoke something of the feel of the stress, urgency and effort of the war-bands of the Island led by an Arthur figure in pursuit of their formidable quarry across the whole of southern Wales. What distinguishes this native prose-tale from the subsequent great Arthurian Romance-cycles is its vivid sense of the particular, of locality and site. The exact topography and terrain is in strong contrast with the vague and generalised topography of the Romances. Though the theme itself is a common mythological theme stretching back to remote pre-history, here in this Welsh tale, its setting is a knowable, factual, precisely defined tract of country. In short, for all its marvels and numinous powers, its many strata, its narration "proceeds from the known to the unknown" – a sound aesthetic principle.' What D. says of *Culhwch and Olwen* could be said of his own treatment of topography.

80   **the dog Toby:** 'Yes, certainly, "dog Toby" from the book you mention (*Tristram Shandy*: wrongly, again: for it is 'Uncle Toby' – Toby is the Punch and Judy dog), but also because so many dogs were called Toby when I was young, and as with the John Peel hounds mentioned, it, Toby, and such-like pet dogs, no less than great Argos and Cerberus etc., could not be but for the mesolithic developments' (D.).

flew'd sweet thunder: *Midsummer Night's Dream* 4.1: '. . . I never heard So musical a discord, such sweet thunder . . . My hounds are out of the Spartan kind, So flew'd, so sanded; and their heads are hung With ears that sweep away the morning dew'.

From here (**And over the submerged dryad-ways**, i.e. forests) to the end of the section the thesis is recapitulated and taken to its climax in the culmination of the 'How else' argument, 'How else' (p. 82) the Eucharist. To this we return in the last section of the poem (p.243), 'How else be coupled of this Wanderer . . . if not by this Viander's [supplier of bread and wine] own death's monument'. There the argument is finally re-inforced by the poet's contradiction of Milton (in the *Hymn on the morning of Christ's nativity*): Anubis is *not* to haste, for he leads to a 'Lord's body'.

First, **his ray searches** W.J.K. suggests ('tentatively', but, to my mind, with good reason) that 'neoliths' in 'the polished neoliths' may be a slip or misprint for 'eoliths'. 'Eoliths' ('dawn-stones') are the earliest chipped flint instruments to be found, in alluvial deposits: whether they be man-made or naturally chipped hardly signifies, for when D. was writing they were generally accepted as being the latter. To read 'eoliths' avoids the unnecessary and awkward repetition of 'polished neoliths' and 'neolithic loves', and restores the chronological progression of eolithic, neolithic long barrows, bronze age round barrows, through which his ray searches for the recognisably human and so potentially divine. 'hallows' is here a noun, the *beati* who handled the pitiless bronze: that last phrase, pitiless bronze, being aptly the Homeric *nêlês ckalkos*. Then urn-burial and the burial sites of the Terramara villages. It is possible that D. had Sir Thomas Browne in mind when he wrote of urn-burial. The preceding page, 79, has what sounds uncommonly like an echo of a sentence in *Religio Medici*. D.'s 'nor is it in the mind of this flesh to practise poiesis ex nihilo' recalls Sir Thomas's 'Certainly there is no happiness with this circle of flesh, nor is it in the optics of these eyes to behold felicity' (1.43).

Cis-padane marls: see *Ana.* p.55. (For 'Terramare' read 'Terramara' or 'Terremare'.) The lay-out of these 'lake-dwellings on land' is taken as the model for the original Rome (*Roma quadrata* on the Palatine) and of the Roman camp. See *The Sleeping Lord*, p.79. Here Vergil is mentioned explicitly (his *Mantuan*), being a native of the Po valley. The 'his' and 'he' still refer to the recurring incarnate God of this section, whose 'perpetual light' or 'new light' illuminates the invisible through

81 the visible. No religion, says D., no artefacture. No Terramara culture, no Aeneid. The *Oxford Classical Dictionary* briefly and conveniently indicates how what D. drew from Stuart Jones about the Quadrilateral Plan needs to be qualified – as D. anticipates in his 'General Note to Section 1'. This passage is elaborated in 'The Wall' (*The Sleeping Lord*), pp. 11–12 in particular). D.'s source here was Dawson, again, especially pp. 334–6 of *The Age of the Gods*.

daily, at the Stone: all the fore-times lead up to the daily re-enactment of the Christian mystery at the stone of the altar when all ('memento etiam') are remembere.d 'servos': D. uses the old form of the nominative, for *servus*, as Vergil, just mentioned, also archaises.

Memento. etiam: the prayer continues 'Domine, famulorum famularumque tuarum [and D., we may note, included both masculine and feminine, *beatus* and *beata*, on p.77] qui nos praecesserunt cum signo fidei', 'Remember also, Lord, thy servants, both men and women, who have gone before us with the sign of faith'; and 'Nobis quoque peccatoribus', 'to us sinners, too, grant some share and fellowship with thy holy apostles and martyrs, with John etc.' Both prayers are from the Canon of the Mass. In the Tridentine Mass, the silence of the Canon is broken by those three words, *Nobis quoque peccatoribus.*

some part . . . like John: 'some part' (see note 1 on the next page, 82) is taken literally (*partem aliquam*) from the prayer quoted. 'like John is': 'Yes, a deliberate colloquialism contrasted with "as" is Felicity. More dapple. Also one can, if one like, read Felicity as a play on "felicity" and read it as meaning "As John is, which it is felicity to think of". Just as a secondary idea.' (D., in a letter to D.M.C., who objected to the colloquial 'like'.)

82 **the naiad her habitat:** gave the river-nymph the river to dwell in, the flow of clear water being not only the most elementary human symbol but also the first (in Baptism) 'outward sign of inward grace', 'his proto-sign': the prelude, too, to the significant bread with which the section ends.

dark humus spread: this, for which we must thank the

'essential and labouring worm' is what the earth's long history **82**
has led up to, the possibility of agriculture – and so culture –
which can produce *his* barlies, so that in 'your Bread' the 'efficacious sign' may be held up. The argument here reaches its
conclusion, 'How else . . . should his barlies grow . . . ?' 'Yes,
I did read Darwin on the Formation of Vegetable Mould
through the action of worms, for *all* Darwin's works were in
Mr Carlile's house [Northwick Lodge, Harrow-on-the-Hill].
See note on p.82 of *The Anathemata*. A pity old Darwin did not
have a glimpse of what even Milton, in his blindness, gave a hint
at'. (D., who thus himself draws attention to his variation on
'exact day-labour, light deny'd' in Milton's sonnet on his
blindness.)

saps micro-workings: cf., as suggested by the idiom of the
trenches, the great rat passage in *In Parenthesis*, p.54, 'his creature of air' must be primarily man, but also all those creatures
which, with man, share this atmospheric need.

Looking back at this first section, we may admire the statement
of themes, their repetition in various forms, and their interweaving, which remind us of the construction of an elaborate
piece of music, the first movement of a symphony, or the emergence of a pattern on the loom.

Thus, the epigraph at the head of p.49 introduces the theme
of the cosmic cycles, to be repeated on pp. 54, 55–8, 63ff.,
66–74. This is blended with the second, 'ritual', theme, the
'groping syntax' and 'pre-application' we meet at the very
beginning, to re-appear on pp. 59, 74–7 (the pagination is only
approximate, for there is considerable overlap). These two
themes are closely linked, for the development of man-the-
artifex is described as parallel to the development of Tellus
the bread-giver. And that again leads (p.51) to the theme of the
'upper room', the symbol of the bread, and the offering of self
to self.

Accompanying this is the ship theme (to re-appear in later
sections of the poem). Embedded in the evolutionary or fore-

82 time themes, we have that of the hill (itself linked with the upper room and the associated hill and sacrifice), both the naturally formed hill and the 'gammadion'd castle'. (We may note, too, that this – being centred on Troy – will lead into the ship-and-voyage themes, through Aeneas, Rome and Britain.)

The human half of the evolutionary themes introduces that of the shepherd and the care for *all* his flock, and this again leads back to the ritual, with the remembering of all that have gone before – taking us back, in fact, to the inscription which faces the opening of the poem. We now see how well the key fits, which we are given on p.45, in the form of the endless circular story of our childhood, 'It was a dark and stormy night . . .'. This will have become even more apparent by the end of the last section, when we shall return to the 'How else' argument of pp. 75–9, and conclude with a re-affirmation of continuity from 'him making this thing other' (in the opening line of the poem) to him who was 'recumbent at the garnished supper' (on the last page).

II

MIDDLE-SEA AND LEAR-SEA

The first section of the poem has followed the evolution of
sacramental man within the geo-physical development of the
earth. It both began and ended with the institution of the
supreme sacrament of the Eucharist in the Upper Room at
Jerusalem. It drew particular attention, moreover, to human and
terrestrial in the west, with a final concentration on the islands
of Britain. The west, and those men for whom the Mediterranean is the Middle Sea, are examined in more detail in this
second section, and we follow the diffusion of culture along the
sea-routes from the eastern Mediterranean and the lands adjoining it to the western extreme of Europe. Included with this is an
account of the emergence of the principle of order and organisation typified by Rome (itself, by the dialectic innate in the
universe, containing in its own aggrandisement the seeds of its
own destruction). Once again, both the starting-point and the
end are the sacrifice and sacrament that begin and end 'Rite
and Fore-time'. This is made clear by the dating with which the
section opens, some twelve hundred years since the fall of Troy
(which gives us a date near the beginning of our own era),
and the concluding words, 'Did he berth her? and to schedule?',
where the voyage which is thus safely completed is a metaphor
for the salvation of man by 'Christ the voyager' and the
'schedule' is the 'appointed time' of the Scriptures.

Middle-Sea: the Mediterranean. **Lear-Sea:** the English
Channel, and more especially the western approaches. In the
Irish mythological tradition we have Manannan mac Lir, 'a
renowned trader who dwelt in the Isle of Man. He was the best
pilot of the western world. By his sky-science he knew the times
of the fair weather and the foul and the changing of the seasons.
Hence the Scots (i.e. the Irish) and Britons called him a god of

84 the sea and hence they said that he was son of the sea, *mac lir*.'
(See Dillon and Chadwick, pp. 190-1, Rees, p.31).

In Welsh we have the corresponding Manawydan son of
Llŷr: hence the title of D.'s watercolour, 'Manawydan's Glass
Door', reproduced by Robin Ironside. Writing, in *Epoch and
Artist*, pp. 44–5, of the mixture of legend and history that
surrounds the early monarchy in Britain, D. says, 'And behind
such figures of true historicity, however overlaid with pseudo-
history of all sorts [e.g. Ambrosius Aurelianus, Magnus
Maximus, Cunobelinus: Emrys Wledig, Maxen Wledig,
Cymbeline] there are other figures such as Lear, who is said to
equate [a verb which is indeed the maid-of-all-work in such
discussions] with the god Nodens or Llud, called in English
Lud, a Celtic deity of the elements, so of estuaries and harbour-
age and port, so made to serve as the eponymous figure of the
port of London.' On *Ana.* p.97 we have the spelling 'Leir' ('when
he stood into Leir's river', i.e. the Thames), so that, for all the
vagueness and fluidity of identification, the Lear who ultimately,
through Geoffrey of Monmouth (Book 2, cap. 11) became the
Lear of Shakespeare, may very well give his name to the sea of
the Celts, into which will sail the trader from the Mediterranean whom we meet in this section.

D. comments on this, but writing, in fact in connection with a
later passage (in 'Redriff', pp. 119♦20, where the shipwright
says, 'Tell the Wop, to-go-to Canute . . . though he's many
times before *his* time') as follows:

'Apart from the straight quotation from Shakespeare's *Lear*
(Act 3. sc. 2) used on the title-page of *The Anathemata* and
in a sense meant to apply to the whole work, *This prophecie
Merlin shall make for I live before his time*, said by the Fool,
as he was supposed to be of Lear's period whereas "Merlin"
was thought of as a figure of Arthurian romance stemming in
Shakespeare's thought from Geoffrey of Monmouth – it was
brilliant even for Shakespeare's brilliance to hint at the notion
that 'Merlin' and so Arthur lived in that wholly indefinable age
of mixed legend, history and genuine 'mythe' (I adopt the word

you tell me Conington used) [I fear that in fact Conington, **84**
Vergil's Victorian editor, did not mean by 'mythe' what D.
meant by 'myth' or 'mythus'] and made Merddyn the great
magician into a court Fool such as medieval kings kept to
amuse them (in the sense of a vaguely medieval monarch
with dukes & earls, as Kent, Gloucester, Cornwall & daughters
of varying degrees struggling for power) and to call the King
'Lear' – a variant of the Celtic Lir, the father of Manannan
in Irish and Llŷr father of Manawydan in Brittonic Celtic,
cult-figures of a prehistoric Celtic pantheon – and especially
associated with the sea, estuaries, storm and weather, & equated
with Nodens of the silver hand, with Lud, Llŷr Nuadens of the
Severn estuary, who had a special shrine at Lydney (in Gloucestershire) and had fire-rites (cf. the Vestal fires and cf. Brigit)
and quite late-ish [A.D. 364–7] in the Roman occupation of
Britain was given a stone-built temple & as so often was the
practice was worshipped there alongside a typical classical cult-
figure . . . Again I meander, but I wonder if Shakespeare knew
anything about this Celtic sea-god – there is the association of
wild weather and echoes of three daughters in some Nordic-
Irish source I think'. (Sept. 1974.)

The device of using a character who looks forward into history
recurs frequently in D.'s work. A typical example is the following from a MS. draft of 'The Fatigue': 'You want to knock
about with the locals, sergeant – you want to rub up y'r pre-
science and let y'r medals bide – and, as the wise poet 'll
say – for we live before his time – keep y'r metaphysic at the
stir' – which looks forward both to *Lear* and Eliot's 'But our lot
crawls between dry ribs To keep our metaphysics warm'.

There is a companion to the Lear passage in Chaucer, *The
Knight's Tale*, vv. 2031–5:

> Depeynted was the slaughtre of Julius,
> Of grete Nero, and of Antonius;
> Al be that thilke tyme they were unborn,
> Yet was hir deth depeynted ther-biforn
> By manasynge of Mars, right by figure.

84 This must have been in D's mind, for both in *In Parenthesis* and in *The Anathemata* he uses the 'cook scalded' of v. 2020 ('The cook yscalded, for al his longe ladel'), who is also depicted in the palace of Mars.

Such liquidities lend themselves more readily to poetic than to scientific exposition: so we read in a draft for a long poem:

'. . . and speaking of Lear, where's Nuada?
where's the Roarer, or was he
the Strider, or what,
by his shape-shifting name,
is he properly called?
They're all shape-shifters, all a
changeling bunch of amphibious hierarchs
refracted in a misted prism –
there's none stays put in their
changing phantomsphere.
Is he their Lord-Director of the cisterns
with aboriginal command of west approaches?
  But whoever he is, where is he?'

Twelve hundred years: if we take the fall of Troy as having occurred about 1200 B.C., the birth of Christ as 5 B.C. or 3 B.C., and his Passion 33 years later, this date fits in with the date at the start of section 7. See *Ana.* p.184, note 8. The difficulty of harmonising dates later in the poem worried D. more than was necessary. He delighted, however, (as the Merlin incident quoted above has shown) in a reversal of historical perspective. Thus, from the same source:

'Has half Pictland massed unseen to storm this one sector of the Wall under plucked boughs of twelve times sixty Birnam woods, a millennium before an imagined date? Is Vercovicium fort mistook for Dunsinane yet to be?

'Does Clio lark about to that extent? After all, these Muses are all the feminine gender – what greater sport than shuffle the sequences and calculations – disorder all a collated Kalendaria?' – a reminder of Calypso's 'shuffling' we met earlier (*Ana.* p.74).

the Seven grouped Shiners: the Pleiades. The one who **84** 'doused her light' was Electra, whose light was dimmed, rather than doused, because Dardanus, the founder of Troy, was her son by Zeus (see *The Sleeping Lord*, p.12). If you look directly at the constellation, you will probably be able to count six stars. The seventh becomes apparent only if you turn your head a little to one side, when the light will fall upon the outer and more sensitive part of the retina. Others say that the one who doused her light was Merope, in her shame at being the only one to bear a child to a mortal (she bore that admirable and ingenuous hero Glaucus to Sisyphus – hence her name, Merope, or mortal). The seven are Maia, Electra, Taygete, Alcyone, Celaeno, Sterope or Asterope, and Merope. There is an appropriateness in their introduction here, in that their heliacal rising and setting marked the opening and closing of the sailing season in the eastern Mediterranean.

dragged him widdershins: D. follows Vergil rather than Homer; the latter describes Achilles as dragging Hector round the funeral mound of Patroclus. Neither Homer nor Vergil has anything to say about the direction, clockwise or counter-clockwise – with the port or against the port – in which Hector was pursued or dragged: some readers will find Jackson Knight's arguments less convincing than D. did (see *Vergil: Epic and Anthropology*, pp. 211–12,) but no reader, convinced or unconvinced, will be lacking in gratitude to J.K. for the material with which he provided the poet.

his beauties made squalid . . . under his dear walls: it may be well to have the Vergilian passage printed here, with, first, a more or less literal translation, and, secondly, a freer reconstruction: for it was this that, in words D. himself uses in a different context, 'really touched the liver'.

> 'Tempus erat, quo prima quies mortalibus aegris
> incipit et dono divum gratissima serpit.
> in somnis, ecce, ante oculos maestissimus Hector
> visus adesse mihi largosque effundere fletus,
> raptatus bigis, ut quondam, aterque cruento

84.   pulvere perque pedes traiectus lora tumentis.
ei mihi, qualis erat! quantum mutatus ab illo
Hectore, qui redit exuvias indutus Achilli
vel Danaum Phrygios iaculatus puppibus ignis!
squalentem barbam et concretos sanguine crinis
volneraque illa gerens, quae circum plurima muros
accepit patrios . . .'

'It was the hour when for weary mortals their first rest begins, and by grace of the gods steals over them most sweet. In slumbers, lo! before my eyes there seemed to stand Hector, most sorrowful and shedding floods of tears; torn by the car, as once of old, and black with gory dust, his swollen feet pierced with thongs. Ah me! what aspect was his! how changed from that Hector who returns after donning the spoils of Achilles or hurling on Danaan ships the Phrygian fires! with ragged beard, with hair matted with blood, and bearing those many wounds he gat around his native walls.' (Tr. H.R. Fairclough, in the Loeb edition.)

'It was the moment when the first depth of sleep
brings respite in man's rough passage.
My own eyes, too, knew heaven's solace: and yet
I saw my brother Hector loom before me.
Sorrow marked his face, tears his eyes mastered,
his feet pierced for the shameful thong,
his body torn,
as when I saw him torn by Achilles' wheel,
dark with the filth of battle:
my comrade Hector,
who once was proud to bear the golden sulker's arms
and strode in lordship from the burning ships.
But now I saw the draggled beard,
the hair set stiff in blood,
the wounds that tore his flesh ·
in the long fight below our walls.'

many of them gives the Vergilian text a slightly different sense from that given in the literal translation (and in D.'s note 5). Servius, the fourth-century commentator on V., suggests that 'gerens' ('bearing') means 'displaying with pride' his honourable wounds: but it is more suitable for us to connect the wounds with the 'envy and malice' of the Achaeans, who slashed and stabbed the body of the dead hero; their 'laughter was cruel, taunting his stillness: "Gentler to our handling a dead man's peace than raging in battle, firing the ships".' (Iliad 22.372ff.)

neque decor and note 3: it is important that the words are from one of the 'songs of the servant of the Lord', who suffers for the sins of the people, and in Christian tradition is a prototype of Christ (so Matthew 8.17, for example, 'Himself took our infirmities, and bare our sicknesses'). By applying Isaiah's words to Hector, D. is assimilating the latter to the Redeemer, and so bringing him into the very heartland of his thought. This would hardly be legitimate with the Homeric hero, though a case might be made out for the Vergilian, Hector's death being seen as the price paid for the foundation of Rome. The poet, however, makes his own Hector, his own Helen, his own Arthur, and even his own Nelson. (In note 3, for '*et*' read '*ei*'.)

In Homer, Hector's body is incorrupt and unblemished, through the care of Apollo – and, since Pope's Iliad is open before me, I must quote from it, for the sake of at least one line:

'For Phoebus watched it with superior care;
Preserved from gaping wounds and tainting air;
And, ignominious as it swept the field,
Spread o'er the sacred corse his golden shield.'

What centuries less: not, in fact, since the golden age of 85 Saturn's reign in Italy, before the coming of the Trojans, although this is the first sense that suggests itself. Note 1 makes it clear that 'Saturn's tellus' is no more than a synonym for Italy: it is how many centuries less since the 'sign-years', the years after the coming of Aeneas, the foundation of Alba Longa and then of Rome, with all the 'signs' and wonders that accompanied them (the 'palladic foreshadowings' of p.50).

85 These took place in the 'middle lands' of Italy, i.e. in Latium, as did the historical fact of the Ten, or Twelve, Tables of B.C. 451–50 alluded to in note 4.

Saturn's tellus: the synonym is used for the sake of a Vergilian allusion, Aeneid 8.319ff., where Evander explains to Aeneas how Saturn, expelled by Jupiter, settled in Italy. Then (v.329) 'saepius et nomen posuit Saturnia tellus', 'time and again the land of Saturn laid aside her name'. In the word 'religio' is contained the notion of a bond or restraint, so that there is a complex interplay of meanings in 'even for the men of rule, whose *religio* is rule': the material instrument for measurement, or ruler, the immaterial bond of respect for the sacred, the material restraints imposed by the 'world-orderers', the immaterial notion of order, the most material cupidities of the 'world-syndicate', of which Augustine speaks. The theme of the corruption of 'world orderer' into 'world-syndicate' is elaborated in 'The Wall' (*The Sleeping Lord*, pp. 10–14).

D. could hardly mention Saturn without a memory of the fourth Eclogue (*iam redit et Virgo, redeunt Saturnia regna*) and of the true ancient Italy celebrated in the second Georgic (vv. 167–76), the *magna parens frugum, Saturnia tellus, Magna virum.*

The Augustinian reference recurs on *Ana.* p.88 ('T's a great robbery – is empire'). What Augustine says (*De Civitate Dei,* 4.4.) is: 'Remota itaque iustitia quid sunt regna nisi magna latrocinia? quia et latrocinia quid sunt nisi parva regna?' – 'If you take away justice, what are kingdoms but large-scale robberies? for what are robberies, too, but petty kingdoms?' (It is more convenient if 'latrocinia' may be translated 'criminal gangs') D., it will be noted, changes Augustine's emphasis; the latter introduces the notion of justice, and uses *regnum*, not *imperium*. D.'s 'whose robbery is co-terminous with empire' is a much more devastating criticism. Behind this there lies also a passage from the *Octavius* (25.5) of the early Christian apologist Minucius Felix; a little book from which D. drew considerable material: 'Ita quicquid Romani tenent, colunt,

possident, audaciae praeda est: templa omnia de manubiis, 85
id est de ruinis urbium, de spoliis deorum, de caedibus sacer-
dotum'. 'Everything that the Romans hold, everything they cultivate, all their possessions, are the stolen loot of barefaced robbery; there is not a single temple that has not cost the devastation
of populous cities, the plunder of divine treasures, the slaughter
of priests.'

Stuart Jones (p.16) illustrates the *groma* and describes its use.
'Nothing', he says later (p.226), 'in the public life of the Romans
bears such eloquent testimony to the orderly and practical
spirit which gave them mastery of the ancient world than their
scientific method of encampment.'

even for us: even for the 'megalopolitan' civilised there was
a 'once upon a time', a cultural spring-time, we might say,
of 'mythopoiesis'. 'Wonder-years and wanderers': the same sort
of half-rime as 'grandeur . . . grand years' on *Ana.* p.90.
'Wanderers' should, maybe, be 'wanderer's' or 'wanderers''
– the latter, more probably, though it can be read as, 'Once
there was a . . . once there were wanderers to tell a tall tale.'
'anabasis' suggests to us a going up-country (Xenophon), but
the verb *anabainein* means to mount or go on board a ship,
which is appropriate to Aeneas's journey from Troy to Italy,
to be followed by the movement 'by land' from Aeneas's city of
Lavinium to Alba Longa, built by his son Iulus, and finally to
the 'forechosen site' of Romulus's Rome.

decalogue, dodecalogue: 'the first and only Roman code,
the Law of the Twelve Tables' (Mommsen). Children would
learn in school to chant them by heart, Cicero tells us – as we
used to learn the Ten Commandments – adding, as we might,
with regret, 'but nobody does so now': 'Discebamus enim
pueri xii, ut carmen necessarium, quas iam nemo discit', de
Legibus 2.23.59. To the original ten (451 B.C.) two were added a
year later. They were engraved on copper or bronze (or incised
on wood – accounts vary) and displayed in the Forum. The
originals were destroyed when the Gauls sacked Rome in 390
or 387. With this passage cf. p.50, 'the tokens, the matrices . . .'

beast of gray: the wolf which suckled the twins Romulus and Remus provides a thread which runs through the fabric of D.'s work, both pictorial and poetic: most magnificently seen in the watercolour 'The Wolf of the West' now in the gallery at Newcastle, the detail of which illuminates *The Anathemata*. The wolf is suckling not the twins but the lamb, *agnus masculus, anniculus*. In the background, among many other significant objects, we see Roman and modern artillery (cf. the 'Ram' part of 'Keel, Ram, Stauros'). 'the lily-white pair': 'two and two are the lily-white boys' (in *Green grow the rushes O*). So *S.L.* p.12: 'did the sallow ducts of Luperca nourish the lily-white boys', and *In Parenthesis*, p.203 n.11.

Horsed Dioscuri: the story of Castor and Pollux (*Dios kouroi*, sons of Zeus, by Leda) at the battle of Lake Regillus (B.C. 496), when the Romans, under the dictator Postumus, over-whelmed the Latins, who were seeking to restore the Tarquins, is reminiscent of the 'Mons Angels' of 1914; and in 'working parts' (a musketry instructor's phrase) and 'front-area muck' we have a link with the vocabulary of the Great War and *In Parenthesis:* so, too, 'square-pushing' below.

86 D. uses the present tense in speaking of the impossibility of forgetting Macaulay's rimes; he handed on that torch, for to at least one child he gave a copy of the *Lays of Ancient Rome* with a beautiful inscription on the fly-leaf, which includes Ver-gil's *Tantae molis erat Romanam condere gentem*. In February 1936, when he was living in Sidmouth, he sent a picture post-card greeting from Exeter to Buckinghamshire, signed also by two other close friends. D.'s contribution was Macaulay's 'Pomona loves the orchard, and Liber loves the vine, And Pales loves the straw-built shed [akin to D.'s wattled enclosures], warm with the breath of kine; And Venus loves the whispers of plighted youth and maid In April's ivory moonlight beneath the chestnut shade'.

W.F.B. compares 'a thing seen of many' with 1 Cor. 15.8. 'piscene', which follows almost immediately, lends colour to the suggestion, for it means both the pond or fountain in the market

place and the *piscina*, 'an aperture in the wall on epistle side of an **86**
altar . . . for the disposal of water that has been used for some
sacred purpose' (Donald Attwater's *Catholic Dictionary*).
This emphasis on the sacred character of those who appeared
makes the parallel very probable.

departed myth left ravished fact: i.e. myth or legend (pre-
historical) left historical fact 'on the couch of time'; 'ravished',
because, as D. would say, myth plays old Harry with fact,
and, as the time passes, we are left with the historicity of D.'s
'genuine myth'. For the shape of the phrase, cf. the illustration
facing p.55. Our 'dim-eyed Clio' of *Ana.* p.68 reappears to
record the birth to Rhea Silvia or Ilia of the twins Romulus and
Remus after her 'sacred commerce' with Mars. In 'her', 'she',
'him', we have the characteristic 'no names, no pack-drill'
method of referring to the principals concerned. 'her' in 'found
her nine calends gone' and 'she' in 'O, him! she said' are Ilia;
'huge in labour with the Roman people' is again based on the
Vergilian *Tantae molis erat* . . . referred to above; and 'the
Roman people' looks also towards vv. 276–7, *et Mavortia
condet Moenia Romanosque suo de nomine dicet*, and he shall
raise the walls of Mars and from his own name call the people
Romans.

Strider is most apt (even if the scholars will not accept the
connection of *gradus*, pace, with *grâdivus*) for it has the further
association with the warrant-officer's pace-stick, an instrument
like a large pair of dividers, used to determine the exact length
of the parade-ground pace, and carried almost as a symbol of
office. Cf. *S.L.* p.22, of Brasso, the *primipilus* or senior centurion: 'Some say he was born shouting the odds, in full parade kit,
with a pacing-stick under his cherubic little arm'. D. adopted
'the Strider' as a name for the legionary's Mars, and uses it
frequently, e.g. (again in the *S.L.*, p.14), 'they used to say we
marched for the Strider, the common father of the Roman
people, by whose very name you're called'.

When Juvenal (read by D. with a sharp eye) is expressing his
disgust with the corruption of his day, he looks back, appro-

priately, to the 'squat Georgie' as the god of the simple agricultural community. 'unde Haec tetigit, Gradive, tuos urtica
nepotes', 'How came this nettle-sting of lust, Gradivus, to
poison your sons' sons ?'. (2.128.)

All these details are a reminder that we are travelling down
the years of history. 'How long since . . . ?' (*Ana*. p.86) – we
now have the date B.C. 753 from which to work.

87   **brazen he wore it . . . twin-crested:** Mars was commonly
represented with a twin-plumed helmet ('his mantling horse-
tail') and for 'twin-crested' cf. Aeneid 6.779: 'Viden, ut geminae
stant vertice cristae, Et pater ipse suo superum signat honore',
'can you not see how the twin plumes stand erect upon his
crown, and already his father himself with his own badge marks
him [Romulus] divine'.

murex: the purple dye of the cuttle-fish. 'Aryan': the adjective could hardly have been used at the time this was written
without an awareness of its misuse by the Nazis (cf. the 'panzer'd lover' of *Ana*. p.105). MS. drafts of 'The Hunt' and 'The
Sleeping Lord' make it clear that the poet used the word in its
meaning of 'Indo-European', and particularly of those bodies
of Celts who occupied the British Isles.

Not he: as with 'and how should I' at the foot of the preceding
page, Ilia is answering a question that has to be understood
and is not expressed. 'thorax': cuirass, the Greek word for what
D. generally calls by its Latin name, *lorica*.

the squat Georgie: because (as in D.'s note) Mars was
originally a gêorgos or farmer; 'squat Georgie', moreover, has an
echo of the slang 'squaddy' (infantryman) which, by the
Second World War had replaced the original 'swaddy'. The
inter-relation of culture and cult, agriculture and the arts
(to which we shall be proceeding in a few pages), of Mars the
farmer and Mars the war-god, is neatly summarised in an
unpublished phrase: 'For Athena to gain, Quirinus [Mars]
must till'. The short note 1 to this page is developed in a later
MS, as follows: (a Roman legionary is speaking):

'and that far back a cult-figure called Arctaius, I think, to

whom oblations were made for the soil to yield good harvesting, **87**
but that like our Marmor he suffered the metamorphosis of
ceasing to be tutelar of the bronze plough-share's furrowed and
sustaining line, and became the especial tutelary of the men who
form in line of battle, not to sustain but to destroy.' D. took the
adjective *Gradivus* from Vergil, Aeneid 3.34–6, where Aeneas
prays to the nymphs of the countryside, *Gradivumque patrem,
Gaeticis qui praesidet arvis*, and to our father the Strider, tutelar
(to retain the idiom) of the ploughlands of Thrace; and from
10.542, where, metamorphosed, he is *rex Gradivus*, to whom the
arms of a fallen enemy are offered as a trophy.

got his papers (and note 1): did D. read Warde Fowler's
The Religious Experience of the Roman People? D. brilliantly
represents the Mars of whom W.F. writes (pp. 131–4) as 'a
genuine Italian religious conception . . . the Roman Mars
was the product of life and experience in Italy, and Italy only'.
Before he got his call-up papers he was, of necessity, more than a
farmer – 'I do not see in him only a deity of agriculture', continues Warde Fowler, 'or only a god of war; in my view he is a
spirit of the wilder regions, where dwell the wolf and wood-
pecker which are connected with him in legend: a spirit who
dwells on the outskirts of civilisation, and can with profit be
propitiated both for help against the enemies beyond, and for
the protection of cattle and crops within, the boundaries of
human activity.'

How different is this union of virgin and god (and how
artfully different the poet's treatment) from that which we may
regard it as prefiguring and which appears later (*Ana.* pp. 188–
9): when his Leda said . . . *fiat mihi.*

prevent us continually: 'prevent' must be understood in
the light of the accompanying 'Verticordia' and 'grace', as
when we speak of 'prevenient grace' – 'a grace which moves the
will spontaneously, unfreely, making it incline to God' (D.A.'s
Cath. Dict.). 'Unfreely' may be applied both to the seizing of the
girl and to the fulfilment of destiny. 'Which way should grace
turn matriarch hearts?', i.e. towards her destined lover, or her

87 father's will, who wished her to remain a Vestal Virgin.
The phrase comes from the Prayer Book: (collect for Trinity
Sunday): 'Lord, we pray we thee that thy grace may always
prevent and follow us, and make us continually to be given to all
good works.' – And so Eliot in *East Coker*. So, again, *Ana*. p.240,
'Who prevents the straight crow-flight? Who goes before the
doings of such kind of fowl?'

he first, with his butt-iron: this paragraph describes the
use of the groma (see *Ana*. p.85). 'butt-iron' gains from a half-
memory of the Great War, 'then were butt-heel-irons opened'
(*In Parenthesis*, p.63), the steel plate with which the end of the
butt of the S.M.L.E. rifle is shod, and from which, when an at
times agonisingly stiff and awkward metal trap was opened, oil-
bottle, pull-through, and 'four-by-two' could be extracted.
The literal meanings of 'ample front' take on further depth
from the fact that the adjective looks forward to 'the ample shape
of our Redemption' (*Ana*. p.135). There it is used by the girl
who will shortly (p.145) appear as Britannia, and here it is
used of the girl who is Rome: and both are linked by 'Redemption'. We find, too, in a *Balaam's Ass* draft, 'She's bright where
she walks She dignifies the spaces of the air and makes an
ample scheme across the trivial shapes'. Arcturus is 'constant'
because he never sets and never ceases to watch the Bear (cf.
below, on *Ana*. p.97).

aligned to the southward: Roman augurs looked to the
south, Greek to the north. The 'sacred routine' of the surveyors,
in note 3, derives its sacred character from its association with
the procedure of the augurs, who marked out in this way the
rectangle which formed the templum. This suggests that of the
many references to the coming glory which are to be found in the
Advent liturgy, D. had particularly in mind when he wrote,
above, 'his glory filled the whole place', Haggai 2.7 'and I will
fill this Temple with glory, says the Lord of hosts', for the
Temple of which the prophet, writing in the sixth century, is
speaking is the one which is to be rebuilt after the Babylonian
exile and in which Christ is to teach.

At the intersection of the first two lines ('at the intersected place') the tabernaculum was set up, the tent, whose entrance faced south. **Inaugurator,** in 'the terrible inaugurator' gains great weight from this double sense of the ritually controlled observation and the begetting of the Roman people. I find the further suggested (W.F.B.) association with 'auger' difficult to accept. It could be justified on the ground that an auger was originally the Old English nafu-gar, nave (of wheel) spear (borer) – but, to my mind, this is far-fetched: indelicate, too. 'west . . . West-turn': the emphasis on direction, because the movement of culture and religion in the poem is to the West. For the Roman surveyors, see Stuart Jones, pp. 15ff.

marcher's lurch . . . pelvic sway: most gruesomely reminiscent of the self-satisfied bearing and gait of a certain sort of N.C.O. Cf. the 'buttocked lance-jacks' of *I.P.* p.28. 'Clarissimi': cf. *egregius, Ana.* p.77, used there (as the title is here) 'before his time'.

West-star, hers: the evening star, Venus – but 'and all', i.e. all such 'Virgo potens' figures.

'T's a great robbery: cf. above, on *Ana.* p.85, where a 88 variation, found in a MS. draft, of a different 'sequence', might have been noticed, for the change in wording and emphasis: military force (the eagle) is replaced by commercial force: 'damp Britons make Roman holiday to pile the takings of a syndicate co-terminous with ocean'.

In the second paragraph of p.88 the same date – the time of Christ – is arrived at by a different reckoning, from the expulsion of the Tarquins and the first consular year, B.C. 509, 'half a millenium or so' before our era.

Lucomos (the word is plural, but here an anglicised plural for *Lucomones*): an Etruscan word for king, as we learn from Servius on Aeneid 8.475. 'abasileutos' (which should be plural, *abasileutoi*, but the poet wanted the same ending in the two words), without a king. **A good year?**, he asks, his point being that it was indeed a good year, but why is nothing said of the bad years, when Rome was forced to accept humiliating terms? Those are the 'hidden years'. 'an armaments commission': 'That refers to when the Etruscan power was stronger than Roman & for a while proscribed the necessary matériel without which armaments & the "hardware", as we now, could not be made, imposing "sanctions" (again as we say now)' – for this was the time of Mussolini's war in Abyssinia – ' "That takes you back / and aback./ The Urbs without edged iron / *can you credit it*?" – that was meant to suggest that it was, perhaps, or even *probably*, legendary, but nudge Kleio, she's like to be musing' – the text reads 'apt to be musing': an improvement, for the word-play is improved by being double, in both 'apt' and 'musing' – 'but if she is the muse of History or she whose name is said to mean "She that extols", well, slap her and *make* her extol *all* or *nothing*. She knows perfectly well that the clerks at the record office have managed to delete from the "tapes" the tell-tale Kalends'. (D. in a much later letter, when 'tapes' had become current.)

Behind this must lie the theory (which contradicts the patriotic legend of Lake Regillus) that Lars Porsenna captured Rome on his own behalf, and that the Urbs was 'without edged iron' because he forbad the use by the Romans of iron weapons. (See Scuddard, *A History of the Roman World*, 753–146 B.C., pp. 37–8). So Graham Webster, *The Roman Imperial Army*, 1974, p.24: 'Most of the early Roman weapons had to be made of wood, as the Etruscans at first denied the Romans iron, except for purely agricultural purposes'. Tacitus (Hist. 3.72) speaks of the surrender of the city to Porsenna: not so Livy and the patriotic legend.

89   The date at the head of the page again agrees, i.e. A.D. 30. In the inscription paragraph, 'carried', with its resemblance to 'quarried', may well be used because it suggests 'squared', as when we speak of 'quarry' (i.e. 'carré', square) tiles, or a 'quarrel', the square bolt fired from a cross-bow. D.'s admiration of the splendour of Roman inscription should be borne in mind when considering his views on the 'utile' and 'gratuitous'. He found the same quality of being 'perfect both formally and

for their purpose' in Eric Gill's finest inscriptions and in his **89**
'stone furniture'.

great epigraphers . . . portrait busts: an expanded version
of this (or a version from which this was condensed) appears
in an unpublished MS. It occurs during a conversation between
a group of Romans in Jerusalem at the time of the Passion:

'Maura always says that. She always says that the incised
inscriptions the portrait busts are where we are liveliest plastic-
ally. I'd rather overlooked the inscriptions – we – are – aristocra-
tic – there. It's an extremely interesting thing – one detects a
streak of true refinement there – the spaces *between* the incisions
have such significance in the best examples. Our masons seem
to have a genuine understanding of the alphabet in a kind of
physical way.' Then follows the nursery rime of note 1. Then
'If "and in them the Word is made stone" [as D. says of E.G.'s
work in *Epoch and Artist*, p.301] is what posterity will say of us,
it is some consolation.' There is an oddly coincidental, but
fortuitous, expansion of D.'s 'The Word is made stone' in a
letter addressed by E. G. to his three young daughters in
1925, as they set out for Rome: ' . . . it was the inscriptions I
went to see. May you see the Word where I saw the letters. May
you see the Christian sentence where I only saw the Roman
alphabet.'

One hundred and sixty-seven years: it was in B.C. 134
that Tiberius Gracchus tried to re-distribute the public lands
and so restore the small farmers, overwhelmed by the city
capitalists (the 'syndicate', below) who worked their vast estates
by slave labour. In the next year, he and 300 of his supporters
were clubbed to death by the extremists of the senatorial party.
Here the date does not fit so well, for the answer we get is A.D.
33. The 'waste land' and the Roman investors link the situation
to our own, through the image common to both, 'Pellam's land',
of *Ana.* p.50. The 'vineyard on a very fruitful hill' is from Isaiah
5, which is peculiarly appropriate to the waste-land and Roman
syndicate theme – the eating up of small farms by the great
ranchers; for, after lamenting the barrenness of the vineyard on

which so much work has been done, the prophet curses those who 'join house to house, that lay field to field, till there be no place' that does not belong to them. Moreover, 'my well-beloved . . . made a wine-press therein'; the wine-press or torcular is a symbol of Christ's filling of the wine-cup favoured by medieval poets and by ours (see, for example, Preface, p.31). 'fenced and watered': protection again, as so often, and life.

The turn-over from p.89 masks the break between the last line of 89 and the first of 90.

90 **in came the Principate:** Octavian adopted the title *Princeps* in 27 B.C. because (*v. Ox. Class. Dict.*) of its 'good Republican association'. In 27 B.C. he received the title 'Augustus'; but even if we take the beginning of his principate as immediately after the battle of Actium, when he defeated Mark Antony, in B.C. 31, we are left with the awkward date of A.D. 37. Can 'sixty-eight' be a slip for the more appropriate 'fifty-eight'?

the beginnings of the end: corresponding, a hundred years later, with the 'end of the beginnings' on the preceding page. What is more, it is the beginning of that end which moves the poet to near-despair in *A, a, a, Domine Deus* at the opening of *The Sleeping Lord*. The key-words here are 'megapolis' and 'commodity.' The latter reminds us, as it must have reminded D., of much of E.G.'s writing, and of Marx's 'fetishism of commodities' – 'man-made objects becoming alien and hostile to their creators'. The growth of the megalopolis (and it was from Spengler, we must admit, that D. learnt to apply the name to Rome) will be accompanied by a corresponding poetic degradation, 'the coarsening of the forms'. There is a sardonic repetition in 'grandeur . . . the grand years' of the rime on p.85, 'wonder-years / wanderers.'

W.F.B. draws attention – how aptly – to the Bastard Faulconbridge's railing against 'Commodity' at the end of Act 2 in *King John:*

  'That smooth-faced gentleman, tickling Commodity,
  Commodity, the bias of the world . . .
  This bawd, this broker . . .'

In the following pages, 90–5, we have an artistic history which **90**
parallels the account of the emergence of poiesis given in 'Rite
and Fore-time'. From approximately the same point in time as
has been adopted earlier – the date of the Passion – we now look
back at the Dorian invasion of Greece in the eleventh century
B.C., which swept away what remained of the Mycenean
civilisation, and at the general introduction of iron. 'Dorian
jarls' belongs to that set of terms which D. uses for brute force:
panzer, storm-group, 'the colossal spear-haft in the supposed
almighty fist-grip of his [Milton's] god-damned Lucifer'
(Intro. to the *Mariner*), Norman panzer-gangs, god-damned
bloody Vikings etc. An isolated fragment (from the same
'sequence' as that quoted earlier) points the conflict between
the maze ('gammadion'd castle') with its protective Virgo
potens, and the force of Roman order (it is a Roman who is
speaking):

'. . . so imposed our shape upon the waking minds of men so
insinuated the male principle as to vulgarise & flatten out the
subtle maze – so squared and mapped the meander of our intuitive origins (Aphrodite of the oblique approach, pray for
us, that gave us Aeneas)' – so Aeneas, after all, is recognised –
'the eye and central keep that the quincuncial fosse & fretted
troia cat's-cradle a defence for . . .'.

Nevertheless, western culture is being born, or reborn,
even though (*Ana.* p.91) the jarls of the dark age must still
learn from Egypt, Crete and Asia Minor. There is much history
in the paragraph 'The makers of anathemata . . . and new god-
fears'. We are seldom without a glancing modern reference, and
here we have 'rolled up the map . . . utile . . . specifications . . .
mobile columns' to give us the Napoleonic wars (Pitt on Auster-
litz: 'Roll up that map; it will not be wanted these ten years'),
industrialism and industrialised war.

The age is obscure . . . **dark:** no tautology. D. notes in the
margin, 'O.K. I nearly wrote "but" for "and".' The history of
the period is obscure, and we may compare it to what we genera-
ally call the Dark Ages – but 'at a pinch' they can beat out utile

spares or amulets, and there are 'new god-fears'; and the age
cannot be completely dark so long as there is some vestige of a
sense of the transcendent. This lends point to the 'second
spring' of p.91, and the corresponding vigour of the early
middle age (p.92, 'West-wood springs new' – cf. 'the sap-years'
of p.49).

91   With this page we move both in time and geographically, to the
Aegean and the 'strife-years', the years during which the Greek
city-states were born. The Hittite empire in Asia Minor came
to a sudden and violent end in the 13th century B.C.; so that the
Hittite creatures' are the Syro-Hittites of the ninth and tenth
centuries.

Our Sea: D. could not have used this of the Mediterranean,
in this context, without having in mind Mussolini's pathetic
perversion in his use of *Mare Nostrum*. The phrase, it is true,
was far from being Mussolini's own, but in the days when *The
Anathemata* was being written you could not have said 'Mare
Nostrum' without thinking of the Italian.

Six centuries: half-way to our cardinal date, we are in the
seventh-sixth centuries B.C., typified by the calf-herd (moscho-
phoros) of the text and notes, referred to also in *Epoch and Artist*,
p.276. With 'man-limb stirs / in the god-stones' cf. the earlier,
Ana. p.59, 'man-hands god-handled'. On the preceding page,
90, the age was dark, but the 'inward continuities / of the site /
of place', i.e. the continuance of the notion of worship and of a
place made sacred for and by worship, were, at a pinch, preserved. Then comes the first suggestion of the dawn, where 'very
grey and early in our morning', heralding 'Second Spring', has a
delectable stillness which reflects the scene at the tomb 'upon the
first day of the week, very early in the morning'. With the coming of that second spring, there is a new infusion of divinity or
of the divine creative power, corresponding to the ultimate divin-
isation symbolised in the Resurrection. *Kouros* (p. *kouroi*) is the
Ionic and Homeric form of *koros*, as *koure* is of *kore*, boy and
girl: and Korê, *the* girl, is Persephone.

92   **Transalpine Eleanore** is Eleanor of Aquitaine (romance,

courtly love). She is 'transalpine' to an observer in the Aegean. **92**
She was the grand-daughter of Guillaume de Poitiers, Duke
of Aquitaine, the first of the troubadours, and his heiress.
As her second husband she married Henry II of England. That
she accompanied her first husband, Louis VII of France, on
crusade, and went with him to Jerusalem, gives her a slender link
with Helen of the True Cross. The romantic poet includes her
with two others, beautiful and wayward. With 'parthenai made
of stone' in mind, D. may well have been thinking of the figure
on her tomb in the Abbey of Fontevrault. In any case, her
appearance here is justified by the magic that surrounded her
in the eyes of those poets of whom one cannot be sure whether
they were in love with the Holy Land, Helen of Troy or the
Duchess of Aquitaine.

For Helen as moon-goddess, see Jackson Knight, *Vergil:
Epic and Anthropology*, p.90. It is to emphasise this connection
that we have the accentuation Elenê, Selenê; and the connection
is continued into the Helen of Britain ('the Selenê of Thulê /
West Helen'). Of her D. writes:

'The British origin of Helena (the mother of Constantine)
can now, in every probability, be dismissed as having no historical foundation; nevertheless in tradition she is paramount.
In Welsh legend, or in material mixed with Welsh legend, she is
almost Britannia herself. In that tangled story she passes from
pseudo-history into the realm of true myth' – a revealing
phrase that can only mean D.'s 'myth in the true sense of the
word', a myth that expresses a need for, and provides an object
for, worship. 'We discern her as the eternal matriarch.
In the Welsh secular tale, *The Dream of Macsen Wledig* [used
by D. in *The Kensington Mass*] she is a figure of numinous
beauty, whose Welsh brothers conquer Rome. And in Christian
hagiography she is associated more than any other woman –
except one – with that instrument on the hill "where that young
prince of glory died".' (*Epoch and Artist*, p.44.) See also *E. & A.*
p.195 for Elen Luyddog (Helen of the Hosts), wife of Macsen
Wledig, the usurping emperor Magnus Maximus: of whom Kip-

ling wrote with some of the re-creative sympathy which gives
vigour to D.'s Roman pieces. In this connection D. speaks of
the 'need to posit some kind of archetypal "Elen" from remote
Celtic antiquity to account for the numinous power and splendour' attaching to her. D. returns to her in note 3 to *Ana.* p.131.
It begins to be apparent that what he means by 'true myth' is a
correspondence with and a poetic expression of what Jung
would call an archetype. The *Dream*, put to such good use by
D., is a short, gem-like, story in the *Mabinogion*, much less
strange to those whose taste has been formed by continental
romance than many of the other stories : beautifully incorporated
in *The Kensington Mass.*

Agelastos Petra: cf. *Ana.* pp. 56, 58, 104, and a longer comment on *Ana.* p.230.

The vigour of this spring-time will not be seen again, 'not
again, not now again' until the 'sap-years' of the early middle
age, when we shall see the great stone-carving of the French
cathedrals. 'Gallia Lugdunensis', one of the four provinces of
Roman Gaul, stretching across the middle of France from
Brittany to its capital Lugdunum (Lyons), founded as a Roman
colony in B.C. 43. 'Faustian': see Spengler, vol. 1, p.183. As D.
uses 'Faustian' of the spring-time in the west, so might he use
the Nietzschean-Spenglerian 'Apollinian' for the classical
spring which he has just left. The impossibility of reconciling
Spengler's basic thesis of the isolation of cultures with D.'s
monism is well summarised by Christopher Dawson in his
Progress and Religion, pp. 31ff.

93   **the Word is made stone:** applying the phrase used of
Roman inscriptions (*Ana.* p.89) to Gothic carving.

The second and third paragraphs are a curious interpolation.
The poet wonders whether such strength and innocence will
ever be found again: in, before, or after all the terrible vicissi-
tudes of human history. ('Loops', maybe, should be taken in the
sense of a loop in a railway line, a divergence from, and return
to, the main line of development.) The answer is *Spes*, hope.

before the prides . . . falls: another double or treble

word-juggling. Pride normally comes before a fall, and so in **93**
man's history. But shall we see the Delectable Kore again before the prides? shall we see her after the falls? Again, the
words can be read to mean 'before, i.e. first (come) the prides;
and after, i.e. secondly (come) the falls'. 'happy falls' contains a
further play, for the fall of man was a *felix culpa*, a happy fault
(or fall) because it made possible the choice of the Virgin and the
Incarnation.

Spes: from that favoured source, the *Vexilla Regis* of Fortu-
natus, *O Crux ave, spes unica*, our single hope. 'answer me'
should be taken closely with 'Spes', for hope is being begged
to answer (and 'how right' she is); but she says that she is
blindfold, and 'blindfold's best', because hope like Justice
is best with bandaged eyes. 'I admit that "Hope" is not the
same thing as Justice, but near enough for my purpose here, and
after all there is that tag about how a religious prays best when
he does not know that he is praying, and in "art-works" also
"blindfold's best" as often as not'. (D. August 1974.) The
anchor has long been used as a symbol of hope ('The Hope
and Anchor' is a common name for an English public-house). It
is a Christian symbol, too, for the stock and shank form a cross.
Hope, therefore, is asked where she thinks the flukes of her
hook (anchor) will hold. (Hebrews 6.18: We have this as a sure
and steadfast anchor of the soul, a hope . . .)

from the feel of things: i.e. not by arguing from cause to
effect, but by a 'flair' (derived, I fear, from Spengler) 'which
enables one to read a whole life in a face or to sum up whole
peoples from the pictures of an epoch', (vol. 1, p.183). Without
serving two masters, we may, like the poet, at times make
friends of the ubiquitous German.

With **Down we come,** we return to Greece, in the fifth
century B.C., the 'skill-years', when the name of the sculptor
can be attached to a carving ('the signed and fine grandeurs').
Yet technical skill is coming uncommonly close to destroying
the very 'god-handling' it has made possible.

the signed and fine grandeurs: speaking of the foundation **94**

94 (traditionally in the year 496) in Rome of the temple of Ceres, Liber and Libera (i.e. Demeter, Dionysus and Persephone in a Roman form) Warde Fowler (*Religious Experience of the Roman People*, 1911, pp. 256–7) says:

'There is one curious fact in connection with the temple that in my opinion goes far to prove that the traditional date is not far out. Pliny tells us explicitly that the two Greek artists who decorated the temple, Damophilus and Gorgasus, inscribed their names on the walls, and he added that the work of the former would be found on the right and that of the latter on the left. (Pliny, N.H., 25.154) Nothing more is known about them; but I am assured that the fact that they signed their names and added these statements suits the character of Greek art in the archaic age 580 to 450 B.C. No signatures of artists are known earlier than about 580; then comes a period when signatures are found, sometimes with statements such as these. And lastly, about 450, we begin to find simple signatures without any other words.'

It's a nice thing, as in Wellington's comment on Waterloo, to the effect that it was as close-run a thing as ever you saw. So the nicety of art, and the nicety of the situation, suggest the nicety of strategic dispositions: cf. *Epoch and Artist*, p.161. where the art of strategy is used as an illustration.

One hundred and seventeen Olympiads: in other words, if we look back from our original point in time, c. A.D. 27–30, we are somewhere in the middle of the fifth century B.C. An Olympiad is a period of four years. 468 years before A.D. 30 is B.C. 438. This is a little late, but not late enough to signify. The 'he' of 'he contrived her' is the Athenian sculptor Pheidias, and the reference is to his ivory and gold statue of Athene ('chryselephantine'). The statue, however, was made before 432, for in that year Pheidias was accused of misappropriating the gold. The colossal Athene stood in the Parthenon ('her Maiden's chamber'). 'Of good counsel', 'tower of ivory', and 'house of gold' are all titles of Our Lady (*Mater boni consilii, turris eburnea, domus aurea*). D. himself made a copy, still in existence, of the well-known painting 'Our Lady of Good Counsel'. **94**

enough and to snare: 'to snare' has a double sense, as applied to academic sculptors (see *Ana*. p.60 and D's comment on 'O the Academies'), and as applied to those who lose their hearts to the Parthenos – and at the same time retains some of the force of the word ('spare') for which it is substituted.

Marathon salvage: the vast statue of Athene Promachos (battle champion, front fighter, as in the Iliad and the dedication to *In Parenthesis*) which the same 'he', that is Pheidias, cast from the bronze gear captured from the Persians at the battle of Marathon in 490. It stood on the Acropolis, and the gleam of the spear-point could be seen by seamen as they approached Cape Sunium, the southernmost promontory of Attica. ('There's where her spear-flukes / pharos for you', p.96. See Pausanias, 1.28, with Peter Levi's note to his translation, 1971.) 'without', i.e. in the open, between the Propylaea and the Erectheum. In saying 'without' D. may well have had in mind the use of the word in such names as 'St Paul's without the walls' (of Rome), and so often (see section 5) of London churches.

Again, in addition to her own titles (*Polias*, guardian of the city, *Promachos, Tritogeneia*, Athene shares Mary's (of *Uranos*, of heaven; both Queen and goddess of the elements; *Virgo Potens*; star of the sea). The meaning of 'Tritogeneia' as an epithet of Athene is not clear: 'Trito-born', i.e. born of a lake or stream of that name; 'third-born'; 'thrice-born'; or (which suits D.'s admired 'Minerva Iovis capite orta' Minerva born from the head of Jupiter) head-born. D. makes use of this last derivation from *trito*, said to be an Aeolic word for *kephale*, head, later in *The Ana*. p.221 and n.3. Elsewhere he writes 'But as Minerva stands here for Eternal Wisdom & so accounts for the Eternal begetting of the Logos *ante omnia saecula*, and as Our Lady is called Seat of Wisdom, the suggested definition *Minerva Iovis capite orta* covers both the Eternal timeless begetting *and* as an aside the earthly begetting in Liknites cave [for which see note to *Ana*. p.97] of Bethlehem.'

The typography is confusing in the last paragraph. She, Athene, is Virgo Potens, and her alerted armament ('alerted' both because 'erect', above, and because she watches unceasingly) is a land-mark for those following a course at sea. We must supply a full-point after 'sea-course'. She is Polias, i.e. of the city (and so of the land), *but* she is also Tritogeneian, i.e. (falling back on the water-born derivation, or because her divine birth extends her empire to the sea) she is also of the sea, and so serves as a sea-mark or star of the sea.

We now meet our first sea-farer. He is half trader, half pirate; he could possibly be an invader. He is of an older race than the Greeks into whose waters he is sailing, for he is 'Pelasgian', a word the poet uses for an earlier indigenous race. He could well be (for the historical setting is sufficiently fluid) as the man who in Odyssey 15 kidnapped the child Eumaeus, sailed with him to Ithaca and sold him to Laertes. That on the next page his 'top-tree boy' sights the spear-point of the goddess does not necessarily imply that this voyage takes place after the erection of the statue, for we may invoke the 'we live before her time' principle. The vessel approaches Attica from the Aegean. They round Sunium and turn into the Saronic Gulf, and continue on a westerly or north-westerly course. This must be so, for their position is such that the island of Salamis obscures Eleusis on the mainland of Attica, and Aegina is to port. Again the typography is confusing. The sense is: right ahead of the vessel, beyond Salamis, Eleusis is hidden; to port, lies Aegina.

D.'s co-ordinates are accurate. The position of Aegina (the town itself, which is at the western end of the island) is 37.44 N. 23.30 E. Their course is now due north, or perhaps a little west of north, and they can see the 'spear-flukes' 'Three points on the starboard bow', i.e. the statue is on a bearing of 33 3/4 degrees, or N.E. by N. They can see, ahead, Phaleron, the old port of Athens.

95   Meanwhile the sun has climbed to, and crosses, the meridian ('his celestial influence gains'). The time of day and the season coincide with the first Good Friday (sec note 1 to the next page,

96) and as the sun begins to sink to the south-west, over the **95**
mainland of Argolis, suddenly the weather clears, and the
outline of the ship ('the build of us') appears as a shadow on the
water, with (p.96) the shadows of the gulls perched on the yards.
Before it was not *blue* Aegean, the italicised *blue* emphasising
(so D.) that 'the Aegean was not always "blue" or calm, but
stormy and dangerous'. As the weather clears, at the foot of
p.95, the waters are 'blueing'.

loomings and dippings: the former in the sense of indistinct appearance, the latter in that of 'her yards dipped'.

Low, raked: it is hardly profitable to try to determine just
what type of ship D. had in mind ('Long Serpent', for example,
suggests the sort of vessel later used by the Vikings, and has an
Homeric ring, too). There was a great difference in antiquity
between the slim war vessel, which was primarily a troop-
transport carrying fighting men who served as rowers, as in
Homer's 'black ships' – D.'s 'marines' of *Ana.* p.105 – and the
much broader-beamed cargo vessel. And this man is surely a
trader.

tanged Salamis: the map shows the 'tangs' at the eastern
and western ends of the island. Since an early meaning of 'tang'
is the tongue of a snake or the sting of an insect, and since the
Persians in the year 480 suffered so heavy a defeat by being
lured into fighting the naval battle of Salamis in the narrow
waters enclosed by the tangs of the island, it may not be over-
fanciful to attach a double meaning to the adjective.

Cleruchy island: Aegina, so called because, after many years
of war with Athens, the Aeginetans were expelled and the island
was divided among Athenian *klerouchoi*, persons who received
an allotment of land but remained Athenian citizens. The name
is here a harmless anachronism, for the poet stands outside the
history he describes – and Salamis has reminded him of Athenian naval power, which overwhelmed the Aeginetans, who had
been the bravest of all in that battle.

his celestial influence gains: the sun (see above) is climbing
to the meridian. 'atmosphere . . . water-sphere': we had a

similar repetition on p.69. 'the wide sinus': the Saronic Gulf. Why *sinus*? for the sake of the double interlacing of the Shakespearean memory (sea-change) and the vowel-changes in 'wide-sinus' – 'sea-hues'. 'Cenchreae', on the east coast of the Isthmus of Corinth, the western extremity of the Gulf. 'his chariot': the chariot of the sun. Cf. *The Kensington Mass*, p.11, 'Brazen-faced Phoebus / had not as yet / in his quadriga / climbed to the horizon rim' of the sun rising. 'tangent' not only, perhaps, because the rays of the sun are seen as leaving the sphere at a tangent, but also because, the overcast having cleared, they can now touch the vessel.

96   **What bells is that . . . the sun in the Ram:** six bells in the afternoon watch (1500 hours), the hour of Christ's death.

'Mars' Venus-Day': a Friday in March, with the moon at the full and the sun in Aries.

A great deal depends upon these three lines. The coincidence of the moment of the death of Christ with the moment of the safe arrival in port of the master of the vessel (in time of day, day of the week, and season, but not, of course, in the same year) shows that the master is indeed a symbol of Christ guiding man to his haven. Nevertheless there is no Christification of the man himself. He is given epithets taken from those given to Christ (e.g. *Ischyros* on the next page), but he remains a type of the skipper in R. H. Dana's *Two Years Before the Mast*, 'Frank Thompson, all the way from "down east". I've been through the mill, ground, and bolted, and come out a regular-built-down-east-johnny-cake'. He is taken, too, as will be apparent when similar figures enter into later parts, from Chaucer's Shipman, as described by D. in his *Introduction* to Coleridge's *Mariner*, pp. 33–4.

pharos . . . day-star: 'pharos', literally 'lighthouse', from the island of Pharos, off Alexandria, the site of a famous light. There is an Odyssean link in the use of word (for D.'s tentacles are ever reaching out), in that it was at Pharos that Menelaus was held up on his way home from Troy, and it was there that he had news of Odysseus, which he passed on to

Telemachus (Odyssey 4.355ff). 'day-star for the sea', an embroidering of the similar passage at the foot of p. 94. 'pelagios',
of the ocean, but also with a suggestion of 'Pelasgian'. 'caulked',
like the later 'pickled', has a double sense ('caulk' is, or used to
be, nautical slang for a shot of rum): toughened, and the sense
so boldly expressed (*Ana.* p.182) in 'the ancient staggerer, the
vine-juice skipper'.

This master is either a Phoenician or from Colchis on the
Black Sea, the destination of the Argonauts. 'queen of the sea-
marts' (which should be taken with Tyre, not with 'Lady') shows
that he is a trader. 'Grogram': 'Old Grog' was the nickname of
the eighteenth-century Admiral Edward Vernon (from his habit
of wearing grogram trousers) and 'grog' is named after him,
because it was he who ordered the issue of rum (now disgrace-
fully abolished) to be diluted with water.

Now that they have made Phaleron, this first voyage to be **97**
described has ended. The reader might be deceived and believe
that the master in the next voyage is the same man, whereas a
completely different voyage is about to be described, taking
place at a completely different time.

D. writes: 'What is said on p.97 *gives the impression* that
having unloaded or done his business in the port of Athens, the
ship's master took his craft south, down the narrows up which
he had come and so out into the Middle-Sea west to the Pillars
of Hercules & thence to Britain. *I had not intended that at all.*
But such sentences as "there's avers he's wintered with
Cronos . . ." and all the rest of p.97 & indeed the continuing
pages . . . give the impression that it was the same "lime-juice
skipper" as he who had rounded Sunium'. D. goes on to say
that although the matter is of no great consequence, it may have
given rise to the notion (mentioned earlier) of a non-existent
'mystic ship'.

A break might well come, and be represented typographically
by a couple of white lines, between 'Ischyros with his sea-boots
on' (note, incidentally, the negro spiritual) and 'There's those
that avers'.

97   **knar,** knot in wood, is a fine word for a man described in terms of tough timber. Cf. Chaucer's 'He was short-sholdred, brood, a thikke knarre' (Prologue 549, of the Miller).

He's drained it again: i.e. a self-consumed libation, generally (as on *Ana.* p.172, where the same words are used) at the start of a voyage, but here, and on p.182, in thanksgiving for a safe passage. *Iacchos:* Dionysus, associated with the vine, and the centre of a vastly complicated mythology. 'He' is a duffle-coated Dionysus and strong, ('ischyros'). As the poet associates the waking of Liknites (the new-born god cradled in a *liknon* or basket-shaped winnowing-fan) at the feast of Dionysus with the birth of the child cradled in a manger at Bethlehem, so with equal boldness he here associates the master of the Phoenician trader with the God who on Good Friday is hailed as Hagios Ischyros – holy, strong – and Hagios athanatos, holy immortal. This reinforces the metaphorical identification with Christ introduced, on p.96, by the reference to the day, hour and season.

There's those that avers: the earliest fragments we have of a navigational manual (preserved by Avienus in the fourth century A.D.) dates from about 500 B.C.; so that at a very early age there may well have been stories of voyages into the North Sea and so to Thule (the Shetlands).

under Arctophylax: in the high northern latitudes, under the circumpolar constellation which we now call Boötes, the Ploughman, and which the ancients called Arcturus or Arctophylax, the bear-warden (we retain the name Arcturus for the brightest star in Boötes). *with Cronos,* because, according to one story, after Cronos had been overthrown by his son Zeus he slept eternally on an island in the far far north. In another story (also used by D.) he, in his Romanised form as Saturn, hid in Latium; hence the fanciful derivation of that name, from *latere,* to hide. There his reign was the golden age of peace and happiness.

With **mare, See,** and **Leir's river** D. brings together the three strands, classical antiquity, Anglo-Teutonic (we may re-

member that the North Sea was often called 'The German
Ocean') and Celtic. For Leir, Lear, Lir, etc. see the beginning
of this section.

at hurricano strength . . .: the voyage is not given in geographical sequence. First we have the Thames ('Leir's river),
then the furthest point ('Thule'); then the Channel ('mid-
sleeve') and the western approaches and the Scillies ('where the
seas of the islands war with the ocean'). For the wild weather in
British waters see the storm scene in *Lear* (Act 3, Sc. 2): 'Blow,
winds, and crack your cheeks! rage! blow! You cataracts and
hurricanoes, spout, Till you have drenched our steeples,
crown'd the cocks! You sulphurous and thought-executing
fires . . .' – a source we have already met twice, on the title-page,
and on page 68 ('rotundities').

the wide gusset: the Channel (the French 'La Manche')
neatly seen as a sleeve, the wrist at the Dover Strait, the
'wide gusset' at the western approaches.

the seas of the islands . . . **insulae:** the Irish Sea and the
Channel (the 'French Sea', 'Mare Gallicum') war with the
Atlantic and so white with foam and spray the Scillies, the
islands of King Mark of Cornwall (see note 3 to this page).

to blanch / main and Ushant: an admirable elegance. In **98**
the literal sense 'blanch' is a verb (as is 'white' in 'white the
horse-king's insulae'); the rush of the tides blanches the mainland of Brittany and the island of Ushant; but 'blanch' may also
be taken as an adjective – white – and so represent Iseult
Blanchmains ('main' too, having a double meaning). Iseult of
the White Hands, the Iseult of Brittany whom Tristram married,
for 'he had allmoste forsakyn La Beale Isode'; yet 'whan they
were a-bed bothe, sir Trystrames remembirde hym of his olde
lady, La Beale Isode, and than he toke suche a thoughte
suddeynly that he was all dismayde, and other chere made he
none but with clyppynge and kyssynge' (Malory, Book 8, c.36.)

'Yes, that blanch / main and Ushant was a bit of luck,
wasn't it. I remember wondering whether I could get away with
it.' (D.)

98   There is a similar felicity in 'where Trystan's sands run out to land's last end'. There is the literal sense, that the thick weather extends to Land's End, covering the Cornish peninsula ('Mark's main'), but it is conveyed in an adaptation of the common phrases 'the sands are running out' and 'man's last end'; and these have a special poignancy when we recall Tristan's last end when, as his 'sands were running out', Iseult Blanchmains deceived him, and he turned his face to the wall and died.

Albion: with the poet's characteristic care, is masculine here (*his* screen of brume) as being the son of Poseidon and Amphitrite, and (in one story) the founder of the kingdom of Britain – the country herself (*la perfide Albion*) being feminine. To return to the voyage: the position given in line 4 (45.57N 5.12E.) is the position (not the bearing) of the Lizard, which D. gives even more accurately. Falmouth ('confluent Fal', because two rivers flow into Falmouth Harbour) lies to the north-east, and Land's End lies west. The fog extends from here across the Channel and over the western part of Cornwall. The position 49.40N 5.20 W. is in mid-Channel, as is the next position, further to the east, 49.57N 4.40 W. When they reach the second position, they emerge from the belt of fog, and the Dodman is sighted, bearing a point (11 1/4 degrees) before the beam 'in a north-westerly direction' – as, indeed, it would, for the longitude of the Dodman is 4.49W, west of the ship's longitude by 9 minutes; as they continued up-Channel it would a little before the beam on the port side, for the vessel would be on a north-easterly course, at a distance of some eighteen miles (six leagues).

by whatever card he knew: in whatever way he described the bearing, in days when compass and compass-card were unknown. So, Macbeth 1.3, 'All the quarters that they know I' the shipman's card' – the witches scene which will re-appear in 'The Lady of the Pool' section, *Ana.* p.141.

Then was when the boy at the masthead, who had come from the eastern Mediterranean ('his *thalassa*'), through the

Gibraltar Strait (the Pillars of Hercules), over the Atlantic . . .
was about to sing out: but the poet breaks off, and goes back
over the earlier part of the voyage, which had been a 'weary
time, a weary time' (as in part 3 of the *Ancient Mariner*).
'north-way is Abendsee': to travel north is also to travel into
waters of the evening, of the west. The gap indicated by the
ellipses after 'over the ocean' is not filled until the top of p.102.

D. drew his metaphorical language for the sea from O.E. **99**
poetry, e.g. 'ofer ganotes baeth' – across the gannet's bath –
(Beowulf 1862). Ursula, too, in Borrow's *Romany Rye* (a book
D. enjoyed vastly over many years) speaks of being sent 'across
the gull's bath to a foreign country'.

At times they were becalmed ('lying-to), at other times they
were 'going' or running 'free' (with the wind aft, favouring
them); sometimes 'before a soldier's wind' (often called a 'farmer's wind': on *Ana.* p.175 it is a 'poet's gale' as opposed to a
'navigator's'), a wind dead aft, with which even a soldier can
sail. The southerly wind carries them north, and the south-
westerlies carry them north-east; but, at times, the wind backs
(shifts counter-clockwise) from south or south-west and by
moving into the east, forces them back to the west.

true to a touched stone: the lodestone, whose attractive
properties were known from an early date. Plato (e.g. Timaeus
80c) speaks of the *lithos Herakleia*, the Heraclean stone or
magnet; and it was known that the magnetic property could be
imparted to other pieces of metal or iron-ore by touching or
stroking. The anachronism of suggesting the use of the directive
property of the magnetised needle or stone is hinted at by the
question-mark, as though the poet were saying, 'Was his north
the north of our compass?'. The date of the invention of the
magnetic compass is discussed, most interestingly, in Professor
E. G. R. Taylor's *Haven-finding Art*, referred to earlier.

north, with the happy veer: their heading is now north, for
the wind has veered (moved clock-wise) from east ('easters west
Him') to south. It veers still more so that they can make good a
north-easterly course, towards the Scillies, and then into

Cornish waters. (D's notes explain the 'nine white grinders' etc.)
This, it should be remembered, is a description of the voyage
before they ran into the Channel fog. We may add to D.'s notes
the following from a letter dated September 1947, which provides a link with *In Parenthesis*, p.140.

'I wonder if *nine* has some echo in the idea that the "ninth
wave" is thought of as being higher or more potent than the
other waves. When I was a child on holidays at the sea-side at
Deal or some such place, there was still lingering some idea that
the *ninth* waves was likely to spray its surf higher – a nursemaid
old wives' tale. Cf. page 140 of *In Parenthesis* . . . make brats
too venturesome flop back with belly full and guardian nurse
girls squeal . . . followed *immediately* by and there was scattering
from that maiming all over the shop.' D. adds, in a marginal
note to the letter, 'It was an analogy that came into my mind at
the time, I mean at the time of the action, July 1916'.

nine white grinders: may be interpreted in more senses than
one. The vessel is travelling over the white waves (which grind
rock, timber and even men); she is riding the waves (the daughters of the mill-stone island, Scilly); but behind this is the notion
that she is travelling past the rocks or reefs of the islands, the
teeth ('white grinders'), and those teeth are the daughters of the
mill-stone. 'kouroi': the crew. 'her', in 'the eyes of her' is the
vessel, the bows; a little elasticity will include Igraine looking
towards her Cornish husband.

100   **what belles can she foam:** the 'belles' are those referred
to in n. 5 to p.99: but the word would not have been used were it
not for the nautical sense of 'bells', as on p.96, 'What bells isthat'.
'Morgana's fay-light': both the deceptive mirage, fatal to mariners, reported mostly in the Strait of Messina, and the illusion
personified in King Arthur's sister, Morgan Le Fay. 'abb', weft,
used as a verb. Cf. *Ana.* p.196 'the fine-abb'd Eblana flax' and
The Kensington Mass, p.9, 'fine abbed fair cloths of Eblana flax.'
'worse', again as a verb (i.e. make the current more dangerous)
or the meaning may be that the mist spreads a veil of white
('diaphanes') over the ebbing waters, or, worse, over the flood.

Dis Manibus: 'to the divine shades', as on Roman tombs (hence the capitals), deliberately placed beside the Breton (Celtic) 'menhir' ('long stone'). It was the disaster in 1707 (note 3), caused by ignorance of longitude, which led to the passing of the Act in 1714 'for providing a Publick Reward for such Person or Persons as shall discover the Longitude at Sea', a reward ultimately won, or partly won, by John Harrison. We owe this page to D.'s reading of Professor E. G. R. Taylor.

Caliban's Lamia . . . Hand of Glory: Lamia, the female demon, serpent, or sea-vampire (like Caliban's mother Sycorax, an island dweller) will re-appear (but from her Cornish wreckers' home as a land-vampire) on p.107. 'rung', meaning both 'wrung' and 'stole the rings from'. 'Hand of Glory', 'the dried and pickled hand of a man who had been hanged. If a candle was made from the fat of a malefactor who had also died on the gallows was lighted and placed in the Hand of Glory as in a candlestick, it rendered motionless all persons to whom it was presented. Sometimes the dead man's hand is itself the candle, or rather bunch of candles, all its withered fingers being set on fire . . .' (Frazer, with even more gruesome details to follow.) 'Hand of Glory' may well be a translation of the French 'Main de Gloire', itself a corruption of 'mandragore' (mandrake, *mandragora officinarum*) used as a narcotic and in magic.

where the wolf . . . Mark's lost hundred: where, long 101 before the navigational light, the Wolf churns up the foam over the now sea-covered area south of Land's End. 'hundred', in the sense of a sub-division of a county, rather than alluding to the submerged churches (140, in fact) mentioned below and in note 1.

Back over (and so a few lines later, 'back to'): back, because (p.99) 'easters west him off' and they have to make their way east again; they will, in fact, as it turns out, be carried too far east, as far as the Dodman.

mensae: the altars of the 'unapsed' (because pre-Roman – cf. p.49, 'apsidal houses') churches. In the Welsh word we recognise *ecclesiae*. 'It appears that *such* evidence *as there is*

of "Celtic" churches the east end was not round but square –
as too I think were the Saxon ones – *if* that is true then about
the only nice thing those blasted hateful men the Normans, men
with a veneer of French culture & language, was the apse – I
love the slow turning wall of an apse & of course it was copied
from the Roman basilica, with a mensa in place of the *bema* of
the magistrate.' (D., August 1974.)

The course we are now given is directed, they hope, to Mounts
Bay, the wind being from the south-south-west: the vessel is
'easting' and enters the Channel. 'chop', variant of 'chap' = jaw;
so, 'the entrance of an abyss, cañon, valley, channel etc. . . .
cruising in the chops of the Channel, Anson's Voyages, 1748'
(O.E.D.). The lead and line is one of the oldest nagivational
aids. Herodotus, writing in the fifth century B.C., not so far distant in time from the period of this section of *The Anathemata*,
says that when you approach Egypt from the sea, 'and are within
a day's sailing of the land, if you let down a sounding line
you will bring up mud [adhering to the bottom of the lead]
and find a depth of eleven fathoms' (3.5). Cf., of another seaman,
p.109 'Did he strike soundings . . . ?' '*Our* thalassa', the italic
and Roman alternating with 'his *thalassa*' of p.98. and corresponding 'to *his* thalassa' overleaf.

102   **That was when:** the look-out cried to his towny, thinking
that the land he had sighted was Land's End ('their Golden
Cornu' – maybe they were from the Black Sea?). D. is at pains
in the note to acknowledge the inaccuracy of 'rounded'. To
round Lands End they would have had to approach it from north
of west. 'Cassiterides' (*kassiteros*, tin) the Tin Islands (Scilly)
and Cornwall. 'I have no knowledge of the Cassiterides, whence
tin is brought to us' (Herodotus, 3.115).

Themis . . . Phoebe . . . Telphousa: the last two names for
the ship-boys' sweethearts have associations that obviously
commend them to the poet. 'Themis' seems at first an unusual
choice. She was the daughter of Ouranos and Gaia (Heaven and
Earth), and the mother of Prometheus – a link with the 'Easter
of technics'. (D. might well accept, even if he did not intend,

that secondary connection.) Note 2 to the next page but one, **102** 104, however, shows that he regarded her not so much as the goddess of Right (*themis* = custom, usage, right disposition) as Earth herself: Peter Levi, on Pausanias 1.22, speaks of inscriptions to *Gaia Themis*. Hence 'warm-dugged'.

Phoebe was confused with Artemis, as a moon-goddess: hence 'white' and the delicacy of 'lune'. 'laughless little Telphousa'; laughless, because of the 'cleft in the rock' (cf. 'Agelastos petra,' *Ana*. p.56 and n.), as 'lune' above. Telphousa or Thelphousa is another form of the name Delphi; it is in Arcadia, and is also the name of a nymph, the daughter of the river Ladon. She was deceitful and unscrupulous ('said she'd smile / for tin!' – the schoolboys money), for she had a shrine at Thelphousa, and when Apollo wished to build himself a shrine there, she persuaded him, pretending to have only his best interests at heart, not to do so. (See the Homeric Hymn to the Pythian Apollo). Apollo accordingly moved to Crisa, where he was obliged first to kill the terrible monster, the Pytho. Telphousa has 'affinities' (see *Ana*. p.104 n.4) with Delphi, but they are indirect. See also comment on *Ana*. p.230.

What ship's boy would lose her? rather than lose her he would risk the 'skerry-mill (the 'quern' of p.99), the reef or rock-hazard and the 'granite molars' of the Lamia.

It is instructive to know what passages gave particular pleasure to the poet himself. Thus: '*The Ana*. (102) has a few words that I am conceited enough to like, middle of page

> . . . and laughless little Telphousa
> what shipman's boy could ask another?
> *said she'd smile*
> > > *for tin!*
> What ship's boy would lose her?
> > > the skerry-mill rather!
> rather the granite molars of the sea-Lamia.'

The lines italicised are underlined twice. D. was probably pleased by the rime, too, a device which he seldom uses and for which he seems to have an ingenuous near-envy. And who would not like 'laughless' (remembering 'agelastos') '. . . smile' ?

But Albion's brume: on p.98 'Albion put down his screen of brume' ('Albion', for the white fog and the white island, the 'candida insula' of the inscription facing p.49). As the fog clears they sight land, but they do not see the bay of Ictis (Mount's Bay), for they have gone too far up-Channel. They reverse their course ('go a compass') and turn the vessel's head to the west. If she 'stands scarce six points off the wind', the angle between her course and direction from which the wind is blowing cannot be less than 66 degrees. The wind, therefore, must now be from North-north-west and if it veers, i.e. moves further into the north, they will not be able to stand into Mount's Bay. 'No Service boat', says the Admiralty Manual of Seaman-ship, 'other than the sailing dinghy will sail closer than about 50 degrees off the wind', and this vessel, with its primitive square sail would not sail with the wind even slightly before the beam.

go a compass originated from Acts 28.13 (the A.V.'s 'from thence we fetched a compass', where the phrase is in-appropriate, for the ship in which St Paul was travelling, con-tinued up the coast from Syracuse, across the strait, to Rhegium).

103   **but no!** the wind backs; 'the smiler' (i.e. the smiling, favourable, wind) draws more south, and then still further south, until, still backing, it is precisely (with the help of the Maiden) where they want it, east of south: but, as it does so, it brings wilder weather. The fog goes, but they have 'squall-mist and rain'.

Close-cowled: it is now that we follow on from the ellipses at the foot of p.98. The look-out at the mast-head sees the Dodman to starboard. ('cowled', 'cantor', 'versicle': cf. the 'schola cantorum' metaphor on *Ana.* pp. 63–4). The water is shoaling and they are in danger of being driven onto the rocks – a lee shore, for the wind is in the south-east; and 'each brined throat·chanties' (echoing 'cantor') the prayer to the Maiden who watches over the seas and seamen. 'Goidel's league': the word 'league' is of Celtic origin (Goidelic and, as here, Brythonic Celts). 'Ilissus', a stream in Attica, whence they have come, although the vessel is not the same as that which earlier made the port of Phaleron. 'matlos', so spelt in Partridge, for French *matelot*, and still current in the R.N.

Dis: the god of the underworld. Have they come 'all the way' **104** only to founder in the Channel ('Lear's Sea') – all for the wealth and power that comes from control of the sea, thalassocracy. The word was used by the ancients, and fits in here naturally enough, since 'thalassa' has been used so much. It is interesting that it is first quoted in the O.E.D. from Grote, the historian of Greece, the 'legendary th. of Minos' (in Crete), and other references are to the th. of Phocaea and the Phoenicians, traders and colonisers in the Mediterranean. There is some bitterness in the use of the word, as with 'empire'.

'Wot'ld you do with the bleedin owners' etc., as in 'What shall we do with a drunken sailor . . . put him in the long boat until he's sober etc.' 'over the sea to Dis' as in the Kennedy Fraser Hebridean song. 'Over the sea to Skye' ('Guillaume and Dai, the men of Skye / who channel the waters / hoof-struck from Helicon . . .')

Agelastos . . . cleft: as the Rock of Ages, and (Exodus 33.22) 'I will put thee in a clift of the rock' (which lies behind 'Not a rock to cleft for . . .' in *The Sleeping Lord*, p.101) – and the rock which Moses struck with his rod (Numbers 20.11).

Paphia: Aphrodite of Paphos, in Cyprus, where she landed, born from the sea, her mother, to whom they are apprenticed.

marines: in the sense of mariners, of the sea; but even more **105** because they are fighting men, if necessary, and so belong to Aphrodite's lover Ares (see the account of Aphrodite's affair with Ares in Odyssey 8.266ff). 'panzer'd lover': cf. the armoured Mars (Ares) of *Ana.* p.87. Since Sparta is the capital of Laconia, we have in 'Laconia' a prayer to Helen, among the many others that are 'tutelar'. 'have a native pity' implies that this was originally a Phoenician ship. 'our anathemata': both the prayer offered and the images in the bows. 'for making by her coasts toward this place': from 'making' to place' inclusive should be read as though between commas – 'for, as we made our way by her coasts toward this place, we *did* call her by name'.

In the parts of Liguria about Massilia: the memory of Acts 2.10, 'in the parts of Libya about Cyrene' would hardly be worth recalling, did it not remind us of the imitation, not so immediately recognisable, of Acts 28.13, 'and from thence we fetched a compass' in the penultimate paragraph of p.102. 'the Three Mothers': the 'three aspects of femaleness' of note 2 to the preceding page, and the 'three seated female figures' of *Ana.* p.162 n.7. See also 'Moel of the Mothers', *Ana.* pp. 55 and p. 233 n.1. 'Letters most of all': the Phoenician origin of our alphabet. 'Almost all': not 'to almost all Gallia', but 'recall that we have donated to Gallia almost all that she has inherited'.

106 **Vestals of Latium:** they pray, too, to the Vestal Virgins of Rome, not yet Christianised ('taught of the Fisherman', Peter). D. returns on several occasions to the Christianising of pagan fire-goddesses, e.g. Brigid of Ireland (see *The Kensington Mass,* p.8, *Ana.* pp. 73, 219 n.1). 'Suffragium', rendered here by 'suffrage' is a common word in the Roman liturgy for the intercession of a saint. 'lode': of the lodestone (see *Ana.* p.99, the 'touched stone'), the Stella Maris being both the Pole Star and Mary.

The second paragraph ('You that shall spread your hands') with the accompanying note, is an unequivocal statement of the core of D.'s thought, as manifest in all his writing. For 'memento' see *The Kensington Mass,* p.8, 'Oramus te, Domine', and comments thereon.

Ocrinum is the Latin name for The Lizard, and they are fearful of being driven on the rocks before they can safely round the promontory, 'schisted', with accuracy, for the metamorphic rocks that have a tendency to split or flake. 'White-plumed riders shoreward go' is a characteristic shift of the common metaphor (as in Matthew Arnold's 'The wild white horses foam and fret'), substituting rider for horse. 'The birds declare it', is capitalised to indicate the extreme eagerness of the look-out as he notes the shore-birds, and also because of the importance of birds in augury; but it is not a happy typographi-cal device. Maybe the glance at Psalm 18.1 excuses it: *Caeli enarrant gloriam Dei*, which in the A.V. (Ps.19) is 'The heavens declare the glory of God'. 'fire-rocks', the sedimentary igneous rocks.

her loosed hair for dog-vane: 'dog-vane' is useful for the 107
dog and hunt image, Lamia, the land-hunter waiting for the 'sea-dogs of the hungry sea' of p.105. It is a 'small vane, made of thread, cork and feathers, or buntin, placed on the weather gunwale to show the direction of the wind' (Smyth, in O.E.D.) 'the grain of the gale': again a double sense, for it is both the harvest of the gale for which she is waiting, and the 'run' of the seas, as in the grain of wood, which she is noting. 'scarfed', referring, accurately, to the scarf-joint of the ship's stem. Cf. the antepenultimate line of *Ana.* p.174, 'cogginged', and the 'cog' in a scarf-joint. 'hull's lair' is also an O.E. metaphor. 'Oh how he cons her': i.e. how the master 'cons' the ship in the hazards; but there may be a suggestion, too, that he is 'conning' in the colloquial sense, i.e. deceiving the hungry Lamia who is expecting her prey. The *lamia*, as a bogey for frightening chil-dren, goes back a long way: to Aristophanes, and to Tertullian – '. . . a nutricula audiise lamiae turres et pectines solis', 'heard from nurse about the witch's towers and the combs of the sun'. See T. R. Glover's *Conflict of Religions in the Early Roman Empire*, 1909, p.308.

the old Pelasgian: D. had this much in mind when (see on *Ana.* p.96) he wrote of Chaucer's shipman in his Introduc-tion to the *Mariner*. 'Manannan', the sea-deity (see above on *Ana.* p.70), of the Isle of Man and so of the keys (*claves*), the other keys being those of Peter, the helmsman – and the swordsman, too, of *Ana.* p.53. 'gladiatorial', from the *gladius*, sword, he used in the Garden when he attacked the servant of the High Priest (the 'unwiped gladius' of the *K.M.*, p.11, and the 'Fisherman with the keys'): and 'vicar', as in the Petrine title of Vicar of Christ.

The last three lines, applying to the master and the vessel:

driven by the world-wind (which is the obedient daughter of the sun, for the sun rules the upper air); hove down by the wind (which raises the waves of the sea); pooped by the billow (which is the son of the waves).

108   **the isthmus:** the narrow neck of land between Mount's Bay and St Ives, which would be on the bearing given. 'the eyes of her', the foremost part of the bows, with the apotropaic oculus or eye we have already met. 'bearing nor' nor' west three-quarter west': 'that was meant to be accurate after he had managed to round Ocrinum and make across the darked bay's wide bowl. He sights, owing to a sudden sun-shaft the white mole due over the bows of her just for an instant, but sufficient to tell him that he was exactly on the right course and was "standing in" toward his "port of call", i.e. Ictis, the tin-trade port.' (D. August 1974.)

shipping a sea: D.'s dislike of punctuation and his mistaken reliance on typographic disposition to indicate the correct emphasis confuse this paragraph. We need a point after 'yet he rounds her to', and another after 'her destined haven', for it is a sky-shaft which is 'due over her bow-wash' or at any rate 'brights the whited mole'. After another stop, we then read: 'wind-hauled, the grinders (the wind-driven waves) white the darked bay's wide bowl; white-echeloned daughters of the island mill (cf. *Ana.* p.99 note 1) deploy . . . to the inner shoal'. It is 'he', the, the master, who is 'spume-blind as he 'bears on his port of call'.

'Keel, Ram, Stauros' also ends explicitly with the 'berthing to schedule' which is implicit in the whole poem.

III

ANGLE-LAND

As the poem progresses, there is a greater concentration of time
and place. *Rite and Fore-time* gave the emergence of the earth,
with the vast swings from cold to warmth and from warmth
to cold; the emergence of the earth as mother, and of her child,
man, his cult and artefacture. *Middle-Sea and Lear-Sea*
narrowed the line of development, to the source of western
culture in the near East, the Aegean, Greece and Rome; and
then centred on the opening of communication, by means of a
Levantine or Aegean trader, with the islands at the extreme
west of Europe. That voyage ended in Mount's Bay, Cornwall,
and we may regard it as being continued in *Angle-land*. Some
nine hundred years, have elapsed, however, even though the
skipper of this vessel may be regarded as 'typical', and so sharing
the identity of his two predecessors in *Middle-Sea and Lear-Sea*,
the man who rounded Cape Sunium and took his ship into
Phaleron, and the man who sailed to the 'Tin Islands'. ('Very
good', notes D. in the margin, 'thanks for mentioning the lapse
of time for unless that is realised the reader thinks of it as a single
voyage, with unfortunate results.')

The date of the voyage in this part is determined by the
reference to the Anglicizing of the Romano-British population,
and must therefore be placed somewhere after the middle of the
fifth century of our era. Time, however, passes swiftly as the
ship moves up-channel and into the North Sea, so that we can
look both back to, and forward to, Trafalgar. The Phoenician of
Part Two found a British island; at the end of Part Three we
are looking at a Saxon land, or at any rate at that part of it which
is Saxon-dominated.

Such dating is useful only as giving the reader a starting
point from which he can orientate himself. It does not mean

110 that the progress of the poem conforms to a temporal scheme as does *In Parenthesis*. (D. has underlined that sentence, and a long marginal note, elaborating that quoted above, starts 'Da iawn! . . .') In *I.P.*, the poet is himself involved in the succession of events, and there must of necessity be a continuous passage in time from Christmas 1915 to July 1916. In *The Anathemata*, the poet and the reader stand outside, and when the former speaks of a place or a process (navigation, for example) he may look at it in any part of history, past, present or future; and it is these linkages which constitute one part of his peculiar craft.

It will be noted that the place-names start with 'Vecta Insula', i.e. the Isle of Wight, and that we then move to the Dover Strait (starting with the 'East Road'). This latter is marked on the Ordnance Survey's Map of Britain in the Dark Ages, to the east of Dungeness. All the names that follow (and this first) are marked on the Admiralty Chart no. 1046, and referred to in the *Channel Pilot*: South Sand Head (south-western extremity of the Goodwin Sands), The Gull ('The Downs and the Gull Stream, its continuation north-eastward, is the channel bounded westward by the banks fronting the coast between South and North Forelands, and eastward by the Goodwin Sands . . . The southern part of the Sands is known as South Calliper and the south-western extremity as South Sand Head . . . The Gull Stream is the usual passage to the North Sea or the Thames estuary from the Downs, and vessels navigating between the English Channel and the Thames generally use it in preference to going outside Goodwin sands . . . The Brake fronts the coast between the Small Downs and Ramsgate.') The Foreland of the text is the North Foreland. 'The Elbow, with a least depth of 19 feet, is a sandy ridge situated about 2 miles eastward of North Foreland.' 'The Oaze, a shoal lying about $1\frac{1}{2}$ miles west-south-westward of the Mouse...has depths of from 6 to 14 fathoms.' This channel lies a little to the northward of the Kentish Flats, but the Flats mentioned in the text must lie between the east coast of Kent and the Brake.

With the Dogger Bank and Well Bank, we are up into the North **110**
Sea, off the Yorkshire coast. The course is then marked by rivers,
until we run out into the northern ocean – in Cronos-*meer*, into
which all rivers flow. The Ordnance Survey map of Britain in
the Dark Ages shows first the thick clustering of cremation and
inhumation sites in Kent, followed by a long series of them up
the east coast, until we reach the Pictish symbol-stones, from the
56th parallel northwards: the river Spey, in particular ('Spey
of the symbol stones', p.115) is marked all along its course by
these stones. A similar voyage is described to the Lady of the
Pool by one of her lovers, 'the cruising old wicing', pp. 199–200.

The reader will already, in part two, have felt that the *Rime
of the Ancient Mariner* was in the background (e.g. when the
vessel runs into thick weather at the entrance to the Channel);
here the Mariner comes closer in both feeling and language,
with the 'kindly *numen* that headed him clear' (p.110) and the
'brumous numen' on p.111. The connection with Coleridge and
the Albatross vessel, subject to the Antarctic spirit and directed
by the 'seraph-band' becomes more apparent to a reader of D.'s
Introduction to the Rime. A study of this long essay brings out the
importance as material for his poetry of the argonaut theme, and
reminds us that the voyages in *The Anathemata* stand for much
more than an expansion of culture and civilisation; the key lies
in the first introduction of that theme in what one might call
the 'cenacle-ship' (pp. 52–3), with the capital initial in the
question, 'Who d'you think is Master of her,' – where, too,
we may well note the use of the present tense. 'Could this', D.
writes in the margin, 'be expanded a little either here or somewhere for if chaps no longer know who figures in classical
mythology then still fewer know what *cenacle* means'; he then
refers to the *S.L.*, p.108, speaking of how Melchisedec foretokened the oblation in the upper room, but that may wait
until we reach p.230 of this poem. *Cenacle* (*cenaculum*), dining-
room, upper room: a humble word covering, too, the dwellings
of the poor – and used, too, with almost the wry affection with
which a man speaks of his 'billet'.

110   The importance of the cenacle-ship must not blur for us the separate identity of the vessels engaged in the different voyages described in the poem, voyages that are separated, too, by long intervals of time.

Collingwood and Myres, *Roman Britain and the English Settlements* (first published in 1936, second edition 1937, and often reprinted since) was much used by D. and will prove of great value to the reader of this section.

The first two lines determine time and place. The Isle of Wight is referred to by its Roman name, **Vecta Insula,** but it is already a Saxon or Jutish island (**gavel-kind,** – the word is not Celtic – system of land-tenure and division) *Igland* = O.E. iegland, island. For **strike soundings,** see on p.101. The modernity of the phrase is repeated in 'his second mate': the poet is thus able to look back through a whole range of historical development and cult-figures. Thus *Fortuna* is not merely a use of the Latin name, but involves her importance (indicated by her many titles, Fortuna Publica, Fortuna Populi Romani, Patricia, Caesaris, virginalis etc.) in Roman religion, and her identification with the Greek *Tyche*, often (and happily) represented with a steering oar or rudder, as being the guider of destiny. 'It had also', adds D., 'a Welsh interest for me, because *llyw* is the word for rudder & the last Llywelyn is affectionately called *Ein Llyw olaf* which is always translated "our last native prince" – but how much more potent as "rudder".'

clean oblation: was their passage through the many hazards the fruit of skilled pilotage or of the sacrifice of an unblemished victim? 'Clean oblation' is a reminder of the Canon of the Mass (*sacrificia illibata, hostiam puram* – unblemished sacrificial offerings, a clean victim), so that there is a bringing-together of Christ the offerer-and-victim and Christ-the-Master; and, at the same time, of other oblations offered for safe passage, one of the most appropriate (since our attention has been drawn to Herodotus and Egypt) being Menalaus's sacrifice to Poseidon that enabled him (in Odyssey iv) to sail home from the Egyptian island of 'Pharos' – not to mention, of course (with the sea-born Aphro-

dite about to be mentioned) the oblation at Aulis when the fleet **110**
was assembled to sail for Troy, and D.'s conflation of Aphrodite
and Iphianassa.

that sheered him: the transitive use of the verb (to direct
a vessel obliquely) is well established as a nautical term.

Sea-born and Sea-star: both Aphrodite and Mary. 'And
this star was not only precious because it was the sailor's star
or Star of the Sea, that never moved; it was also by tradition the
Star of Mary' (E. G. R. Taylor, *The Haven-finding Art*, p.100
with many other references to the same). We could have noted
earlier (pp. 103–5): the maiden, the sailor's star, stella maris,
and (here) 'whose own . . . the pious ('pious' as Latin *pius*)
'matlos are'.

a whim of Poseidon's: the unpredictability of the god who
keeps the western approaches is Homeric, and keeps alive the
Mediterranean starting-point of the voyage. In 'preclear', the
'pre' is intensive, a characteristic borrowing of Latin *praeclarus*
(D. could not resist the 'invisible' wind in 'preclear' *visibility*.)
'Dogger' goes with 'bank', as 'Well' with 'mound' (cf. **deeped
. . . Oaze**, above, with note): followed by the double meanings
of **sheet** and **shroud**. (There is a danger here of spoiling the
delicacy by crude explanation, and I apologise if I irritate any
reader by such explanation. It is difficult to know what is seen
and what is not. For example, the parallel between 'God speed
the plough, long life and success to the farmer' and *they speed the
coulter deep*. So, too, with *once did quilt Boudicca's royal gwely*
and 'once in David's royal city', and with *from Schleswig over the
foam* and 'to Noroway, to Noroway over the foam' – with which
last cf. p.200, *to Noroway o'er his faem*.)

the cinque masters of lodemanage: adds the Norman and
Anglo-Norman to the Saxon. The cinque ports (and with their
introduction we have a careful geographical progression) were
the chief providers of naval vessels, and formed a confederacy
of those who interests lay in the North Sea fisheries. The 'head
ports' were Hastings, Sandwich, Dover, Romney and Hithe,
to which two others, Rye and Winchelsea, were added later.

'lodemanage': pilotage – O.E. *ladmann*, guide. ('Heavenly word is not *Lodemanage* – especially when one connects it with "lode" as in lodestar.' D. in margin.)

111   **Past where they placed their ingas-names:** (with which cf. 'south hams and the north tons', last line of p.113) the Anglo-Saxon primitive patronymic or group-termination place-names. See Collingwood & Myres, p.368 (where the context is Sussex. with the Haestingas, but the principle is the same when applied to the east coast described in *The Ana.*): 'It may not be too fantastic to see in the distribution of three types of place-names in Sussex the slow expansion of the original folk [i.e. the South Saxons]: in the *ingas* names of the coast plain, the river valleys, and the fertile strip of dry land along the northern base of the chalk escarpment the earliest settlements; in the *hams* which follow so strikingly the course of the river valleys into the Weald a symbol of the next stage; and finally in the *tons* with their fine disregard of the facts of geography an unconscious record of final domination over the forces of nature.' (See their map, after p.456, and the Ordnance Survey's Britain in the Dark Ages.)

   speed the coulter deep: see Collingwood & Myres, pp. 28, 68, 442 on the introduction of the heavy, Gaulish plough which could turn the sod, a task too difficult for the 'light and primitive type', used to cultivate the small Celtic fields, 'which merely furrowed the surface of the soil'.

   To this should be added a note in Stenton's *Anglo-Saxon England* (much read by D. – first edition 1943, third edition 1971) p.318, which concludes that 'Regarded as a whole, these (ingas) names are clearly too vague in sense to be of much use for the reconstruction of early society' although (*ibid.* p.18, note 2) 'their archaic character and therefore their value as evidence of early settlement' is established.

112   **the south-west wall of the chester** (i.e. Caister-by-Norwich) ... *his VERBUM*: the turn of the page from p.111 masks the fact that the poet is still speaking of the invaders' burial sites 'It was the mixed settlers from Schleswig or Elbe-mouth to

elsewhere who, at all events in the earlier stages, avoided dwell- **112**
ing in the (presumably) "sacked" or anyway partly despoiled
towns, but also avoided burying their dead (there), for fear of
raising the "ghosts" of Romano-British inhabitants (**'an Icenian
Venta's Brettisc ghost'**: i.e. the ghost of a British inhabitant
of Venta Icenorum, the Roman name for Norwich) – or more
because the Bret-Wealas, alive or dead, might "call up" spirits
from the vasty deep of the Roman thing of which, after all, they
were part.' (.D., Sept. 1974.) Archaeologists, D. adds, may very
well have now abandoned the idea of the invaders' fear of burying
their dead within the orbit of British towns, but it was certainly
accepted when *The Ana.* was being written, so that its use here
is perfectly justified.

We have an interesting example here of the poet's hoarding
of a phrase, which is then re-fashioned and, by a slight adjust-
ment, given that twist which adds the necessary brilliance:
'without the orbit, if but a stone's throw' must have originated
in Collingwood & Myres, p.453, 'the Angles who cremated their
dead within a stone's throw of the Roman walls of *Venta
Icenorum*'.

In another letter of about the same date, D. speaks of the poet
as rightly using the archaeological, scientific, historical, theories
or facts accepted in his own time, however much they may be
modified by later discoveries or investigations. This applies on a
wider scale to the diffusion of culture by sea-voyages (the
extreme 'diffusionist' view being extended to trans-Pacific
voyages) which is assumed in *Rite and Fore-time*, and which has
(I imagine) been shaken by radio carbon dating. D.'s principle,
however, holds good: see, in particular, the 'General Note to
Section I' (p.82) and what D. says about 'thalassic journeyings'
in the note that accompanies the 'Argo' record of his reading
from *The Anathemata* and *The Hunt* (PLP 1093).

The 'he' of line 4 is one of the newcomers. He reckons out or
puzzles out (O.E. *tellan*) the unfamiliar Latin. *Runes*, because
of their association with northern Europe, and Odin in particular (cf. p.225, 'Who made the runes would read them'), and

112 because of the atmosphere of secrecy and magic that surrounded them (O.E. *run* = secret). 'Rune', like 'wattle' and 'bangor' is ever in D.'s mind: so that Calvary (p.240) is 'rune-height' and in the *K.M.* (p.13) we meet 'the Galilaean runes'. D. connects this with the barbarians' fear of writing: 'just as a few centuries later the "Vikings", while bringing fire and sword to the Anglo-Saxon towns and habitations had a dread of any writings for these they thought had a magic power as "runes" of some potency which they could not understand, hence when they sacked monastic houses they put the parchments into wells or other places containing water. This, I understand (or understood) is proved from Irish evidence where illuminated MSS have been thrown into wells & astonishingly enough have been retrieved with the ink script & illuminated work still intact & the colours still quite bright – it sounds impossible but is, in fact, known to be true.'

'I wrote' (quoting D. again) '*IAM REDIT ROMA* because on some of the Roman [military] *signa* (I *think* it was a cohort signum) the flat palm (with sometimes an *oculus* painted on it I'm told) anyway this lifted palm his Verbum is the Verbum that conquered the world, or those whose mighty power disciplined the "schoolboys" through the known orbis.' Two trifling addenda to that quotation: first, behind 'Iam redit Roma' must lie 'Iam redit et Virgo' from the fourth ('Messianic') Eclogue, hinted at by the reference to the Sibyl at the very beginning of the poem: secondly, D.'s source, Stuart Jones, pp. 210–15, attaches the *signum* to the maniple and not to the cohort or the century; each maniple 'was provided with a standard or signum by which its evolutions were directed . . . at the top of the legionary standard [i.e. the standard of the legionary maniple, not the ensign or 'colours' of the whole legion, which after the reforms of Marius was always the eagle] we find sometimes a small flag or *vexillum* with an oval shield fastened thereon, sometimes an open hand (which has been explained as symbolical of fidelity and therefore appropriate to such legions as bore the title *pia fidelis*, but is perhaps merely a talisman to

avert ill-fortune.)' Each of the ten cohorts in a legion had three   **112**
maniples, with two centuries to the maniple, so that the maniple
might be taken as more or less the equivalent of a company.

Graham Webster (*The Roman Imperial Army*, 1974) illustrates the signum with the flat open palm, from Trajan's column,
and comments: 'Does it signify the hand of comradeship or
depict a military salute with arm upraised, or would it be too
fanciful to imagine it stretching out towards the gods, claiming
divine protection?' (p.139.) In view of the time when D. was
writing, or the poem was fermenting in his mind, the dictators'
salute must surely have been in his mind.

Tertullian, himself a soldier's son, sarcastically points out
that 'all those rows of images on the standards (*in signis*) are
but ornaments on crosses. Those hanging of your ensigns
(*siphara illa vexillorum*) and banners are but robes (*stolae*)
upon crosses.' (Apology 16.8.) D., with a sharp eye for *signum*
and *vexillum*, hints at the parallel in kindlier fashion – as often
in both words and drawing.

The capitals of VERBUM may encourage us to elaborate this
phrase. The 'lifted palm' is a *signum*, and sign and word have a
special connotation for the poet. This is brought out by Walter
Shewring in his essay 'Art in Christian Philosophy' (*Making
and Thinking*, Buffalo, N.Y., 1958, p.24): '. . . as St Thomas
says, "the Catholic faith calls Almighty God not only *Creator*
but also *Maker*, for making properly belongs to an artist who
works though his will. And because every voluntary agent works
through a concept of his intellect which is called his *word*,
and the Word of God is his Son, the Catholic faith confesses of
the Son that through him *all things were made*". Differing
infinitely from human modes by a generation without becoming
and a consubstantiality of nature and essence with the conceiving
intellect, God the Son is nevertheless the true archetype of the
word in the human artist's mind.' That argument should be in
the mind of every person who considers or discusses D.'s use
of those key-words.

Added pungency is given to this 'runes' passage by that to

112 which D. refers indirectly in the quotation above: in *The Wall*
(*S.L.*, p.11) – where the neutralising of the spell is seen from the
other, the Roman, side. 'Erect, crested with the open fist
lifting the palm that disciplines the world, the signa lift in
disciplined acknowledgement, the eagles stand erect for Ilia

> O Roma
> O Ilia
> Io Triumphe, Io, Io . . .'

– but there the Roman order is degraded for the profit of the
city's capitalists and rabble.

horror-coat: the O.E. *here-byrne* or war corselet. So Beowulf
(v.1443) puts on his 'here-byrne, hondum gebroden' (the
links interlocked by hand); and we still use 'byrnie' for mail-
coat. The move from 'war-coat' to 'horror-coat', suggested by
the similarity of 'here' and 'horor', gains strength from 'horridus'
as a favourite Vergilian epithet for war and the things of war
(spears, a battle array). So the Sibyl says to Aeneas, for example,
(Aen. 6.86–7), 'bella, horrida bella . . . cerno'. It is the corresponding German *Panzer* for mail-coat (in addition to the more familiar use in modern military vocabulary) that gives a savage
touch to the 'panzer'd lover' of p.105, the Norman 'panzer-
gangs' etc.

D. did not reject a further, chance association of 'horror-coat'
with the Ghost in Hamlet, suggested partly by 'I saw young
Harry with his beaver on' in *In Parenthesis*, p.xiv., with D.'s
memory of the incident in which those words were used
(recorded elsewhere). The accuracy of the quotation (beaver
on, not beaver *up*) was a reminder of the Ghost, and 'in his
horror-coat standing' brought back Hamlet's quills upon the
fretful porpentine – transferring, so to speak, the bristling of the
frightened person's hair (which 'stands') to the frightening
horror-coated visitant. For the Ghost of Hamlet's father was in
armour ('panzered'), was he not ? – 'What may this mean, that
thou, dead corpse, again in complete steel, Revisit'st thus the
glimpses of the moon' – and, a few lines later, 'and we fools of
nature so horridly to shake our dispositions'. So, war, armour,

byrnie, fear, are horrid, are horror, and the reader, when re- 112
creating the poem by reading it, is entitled, within reason, and
even obliged, to add what comes to him from his own harvesting. The link between D.'s war-scene in 1916 and, the Anglo-
Saxon invader's fear of the British ghost lies in 'Then saw you
not his face? O yes! my lord; he wore his beaver up.'

In a MS. draft of another 'sequence', 'horror-coat' reappears
as the 'fragile haubergeon' of human nature assumed by the
incarnate God: the notion, borrowed from *Piers Plowman*,
which is used in the inscriptional poem 'Cloelia, Cornelia':
Thus:

> 'What horror-coat had he on
>   at his Caersalem Camlan
> when he jousted alone
>   in the lists of Skull Mountain
> His only habergeon
>   was what clerks call *Humana Natura*.
> Who wove him that frail lorica
>   if not puella, Fons Amoris,
>   the gladius-pierced Mother for us?'

'Cloelia, Cornelia', it is clear, was extracted from a much larger
quarry of material – like all the other short pieces.

Past where the ancra-man: (the anchorite – O.E., but, we
may observe, through the Latin *anchoreta*). We are now off the
Lincolnshire coast, with St Guthlac feeling his way up the
river Welland, with sounding-pole, to found the monastery of
Crowland in the year 716. Prof. Taylor (*op. cit.* facing p.52)
reproduces a 12th-century miniature representing this.

deeping his holy rule: again in a double sense, of carrying
the monastic rule deep into the fen country, and of dipping the
sounding-pole or rule. 'Fiendish' is explained in the note on
diawliaidd, but there is also a pleasing variation, in the use of the
Anglo-Saxon word (*feond*) in which there is also a suggestion of
'fen'.

Geisterstunde: midnight, the very witching time of night
of *Hamlet* (3.2 394) 'When churchyards yawn and hell itself

112 breathes out Contagion to this world,' on the night of All
Saints Day as it passes into All Souls. There may well, however.
be a confusion with the particularly Celtic (see Frazer) celebration of Hallowe'en.

A letter of D.'s is useful at this point: the direct reference is to
p.113.

' "Townsmen gone wold-men" [Lincolnshire *wolds*] and
"citizen gone outlaw" do not evoke the extraordinary mix-up
of the break-up of the phenomenally mixed mess-up of Celtic,
Teutonic and Latin elements of the early dark ages which I was
trying to express. The fractured and fused forms, the hyphenated
words such as *dinas*-man and (p.112) "Crowland-diawliaidd'
etc were merely an attempt to get *something* of this historic
situation. It had to be halting, broken and complicated and
Babel-like – I think. At least that was the only way *I* saw of doing
it. A somewhat germane example: had I written "Wealcyn"
(113) it would have been a straight A.S. Anglo-Saxon word
taken from any Anglo-Saxon document, a dead word, a student's
word, but by hyphenating "Weal" with "kin", the word can
be made to take on a certain life, because we still use the word
"kin" and cannot see it without thinking of "kith", whereas
"cyn" is remote and anyway is pronounced kune or something
like it (kun ?). Alternatively had I just translated the whole word
and said "Welshman" or "Welsh folk" these would have given
no historic undertone, or, in the case of "Welsh folk" rather
bogus, or "poetic" or dated feeling'.

It is this mixture that is described in the form of question.
The 'going wild' of the Romano-Celts comes up in the various
examples of **Romanity gone Wealisc;** in the general disorder,
the Romanised town-dwellers have been forced back into a life
of hunted and hunter. There is great care in the choice of words.
Thus, *Is Sylvanus* (the man of the woods) *Urbigena's son* (son
of the city-born)? *Has toga'd* (city-suited) *Rhufon* (Romanus),
become the hunting and hunted *Actaeon* – where we may note
the crafty half-disguising of the hunter's 'Gone away!' in 'gone
Actaeon . . . come away'. 'bogle-baragouinage': goblin-

gibberish; see the O.E.D. for the possible Breton origin of the 112
word.

Wake is used in 'the sense of Hereward "the Wake" but not
of Hereward but of mixed fore-types of Bret-Wealas and others
who as civic life caved in sought out a life in forest or fens . . .
not of Hereward or his men who gave those damned Normans a
lot of trouble by their alertness in the Fen country, by the armed
"wake" or vigil,or watchfulness that only the skill and determination of the Conqueror's *panzer*-gangs could overcome. Which
reminds me of another passage where you mention my use of
the Jerry word Panzer. Do you suppose Adolf and Co. delibera-
ately used the word Panzer Division for tank or armoured corps
to revive the use of *Panzer* which meant mailcoat in the Nordic
tales ?'.

John Collier's *Tom's a-cold* (the *Lear* connection is an odd
coincidence with the quotation, on the title-page of *The Ana.*,
from the storm scene in *Lear*) was published in 1933, and was
read by D. with pleasure and interest. This, too, describes
a breakdown of civilisation, but one imagined in the future, in
which something of the feeling of this passage is reflected.

the bittern's low aery: a typical oxymoron, which ceases
to be such when the derivation of the word 'aerie' is examined,
though it has come to be associated with height. There is a
curious mistake in the introduction of the bittern, though, as it
turns out, a *felix culpa*. Speaking of the British who had had to
take refuge in wild places, D. says, 'had they been further West,
in mountainous lands, the bittern (still surviving in Wales)
[though this, I believe, is not true; the bittern is a comparatively
rare summer visitor to Norfolk and Suffolk] would have had no
need to build his aery 'low', but high. It was an echo, *only a
very faint echo*, from that passage in *In Parenthesis* (p.54) of how
the speckled kite of Maldon & the crow have, like us, "condescen-
ded to dig in". *But I was wrong in thinking that*, for it appears
that the bittern has his habitat in marshy low-lying country,
bog-land and the like – so much for false ill-founded analogies!'
It is, however, most appropriate for it is 'skulking, solitary and

usually crepuscular, hiding in reeds by day . . . Habitat: dense
reed-beds in fens . . . nests among reeds' (Peterson, Mountford
and Hollom, *Field Guide to the Birds of Britain and Europe*).

113   **Patricius gone the wilde Jäger:** (*die wilde Jäger*, the wild
hunt or the wild huntsman) another variation of 'Rhufon gone
Actaeon', romanised 'gone native', with the advantage that the
'Wild Hunt' appears to be Teutonic in origin, though many
countries have their own version of the legend. The huntsman
rides at night, accompanied by the ghosts of desperate criminals,
and it is fatal to approach him or to join in the chase or the
hallooing. Herne the Hunter is an English version, described in
The Merry Wives of Windsor, Act IV, Sc. 4. There is a further
link for D. in the command the Wild Huntsman exercises over
the elements: the storm and howling that accompanying him
fit in with D.'s concern for the storm scene in *Lear*. Cf. Frazer's
Golden Bough, Part VI, p.164: 'Another witching time is the
period of twelve days between Christmas and Epiphany . . . a
thousand quaint superstitions cluster round that mystic season.
It's then that the Wild Huntsman sweeps through the air, the
powers of evil are let loose, werewolves are prowling round and
witches work their wicked will . . .'

   Gens Romulum is difficult to interpret unless we take
Romulum to be a contracted form of the genitive *Romulorum*,
i.e. of the adjective *Romulus*. Horace addresses Augustus as
'optime Romulae Custos gentis', and Jackson Knight did not
object to D.'s use of the contraction, but here we have the harsh-
ness of the use, also, of the adjective as noun. D. was determined
not to say 'Gens Romulea' or 'Romula': and '*gens Romulorum*
would not get what I wanted'.

   That was written in 1974. This is only a small matter, but I
add a couple of extracts from letters written 21 years earlier
(in 1953, to Desmond Chute), as an indication of D.'s constant
care for exactness. 'Before I forget; *gens Romulum* is now *gens
Romula*. It seems to be the only possible form. I wrote to a
"latin wallah" of some eminence about it and although he is
very "undonnish' and prepared to make all allowances and sees

the value of the ending *um* within the context [what secret ray of **113**
illumination did he have ?], he says that it won't really work and
that *gens Romula* is all one can do. So *gens Romula* it shall be.
Relieved to get it settled, but sorry to lose the sound value. He
had himself noticed it, but thought it might be possible, but on
going into the matter decided that it wont work.' A fortnight
later, however: 'Yes, that damned old *Romulum*. I think I shall
stick to it after all! I cannot see what is the matter with it
taken as a contraction of Romulorum, the gen. pl. of the adjective *Romulus*. With the sign ûm it is surely unassailable.'
(So far as I know, the circumflex never appeared in later
printings.)

wold, akin to German Wald and West Saxon *weald*, because
we speak of the Lincolnshire wolds.

from Lindum to London: Lindum = Lincoln. Cf. p.167,
'as though he walked the solid causey over m' dancin' Lady
Lea', with the reference in the note to the song 'London Bridge
is broken down, Dance (over) my Lady Lea'. Speaking of the
'problem of Romano-British survival in the areas of primary
Anglo-Saxon settlement', the Ordnance Survey *Britain in the
Dark Ages* says, 'The decay of the road system must have been
early and severe when bridges broke, engineering works failed
and major arteries lay for long in debatable lands.'

Hausname: as on p.59, 'Who were his *gens*-men or had he no
Hausname yet . . . ?' The river *Yare* runs into the sea at Great
Yarmouth, having passed close to Norwich, 17 miles to the
westward. The map shows inhumation, cremation, and mixed
inhumation-cremation cemeteries along the course of the river.

the Waltons: Walton-on-the-Naze, Essex; and Walton
Castle, Suffolk (Portus Adurni, possibly), one of the ten forts
for which the Count of the Saxon Shore was responsible; now
destroyed by erosion.

what's the cephalic index: in other words, are they mermaids (English – Middle English), morforynion (Celtic) or
the classical sirens ? Shakespeare's language is so much part of
the poet's raw material that we are inclined to overlook it when

113 it is not so plain as it is here and, as it is so often, in *In Parenthesis*. *Ned Mizzen*: as Ben Backstay (p.141) and both Ned and Ben (p.155), Tom Bowline (p.118) and (in correspondence) William Taplow.

the low low lands: a favourite folk-song, with Holland transferred to the Holland 'division' of Lincolnshire.

> 'Twas just when my love was to marry me,
>> That night he lay on his bed;
> The captain came to his bedside,
>> These words to him he said:
> Arise, arise from your sleep, young man,
>> And come along with me, with me,
> To the low low lands of Holland,
>> To face your enemy.

And it ends, I fear,

> Until the day that I shall die
> A maiden I shall be,
> Since the low low lands of Holland
> Depart my love and me.

the **Welland,** on which stands Crowland, runs into the Wash; *the Soke*: the Soke of Peterborough, which city now stands on the Nene; *new to old Nene:* the pun is justified by the artificial alterations to the course of the river in the fifteenth and eighteenth centuries. The Ordnance Survey Dark Ages marks the Old Nene.

gens Julii: corrected in later printings to *gens Julia*. Is the use of the adjective here connected with the insistence on the use above of the noun *Romulum?*

Woden's gang . . . Wuffingas: an embroidery on Nennius and Bede, through Collingwood & Myres (p.390): 'If we add to this amalgam the suggestion of a not inconsiderable British survival, at any rate in the Brandon area of West Suffolk, it is perhaps easier to understand how the Wuffingas found it advisable to trace their descent from Caesar as well as from Woden (Nennius, Historia Brittonum 57), and to follow the reasoning which led the greatest of their number, Raedwald, when the tidings of Christianity reached him, merely to add a Christian altar to the pagan temple where already, perhaps, he attempted to syncretize the religious diversity of the people.' (Bede, *Hist. Eccles.* ii.15.) D. in a letter, uses the analogy of rulers of African states 'togged-up in field-service khaki, red tabs, rows of medal-ribbons etc.'

Wealas (note 3) – misprinted *Waelisc* for Wealisc on the preceding page: from Volcae, a Gaulish tribe on both banks of the Rhone, which appears in Livy, 21.26, attempting to prevent Hannibal from crossing the river. Teutonic tribes which came into contact with them and regarded them as 'foreigners' transferred 'Volcae' to all foreigners.

the south hams and the north tons: the endings of place-names conveniently introduce the O.E. throp, thorp, farm, village, and so the Norfolk village where Nelson was born, and **114** so the Trafalgar passage ending with 'worsening weather'. 'Him whom Nike did bear' has a complex of meanings: that victory was his mother (as Thorpe 'bore' him), with which meaning we cannot fail to have in mind such things as the winged Victory of Samothrace ('I'm glad that the winged Victory of Samothrace came to your mind because I was thinking of her when I was writing that passage – that Academic winged Nike of Samothrace is a *real* caulker', D., with a revealing mis-spelling.) – then the meaning that victory was his guide; and that it was in H.M.S. Victory that he met victory and death. **her tears at flood** is parenthetical: typographic arrangement again failing to serve as pointing.

the forebrace bitts: the following from one of the last letters written by D., in answer to greetings for Trafalgar Day (October 21) 1974; and received the day after his death: 'Seeing we are on the subject of Trafalgar I can't resist a matter (Mike Richey would laugh at this because from time to time I've mentioned it) You know the account says that when Nelson was hit by a musket shot fired from the maintop "platform", or anyway from the lower mast-head where cross timbers formed a "fire-bay" for marksmen to pick off targets from their high

114 perches but at mortally close range, for, unless I've got that
wrong too, there was between the *Victory* and the French ship
a little leeway – But that's not what puzzles me. Nelson was
pacing the quarter-deck when he fell, but a few moments
before one of his officers had fallen & the account says that the
actual spot was scattered with fragments of timber from the
"*fore-brace bitts*" i.e. the heavy baulk of timber to which were
belayed the braces (of cordage) of the *fore-mast*, or rather the
yards of the foremast to which the formast sails were bent (in
margin: I understand that Quarter-deck derives from a time
when a "half-deck" extending over half the length of the vessel
had above it a much smaller deck right in the stern roughly
covering a quarter of the ship's length. That makes sense of the
word "quarter-deck"). Bitt or bitts could be used nautically of
other contrivances, but it is obvious in this context of Nelson
on the quarter-deck & the scattered fragments of the "fore-
brace bitts" that what had been hit was one or both of the heavy
uprights that supported and were part of a heavy cross timber to
which was belayed the cordage of the fore-mast yards and so
determined the manipulation of the sails of that fore-mast.
Generally speaking, rightly or wrongly I say sometimes to
myself Remember "braces" go aft, "stays" go forward, &
shrouds go from beam to beam or rather from mast to outboard,
beyond top-strake, and made fast by heavy-sheaved blocks &
dead eyes to wale above where her bulwarks "tumble home" (in
margin: what a *perfect* term to express the inward inclination of
a ship's bulwarks) – I fancy her shrouds are set *very slightly*
to aft of the mast they supported but this is purely from memory
and may well be wrong. I've still not come to the question that
no doubt has a perfectly simple answer. If the timber called the
"fore-brace bits" was on the quarter-deck, that is far to the
stern of the great vessel, from all time the place of command
and helm & admiralty – part, in medieval vessels of the After
Castle – are we to suppose that the cordage of the fore-mast
ran the whole or a large part of the whole length of the *Victory*,
that her hempen sheets had their belaying bitts that far aft?

'If so, where were the braces of the *main-mast* yards belayed – or more difficult still, where were the sheets of the mizzen-mast yards, for braces being part of the "running rigging" run aft, to what brace-bitts were they belayed? Ludicrous question of course and foolish for the answer is, without any doubt, quite simple. But those bloody "fore-brace bitts" that got a nasty one (presumably from a cannon-shot) shortly before the discharge of a mere musket laid "that great Admiral" low on the quarter deck of the "leading vessel of the weather column" still seems odd.

' "I'll thank you Capt Harvey to keep y'r place in line". Do you remember how we enjoyed that.'

Far drawn on away: there is a break between this and the Trafalgar digression. The craft from the Mediterranean is drawn on, far away from the continental shelf, into the high northern latitudes. Lerwick, in the Shetlands, is just north of the sixtieth parallel, and we have been travelling from the fiftieth, in the Channel. The course is held, as river after river is passed, all the way north to the Arctic, the great ocean of Cronos, or great river Oceanus. Thames, Great Ouse (The Wash), Tyne at the end of Hadrian's Wall, Tweed marking the border, Forth that winds along (or is it *minds*?) the waist of Scotland, where the Antonine Wall for a time hemmed in Caledonia, Tummel that runs into Tay, Tay that indeed loops, for it (or its tributary) curls round Macbeth's Glamis, then to swing south and east into the firth.

Dunsinane: 'is here to be pronounced dun-sun-un'. "deploy toward Dunsin'ane". That is I am told the *right* Scots pronunciation. W.S. in Macbeth uses *both* pronunciations, as might be expected of him.' (to D.M.C. Feb. 1953)

Finally **Spey:** the fantastic glacial deposits of the Spey river 115 and valley. 'serpentine mere': Loch Ness, only too obviously 'serpentine', but would any but a Londoner have used that adjective?

The O.S. Dark Ages map shows the series of Pictish symbol stones following the course of the river Spey. See also p.145 and

115 D.'s note, '*this* is the sound of the Findhorn stone!' The Findhorn river runs parallel to, and to the north of, the Spey, enter-
ing the sea at Findhorn on the Moray coast.

With the mention of **Cronos** (with whom the cosmogony of
The Anathemata starts) we leap down to our own day, the
reference to the second world-war, and the doom-laden anticipation of the last phase *of our dear West*; this latter echoing the
apocalyptic tone of the opening quotation from the *Dies Irae*.
And we remember that, in Part Two, we had hardly met 'the
end of the beginnings' (p. 89) before we were warned of the
'beginnings of the end' (p. 90).

Rhenus-flow: the Rhine being taken as symbolic of all the
European rivers that flow into Cronos-*meer*. The German *Meer*
anticipates the German chart, while *whale-roads* and *keel-paths*
retain the Norse metaphors. It is not impossible that, writing
when he did, (mentioning a German naval chart) D. may have
had in mind the escape-route from Norway to Shetland (even
though it is the Orkneys he mentions). 'Yes,' he wrote to D.M.C.,
'probably "grid, quadrate and number" would be better running on in one line, but I know how it was that I broke the line
at "grid". I wanted a slight pause at that word, because I
wanted   quadrate-and-number-on-the-seagreen-*Quadratkarte*
said very much in one breath but somewhat sharply rapped out,
but almost as one word.'

phase: accented 'to emphasize the consonance with the *see*
of *Brudersee*' (*ibid.*)

O Balin O Balan!: there is a peculiar appropriateness in the
choice of the two brothers to symbolise the two fratricidal wars,
in that it was 'by misadventure' that they fought and killed one
another, as did those to whom *In Parenthesis* is dedicated:
moreover, it was Balin who wounded King Pellam 'with the
same spear that Longius smote Our Lord to the heart' and, by
that 'dolorous stroke' caused the land to be laid waste and
'three countries to be destroyed'.

IV

REDRIFF

Redriff: Rotherhithe, formerly 'redrif', Surrey – other medieval
spellings, Rederheia, (Latin), Ruerhee, Rutherhee, Rutherheth:
'landing-place where cattle were shipped'. (Elkwall's *Concise
Oxford Dict. of Place-names*). O.E. *hrither*, cattle, *hyth*, landing-
place, harbour (cf. Hythe).

D. (writing without any books of reference) was under the
impression that the 'Roth' of Rotherhithe had some connection
with 'red'. Of the spelling and pronunciation he writes, with a
pleasing parallel from the Great War:

'I know only that Rotherhythe was usual form in our days
but "Redriff" also was used by chaps who had resided there.
My mother referred to it but as far as I can recall said it was
used more in her childhood and by the locals – *rather* like
"Ypres" & "Wipers" in the 1st War. "Old sweats" used
"Wipers" & I heard one such say to a man of the New Armies,
who had called it "Wipers", to which the Old Sweat said
"Ypres" for you if you dont mind – You weren't out in '14,
nor '15 neither, "Wipers" aint for the likes of you, alright for
me as I were out for Mons & in that show called now officially
"First Ypres".'

It is not often that D. can say of his work that 'it was handed
to me on a plate', but he uses that expression in connection with
one passage ('those lancer-whiskered bloody bucinators' in
The Dream of Private Clitus, S.L. p. 22) where the translation
of Aristophanes, Frogs 966, *salpingolonchypenadai*, as 'lancer-
whiskered trumpeters' leapt to his eye from the page. He might
have used it, too, of Ebenezer Bradshaw, mast-maker and shipwright (signing as witness to his daughter's marriage to D.'s
father, 20 Sept 1888, he describes himself as Mast Maker), of
Rotherhithe – so far, at least, as name, trade and place are

118 concerned; for these three came to him directly from his mater-
nal grandfather, and he seized on them as being perfectly
adapted to this section.

It will be remembered that *Angle-land* opens with a question;
so *Redriff* himself opens with an alternative. The answer to the
former was that the old shipmaster came into soundings off the
Isle of Wight, then made his way through the hazards of the
Dover Strait; but instead of standing in to the Thames estuary,
he held his course northwards, all along the east coast of
England, and then past the rivers and firths of Scotland, until
he came out into the great Ocean into which all rivers run – for
(as we read in the preceding *Middle-Sea and Lear-Sea*) 'There's
those that avers that he's [i.e. the adventurer he typifies]
wintered with Cronos under Arctophylax'.

Angle-land is set in the Dark Ages, and the Ordnance Survey
Map for the period shows first the thick clustering of cremation
and inhumation sites in Sussex, Kent and Essex, and then the
long string that reaches up into Scotland, where the Pictish
symbols re-appear – all of which is reflected in the text. There
is no need to determine the date of *Redriff* with any precision.
It is obviously later than the maritime expansion of England
under the Tudors; the sailing ship is supreme, and the general
feeling of the section is very much that of R. H. Dana's *Two
Years before the Mast* (known to, but not read by, D.), which
was published in 1840; and D.'s grandfather, the real Eb.
Bradshaw, would have been in the prime of his working life
during the decades that followed the publication of Dana's
book. Nevertheless, the poet adopts his own standing-point in
time (as he does throughout *The Anathemata*) and can range
backward and forward at will. Thus we meet flavours from
other periods (eighteenth or seventeenth century *Gangem-land*,
East Mark) and a connection is maintained with even earlier
times by such expressions as 'fair-grained-*ulmus*', 'the old
Jason', and the intensely medieval 'Rootless Tree'. In this there
is no inconsistency or violation of artistic canons, for the shipwright, like the skipper in this and the preceding parts, is both

individual (Eb. B., in fact, is a piece of exact drawing based on **118**
close attention to what D. was told about him) and typical:
thus he can serve to reflect the poet's shifting view-point.

We may note that, as there has been a geographical concentration, which has taken us to the port of London, so there
is now a greater concentration on one particular character.
Short though this section is, the person of the shipwright is
presented sharply and clearly: expressed, moreover, entirely
through this own speech, which does not begin until near the
bottom of the first page, with 'Not for a gratis load . . .'. There
are two strands in D.'s work. Whether they are at once conflicting and complementary, or whether they are only the
former – for they are certainly not only the latter – it is not easy
to determine. The first strand is his love of the Brythonic, and
Romanised Brythonic, culture of the island. This love was self-
conscious and, we might say, artificially stimulated, because,
being cut off from Wales, D. had no roots reaching down into
Welsh ways of thinking and speaking through which he could
draw natural nourishment for his love. He complained that he
'had been deprived of a heritage' and says that, 'It is impossible
to explain the sense of frustration – genuine bitterness, grief is
not too strong a word'. This grief is seen in such places as the
inscriptional poem 'Cara Wallia derelicta', and his frequent
attempts to assuage it by deliberately introducing a foreign
element of Welsh imagery and idiom in the same way as he
introduced naturally the corresponding English.

The second strand is the poet's involvement – unconscious,
natural and uncontrived – in the far richer tradition that came
to England from Greece, Rome, the Saxon and Norman
invasions and France. This is supreme in *Redriff* and in the
following *Lady of the Pool*, in both of which he speaks as one
who is completely at home. He speaks as a Londoner – a
Londoner, it is true, who is aware of the old London symbolised
in the name Troy Novaunt and (in D.'s words) 'feels a kinship
with the more venerable culture in that hotch-potch which is
ourselves' – but one who is so thoroughly imbued with the

118 spirit that came from outside the island that in writing of the 'hotch-potch' he attains an assurance, a certainty of aim, that makes the reader conclude that, for all his love of Wales, he is eminently an English poet. *The Battle of Maldon, The Dream of the Rood*, medieval English lyrics, Piers Plowman, Chaucer, folk-song, Malory, Shakespeare, Milton, Blake, Smart, Coleridge, Browning, Hopkins – these, and the classical world behind them are the homeland of his tradition.

    Cant, Knock etc: for these see the appropriate Admiralty Chart.

    Greenland. Note, with an eye to the title of the next section and the introduction of the lavender-seller, that the Greenland Dock adjoins the Lady and Lavender.

    Tom Bowline: originally Tom Bowling, in Smollett's *Roderick Random*, as a type of the honest seaman. The Tom Bowling in Dibdin's song ('poor Tom Bowling') was Captain Thomas Dibdin, brother of Charles (1745–1814), who wrote the song, and father of Dibdin the bibliophile.

    the drownded Syro-Phoenician: reminds us of Eliot's 'Phlebas the Phoenician, a fortnight dead'; but more important is the quasi-sacrificial death of Palinurus in the fifth Aeneid, torn from the steering by Sleep, to appease the God of the seas. 'Drownded' is by no means the only Dickensian echo.

    The Wop is anxious to sail with Thursday night's tide, even at the cost of scamping the work, 'or the dues 'ld ruin him'. *oil an elbow*: the variation of 'oil' for 'grease, as in 'Elbow-grease' brings a suggestion of bribery ('palm-oil').

    'The background', writes D. in September 1974, 'of the stuff on page 118 about the skipper from Sicily or thereabouts in the Mediterranean was based on an incident of which my mother told me. The vessel from the Middle Sea lay in the Pool of London and sent some message either directly or indirectly to Eb. B., to come with his few workmen as urgent repairs were needed. Eb. B. rowed out with his men to the waiting ship & was taken aboard her & when he saw that there was much more to be done than he had been given to understand & agreed to do the job or jobs, but that it would take that day and the next. This was communicated to the Sicily skipper who became angry and pleading owing to the heavy harbour dues that would arise. Eb. B. said the Harbour dues were not his concern but ... sorry, but this would involve too long a thing.'

lignum vitae: (literally, timber of life, with obvious relevance) one of the hardest of all woods. It contains a waxy resin (guaiacum), which acts as a natural lubricant; and is, or was, (as here) therefore used for pulley-sheaves.

the hound: '*Naut.* A projection or cheek, of which one or more are fayed (a word we meet on p.120) to the masthead to serve as supports for the trestle-trees.' (S.O.D.). *Suky Tawdry:* 119 according to Partridge, 'a slatternly woman in fine tawdry' (lace), and precisely of our period, about 1820–50. But Eb. Bradshaw's use of the capitals brings the expression closer to its origin in St Ethelreda or Audrey (who abandoned fine necklaces for a scarf of silk). Here, however, D. had in mind 'the various Sukey tawdries of the *Beggar's Opera*,' the 'molls' of p. 161. There is another reference to the *Beggar's Opera* on p. 176.

to pile a mint: 'pile' both in the obvious sense, and with an eye to 'pile' as the reverse side of a coin: 'cross or pile' (as in French), head or tail; there is the same sort of side-glance in 'lent of tides'. i.e. forty days of tides, and lent-spring.

for all the gold on his fleece: cf. 'Jason', p. 121.

Trinity Brethren: the Guild of the Holy Trinity and St Clement in Deptford was granted a charter by Henry VIII in 1514, but its origins go back much further into the middle age. There were other Trinity Houses at Dover, Kingston-on-Hull and Newcastle upon Tyne. Their chief concern was, and remains, safety of navigation in coastal waters, including lighthouses and pilotage. 'For the first time [i.e. in the charter granted by James I in 1604] a distinction was made between Elder and Younger Brethren, there being thirty-one of the former, from whom were elected the Master, Wardens, and Assistants, "all the rest of the seamen and mariners" of the guild being Younger Brethren.' (David W. Waters, *The Art of*

119 *Navigation in England in Elizabethan and Early Stuart Times*,
1958, p. 111). The Port of London Authority, on which
Trinity House is represented, was established in 1909, with
general control of the river and docks.

Not for a boozed Murphy's bull: i.e. not for the Pope of
Rome, not even if he issued a bull, written out in the cursive
hand of the papal court or chancellery, with the leaden *bulla*
attached. *boozed Murphy*, not simply because Eb. B. might well
associate the Pope with Irish Catholics, and Irish Catholics
with drink, but: 'That again is wholly derived from what my
mother told me – I owe virtually *all Redriff* & a good deal of
The Lady of the Pool to conversations with my mother, God rest
her. In fact *The Ana* or large parts of it could not have been
made in the 1940s had I not been able to recall things (about
Eb. B. & the Pool of London) she had told me of when I was
a child and then again after my return from the army in 1919
for in that period after the 1st War we conversed a lot – She
did not die until 1937.

'Now Eb. B. was C. of E. & in fact a Warden of the Church
in Rotherhythe but of very radical opinions, anyway he had
among his workmen in his boat-yard where he made masts and
blocks and also small craft, an Irish Catholic named Murphy,
who, like Tim Finnegan, "had a drop of the creature every
morn" – in fact took a good few drops at all times of the day;
but Eb. B. (almost a teetotaller himself) kept Murphy on
because of his good workmanship & general usefulness and
intelligence. Sometimes Murphy did not turn up at the early
hour in the morning but was there for sure a bit late. Eb. B.
evidently had a liking for Murphy in spite of his drinking
habits and his being a Catholic. For my mother told me that
he, Eb. B., would ask my brother (who was born a little before
Eb. B. died, "Where's Mur?" to which my brother (still *very*
young) would answer "Mur boozed", which amused Eb. B.
greatly. So that provided me with "Not for a boozed Murphy's
bull". And moreover gave me also an actual basis for "in curial
cursive and leaded *from the scarlet pontiff o' the West*". For

though, according to what my mother told me Eb. B. was very sparing in his use of oaths or "bad language" (as she called it) of any sort, none the less when really put out (as in the case of the demands of the skipper from Palermo) he would say with much emphasis: "No, I will not, not for you nor any one, *not for the Pope o' Rome*".

'Also (p.121) he used to say when faced with a difficult task "I'll manage somehow, *or dash my buttons*". So, almost all *Redriff* depended upon what I had heard from my mother, decades before *The Anathemata* was being written.' (Letter of 4 September 1974).

Canute . . . Galley Wall: see above, in the note at the beginning of *Middle-Sea and Lear-Sea*. Stow, in his *Survey of London* (first published in 1598), which was much used by D. for the next section (*The Lady of the Pool*), speaks of Canute's ditch (p. 21 of the *Everyman* edition); and see Stenton's *Anglo-Saxon England*, 1971, pp. 390–1.

cis- or trans- Gangem-land: west or east of the Ganges. **120** 'ulmus': elm. 'East Mark oak': Austrian oak, 'goodish' but not so good as English. One of the very few wood-carvings by D. of any size (almost certainly, in fact, the only such), some $3'$ in height, was, I thought, of Austrian oak, from the old church of Fr. Ignatius's monastery at Capel-y-ffin: a carving of St Dominic. I was mistaken: 'The oak St. Dominic was made at Ditchling of bloody hard "heart of island-grown". It was, I mean the oak was, given to me by George Maxwell's father.' (D. 27 Sept. 1974 – Maxwell's father-in-law, 'old Mr Baker', says J.H. – in any case it was 'seasoned in m' neighbour's yard'.)

fay: in shipbuilding, 'to fit closely and exactly to', as in note on 'hound' above.

keel-elm: cf. p. 173, 'the quivering elm on which our salvation sways'. 'Jason': with 'fleece' on p. 119.

the Fault: one of many examples of the insistence on the Redemption as payment. 'aspen transom': the cross-piece of the True Cross, which was traditionally made from willow. 'the Rootless Tree': from *The Dream of the Rood*, v. 30, where the

Cross says that it was 'astyred of stefne minum', 'torn from my trunk (stem). 'Day o' Doom': a reminder of the opening *Dies Irae*. (But for the wood, see Rahner, p.65.)

121   **dash my buttons:** this common old-fashioned expression, used in real life by the mast-maker, occurs more than once in a greatly loved book, Borrow's *The Romany Rye*: first, in the opening chapter, where the postillion, delighted at having his chaise repaired, says, 'If ever I forget your kindness and that of the young woman below, dash my buttons'. The thought of Borrow sent me to D.'s introduction to *Wild Wales*; and, as so often, the first sentence that catches my eye gives a glimpse through a window opening into the poet's mind, ever revolving round the same themes. Thus: '. . . his (Borrow's) long right knocked senseless the abominable tinker, so that Diana Nemorensis, in the person of Belle Berners, cried out, "Hurrah! . . . there's nothing like Long Melford for shortness the world over".' I find it difficult fitly to express the delight of savouring what the poet savoured and recognising his delight.

V

THE LADY OF THE POOL

With this section the voyaging comes to an end, except for the **124**
vessel's safe return to her home waters, of which we are told at
the end of *Keel, Ram, Stauros.*

The skipper ties up in the Pool of London, the stretch of
water, well below the old city, on the south side of which lies
Rotherhithe. He goes ashore, is accosted and entertained by the
lavender-seller who gives her name to this section. On p.124
the poet himself is speaking; the Lady of the Pool intervenes at
the head of p.125, and it is she who continues to speak until the
end, on p.168, when she goes back to her crying of lavender.
The skipper himself speaks only once, on p.141, when he inter-
jects the remark 'For certain this Barke was Tempest-tost'.
D., however, uses the girl as a vehicle for his own thoughts and
images, deliberately attributing to her knowledge and sensibili-
ties that could not be her own.

This skipper is not the same man as the skipper of the preceding section, except in so far as they are both types of
adventurous seamen, for we have moved back some four hundred years or more in time. 'The setting', D. writes to D.M.C.,
12 March 1953, 'is toward the end of the middle ages. There
were a number of reasons necessitating this. For one thing she
(the L. of the P.) had to represent to some extent the British sea
thing which rose only after the end of the 15th century, so that
the figure had to combine the Hogarthian, Turneresque, even
Dickensian worlds with the Catholic world of "Dick Whitting-
ton", Chaucer, Langland, Geoffrey of Monmouth's Trojan-
London myth and so on and so on.' To a reader of Chaucer,
the spirit of his writing and, in particular, the emphasis he and
his characters so often lay on all that is associated with the Cross
of Calvary, are so akin to D.'s own, and entail so marked a

124 similarity of metaphor and image, that the date of Chaucer's death (1400?) is an appropriate central point for what he calls (*ibid*) 'the interpenetration backwards and forwards and up and down' of the many facts and fancies that are transmitted by the lavender-seller.

We may add to this that, while it was Chaucer's London that the master of this ship visited, that London is seen through Tudor eyes; for D. made great use of Stow's *Survey of London*, first published in 1598, from which he drew not only the general picture of the city, but much detail concerning churches, monuments and legends.

The time is late summer ('but a month and less from the septimal month', p.124), when lavender is being sold in the streets; and D. takes advantage of the approach of the feast of the Exaltation of the Holy Cross (September 14) to introduce and embroider upon the churches in which the feast will be celebrated. This serves also as an anticipation of the next section, for *Keel, Ram, Stauros* is a great hymn to the timber of the Cross; and that section, in turn, will naturally suggest the conception of Christ and his birth (*Mabinog's Liturgy*) which were the essential preliminary; and that, again, will lead into the final sacrifice in *Sherthursdaye and Venus Day*: completing the circle, like the great river Ocean which encompasses the world and 'flows back upon itself'.

The lavender-seller starts by speaking (p. 125) of the coming of autumn; it was already 'rawish' on the river, early that morning, even though Crouchmass, September 14th, has not yet come. This leads her into the London churches, and that again (p.128) into the story of her various lovers, introduced by 'Or may I never keep company more with a dunce of a maudlin inceptor'. This young clerk or graduate is the first of her lovers. The next comes in at the second paragraph of p.130: the mason. On p.135 she turns to the seamen, from whom she has learned much. The first is the skipper of the Margaron; the second is (p.137) 'him from Aleppo come/the master of the Mary'. The arrival of the battered vessel is described (pp. 137–9), followed

by an account of the storms through which she had passed **124**
and the wonders that were seen, including mermaids (p.142–5).
This last allows the girl to present herself to our skipper, to
whom she is telling the tale, as Britannia; after which she
returns 'to my tale I regaled my mason with', and tells him of the
Aleppo skipper's encounter with Barbary pirates (p.147) and
'other sharp exchanges' (pp. 148–9).

The crew of the vessel are then described in turn, and D.
(and the girl) take the opportunity provided by the mention of
the Welsh boatswain (p.149) to introduce (pp. 149–54) a number
of Welsh legends. Of these she concludes (p.154) ' 'T were *too*
much. Yet, you could not choose but hear, for as parson say of
Chrysostom, his tongue *could tell !*' The last of the crew to be
spoken of is the second mate, a Scotsman, who is blamed for
the vessel's troubles. The skipper's incredulity leads her into
further memories of nautical adventures (pp. 155–60), Phoenicians, Egyptians, Saxons, ending with a circumnavigation of
Africa. Here the return to the Mediterranean (p.156) allows a
reference to the 'navel of the world' (Jerusalem), and so to Calvary, and so to those who were saved on that hill, and so to a
prayer for the repose of all mariners.

With the last line of p.160 we see that all this series of tales
has been an interlude, for we return to the celebration of the
feast of the Holy Cross with which we were concerned on pp.
127–8. We go back to the London churches; to the legends of the
foundation of London; and end with a farewell to our skipper,
after which the girl returns to crying her lavender.

In this section there is a good deal of what one might call
'lavender-ese', the lavender-seller's corruption or cockneyfied
version of cultured or learned idiom. This is self-explanatory.

Lud: to Stow (at the very opening of his *Survey*), to Shakespeare (Cymbeline, Act IV, sc. 2), to Geoffrey of Monmouth
(III.20) and to the inhabitants of the fifteenth-century London
the master of our vessel is visiting, Lud, who repaired, strength-
ened, and adorned the city, was its second founder; and London
was to them Luds-town. *the Fleet Gate*, i.e. Ludgate, just outside

which was the Fleet Bridge, over the river Fleet, which ran into the Thames at the present Blackfriars. The name Ludgate is not connected with King Lud, but derives from O.E. *ludgeat*, postern.

forest of Llefelys: see the story in the *Mabinogion*.

the twenty-six wards: as described in turn by Stow, within and without the wall. **'kell'** (*kellis*) in the Dunbar verse is the same word as 'caul', a girl's hair-net or head-scarf. 'troia'd', as before, labyrinthine; cf. 'gammadion'd' of Troy, p.56. 'East-Seaxna nasal': a certain nasal quality, particularly in plainsong, gave great pleasure to D. 'I used to love to hear Fr Bernardine at Brockley intone that if he chanced to be deacon at the first Mass of the Nat. ['In illo tempore exiit edictum a Caesare Augusto . . .'] His French accent made the Latin slightly nasal and very strong.' (Letter of September 1974.) There would have been a similar 'vocal pulchritude' in the accents 'heard long since in Alban hill-ways in Latium' (*K.M.* p.7.)

nestle-cock: cockney (M.E. *cokeneye*, cock's egg.) 'nestle-cock polis,' because a child who was suckled for longer than normal was a 'nestle-cock', and the name was applied to the soft-bred townsman. *polis*, for the Greek origin (Troy), *urbs* (for the Roman), *oppidum* (as being more suitable to towns other than Rome), *burh* (for the Anglo-Saxon).

125 The lavender-seller begins. *introit in a Dirige time:* the introit ('entrance') being the beginning of the Mass, and 'Dirige' being the opening word of the first antiphon at Matins in the Office for the dead (dirge), she is beginning to cry her lavender when it is already nearly time to lament the passing of summer: the first frosts will soon be here.

ditty-box (R.N. and cockney) is more immediately from Taplow (Hamish Maclaren's *Private Opinions of a British Bluejacket*), e.g. 'he said you haves nise war ships i thort this is suspicuous i did not know if he was getting At you. says i am not awair if they are partiklar nise i were in one, i were in the black Prinse in jutland, he said were you. god damn it yes i said you do

nor forget this triphul, he said she were sunked if i am not miss **125**
took. Tells him pressisively, arsks if you was rescewed, i thort oh
no i dyed i am a gost, but says yes but onlye by the skin of your
tooth, which what do you find. he says what. says well damn it
what a nise thing to be rescewed but all your cherrissed posses-
suons find a so-call whaterie Grave, to whit i was angery as a
tyger which its kids have been took out of its Very Pors to go in
the zoo, oh was you he said. sais yes i will tell you why specually,
it is this, i were in my old soot for one thing, as further mores
my ditty box did not Flote . . .'.

my fish-eye: we have already met (p.74), in 'brights his
ichthyic sign' a reference to the Christian symbol of the fish,
ichthus, the initial letters of which (in the Greek alphabet) give
Iēsous Christos Theou Uios Sōtēr, Jesus Christ, son of God,
saviour. D. applies this to the Masters of the various vessels
whose journeyings are described, in as much as they may be
seen as typifying the Master (or, more precisely, the mate as his
vicar) in the ship-like upper room of the Last Supper (p.53).
Of its use here he says 'Not so bright as "ichthyic sign" perhaps
because here is an image of more gross a nature – the drunken
[cf. the references to 'Iacchos', 'bacchic'] sodden, tough but
efficient, and, at base, kindly skipper who berths them to
schedule and is thus a type of S. Peter and of our David and
Manawydan the sea-god' (to D.M.C., March 1973).

Later (p.173) we have the 'cod's-eye man'. And this makes it
clear that the image is probably based on a misconception –
but, we must agree, a happy misconception. When living at
Capel-y-ffin D. would often hear the three girls singing. Among
the songs that most delighted him were *Shallow Brown* and *The
Cod's-eye man*. From the former he took 'And who d'you think
was Master of her, but A Yankee mate and a lime-juice skipper';
and this reminded him of the 'cod's-eye man', giving him the
connection lime-juice, vine-juice, Christ, ichthys.

Terry, however, in his *Shanty Book, Part* I (*Sailor Shanties*),
makes it clear that the correct title is 'The Hog's-eye Man'.
'There has been much speculation as to the origin of the title.

125 As a boy my curiosity was piqued by reticence, evasion, or declaration of ignorance. It was only in later life that I learnt it from Mr Morley Roberts. His explanation made it clear why every *sailor* either called it "hog-eye" or "hog's eye", and why only *landsmen* editors ever get the word wrong.' Earlier, Terry writes 'One of the best known of all shanties is "The Hog's eye man"; I have seen this entitled "The Hog-eyed Man" and even "The Ox-eyed Man". Every old sailor knew the meaning of the term. Whall and Bullen, who were both sailors, use the correct expression, "Hog-eye". The majority of sailors of my acquaintance called it "Hog's-eye". Did decency permit I could show conclusively how Whall and Bullen are right and the mere collector wrong. It must suffice, however, for me to say that the term "Hog's-eye" or "Hog-eye" had nothing whatever to do with the optic of the "man" who was sung about.'

The first verse as the girls sang it, went:

> Oh the cod's-eye man is the man for me,
> He were raised way down in Tennessee.
> Oh cod's-eye, oh.
> Row the boat ashore for the hog's-eye,
> Steady on a jig with a hog's-eye oh,
> She wants the hog's-eye man.

The fish, like Brigid's fire, plays a part in D.'s conflation of mythology (in this case Celtic) and Christian truth. So we meet 'the primordial fish that was before them all – long long before, long anterior, and before again, before the early whirling sticks caught the worm of fire . . . who bears the barbed name of Ichthus, the king-salmon of Glevum', who is later 'Ichthus of the three liaisons' i.e. of the three Persons of the Trinity.

The Nore gulls: the gulls coming in over the Thames ('Lear's river') presage a hard winter (a long *Winter's Tale*). It does not take D. long to start using the girl as the medium for his word-juggling.

Was already rawish: she is speaking of that same morning; although the date is still before the feast of the Exaltation of the Holy Cross, it was as cold as November. *Ides*, 13 December, the

feast of St Lucy, an Ember Day. *pontiff Juliuses 'versal colander:*
the Julian calendar, introduced by Julius Caesar in 46 B.C., in
his capacity of Pontifex Maximus.

The mention of the date allows the introduction of the **127**
London churches in which the feast will be celebrated. *Archie's
piscopal Ordo* is one of many similar distortions, the interpretation of which seldom presents difficulty. *Ordo:* the 'Ordo
Divini Officii Recitandi Sacrique Peragendi', Order for the
recitation of the Divine Office and the celebration of Mass, in
the form of an annual calendar. **Two Sticks and an Apple:**
riming slang. This church (St Mary Matfellon in Stow, pp.
376–7) is in the extreme eastern suburbs, as St Bride's is at the
western end of the city, All Hallows at the northern, and the
keelhaws (ship-yards) are on the river, which forms the southern
boundary of the city.

D. borrowed **Shandies,** for candles, from a little child in the
early 1930's. When darkness came early in the winter evenings,
the child would be delighted by the lighting of the candles which
were the only illumination. For Brigid (Bride) see also *K.M.*
p.8.

middle-brook that waters: (and note 7) Stow (from whom
comes the 'long bourn of sweet water' at the foot of the page)
has much to say both about the natural supply of water and about
the construction of conduits and miles of lead piping for the
distribution of good water. Note 6 or 7 should refer to
Apocalypse ch. xxii. 'Pomarary': Stow (p.242) took this to
refer to an apple-orchard. The *pomoerium* recurs in the *K.M.*
p.10, and *Ana.* p.221, where see comment. 'wheat-hill':–
i.e. corn-hill. 'Laidly Worm' should have the reference to the
Apocalypse in note 6. 'Laidly' (M.E.) = loathly; cf. p.168.
This is the dragon or serpent (vv. 3–10) destroyed by Michael.

St Mary Newchurch (**the Great Mother's newer chapelle**),
also known as St Mary Woolchurch, is in Walbrook Ward
(Stow, p.203). St May le Bow is in Cordwainer Street Ward,
and Stow refers to this as New Marie Church. New Neva's Old
Crepel, as note 11 says, must be St Mary Aldermary, and this

127 also is in Cordwainer Street Ward, and is so called (Stow, p.226) 'because the same was very old, and elder than any church of St Marie in the city'. 'Crepel', however, implies Cripplegate Ward, in which stands St Mary Aldermanbury, to which the passage which follows, in brackets, might apply. In that church Stow saw an enormous 'shank-bone of a man', which he took to be one of 'some thousands of carrie loads' of bones removed from the cloister of Paul's Church.

The passage in brackets, however, could equally well, or better, be read as an anticipation of St Paul's, for Stow (p.298, as D. in his note 12) speaks of the discovery of many 'scalps of oxen and kine in the year 1316; which thing (say they) confirmed greatly the opinion of those which have reported, that of old time there had been a temple of Jupiter, and that there was daily sacrifice of beasts'. This will account for the **chthonic matres under the croft** (crypt), with which we may connect, though hardly directly, the **Deae matres** in n. 7 to p.162. **a Maye's Aves:** the May Day carols (as on Magdalen Tower) rising up to the clerestory. 'springan' follows after the colon of 'croft:', as 'luce' follows that of 'sub-crypt:' so that in the two pairs of lines enclosed by the brackets, the second phrase of each pair bears the same relation to the first. The *Aves*, then, rise up to clerestory from the chthonic matres in the same way as the fleur-de-lys rise up from the 'Delphi' in the sub-crypt to the steeple. And this can only mean, I suggest, that there is evidence for, or D. guesses at, the existence, in pre-Roman times, of some sibylline or prophetic priestess at the place on which St Paul's was to be built. From her the lilies of Mary spring to the steeple. 'Flowers' I take to be a verb, and the fleur-de-lys to be the carved floriation that often decorates the ribs of a steeple. I still find this passage puzzling.

A MS. draft of this passage shows that 'Chthonic matres under the croft' was once 'Triad matres undercroft', which confirms the association with the three Deae Matres. 'Delphi' would appear to have come in through an accidental coincidence of sound. D. wrote, 'Sow in sub-crypt / flower de luce the steeple'

(the second line is a tentative reading of what is difficult to **127**
decipher). 'Sow' was discarded in favour of 'delve', which was
itself crossed out in favour of 'Delphi'.

faiths under Paul: the pre-Christian remains referred to in
note 12. **Artemis:** the 'blowing of the buck' is D.'s justification
for transferring the old temple from Jupiter to the goddess of
the chase: particularly since he wished to connect the older
worship with the Christian Virgin. Stow's account of the
ceremony may be of interest (pp. 298–9). 'Sir William Baud,
knight, the 3rd of Edward I, in the year 1274, on Candlemas
day, granted to Harvey de Borham, dean of Powle's, and to the
chapter there, that, in consideration of twenty-two acres of
ground or land, by them granted, within their manor of Westley
in Essex, to be inclosed into his park of Curingham, he would for
ever, upon the feast day of the Conversion of St. Paul in winter,
give them a good doe, seasonable and sweet, and upon the feast
of the commemoration of St Paul in summer, a good buck, and
offer the same upon the high altar . . . Now what I have heard
by report, and have partly seen, it followeth. On the feast
day of the commemoration of St Paul, the buck being brought
up to the steps of the high altar in Paul's church, at the hour of
procession, the dean and chapter being apparelled in copes and
vestments, with garlands of roses on their heads, they sent the
body of the buck to baking, and had the head fixed upon a pole,
borne before the cross in their procession, until they issued out
of the west door, where the keeper that brought it blowed the
death of the buck, and then the horners that were about the
city presently answered him in like manner . . . There was
belonging to the church of St Paul, for both the days, two special
suits of vestments, the one embroidered with bucks, the other
with does, both given by the same Bauds (as I have heard).
Thus much for the matter.'

Quintilis, the fifth month (counting from March), changed
to July by Julius Caesar when he reformed the calendar.

the tunicled martyr's: 'tunicled' because of the 'dalmatic'
worn by deacons.

prills: the verb comes from Stow, p.239: 'on the east side of the same cross (in West Cheape, erected in 1290 by Edward I, marking one of the places where the body of his wife Eleanor rested on the journey from Hardeby to Westminster) . . . was then set up a curiously wrought tabernacle of grey marble, and in the same an image alabaster of Diana, and water conveyed from the Thames prilling from her naked breast.'

long bourn: (with note 14). The reference in Stow is p.179.

128   **painters an' limners:** Stow, however, (p.273) derives the name from its standing 'at the north end of Stayning Lane' – 'of old time so called, as may be supposed, of painter-stainers dwelling there.'

budge-dressers: budge, a fur of lamb's wool, worn with the wool outside. See 'budged owls' on the next page.

buxom: in the original sense of 'obedient'. Cf. 'the pliant puella' in the inscriptional poem 'Cloelia, Cornelia, with the Palmyrene' reproduced in the 1967 David Jones issue of *Agenda*: 'the pliant puella who wove alone the Logos his fragile haubergeon, humana natura.'

as do renown our city: the *Twelfth Night* phrase reaches back to 'memorials' ('I pray you, let us satisfy our eyes With the memorials and the things of fame That do renown our city'); which was precisely what Stow was concerned to do. He lists the monuments and memorials and laments the defacement and destruction inflicted within decades of his own time.

She's as she of Aulis: cf. 'fiat mihi', p.189, and the 'thousand ships' of p.172. Behind the obvious sense of 'not a puff of wind without her' (i.e. the sense in which the Achaeans waited for the wind at Aulis) lies a more profound elaboration – without her pliancy, she would not have conceived of, nor would we have received, the Holy Spirit (wind, *pneuma*). In **her fiat is our fortune** there is a nicely contrived interweaving of 'my face is my fortune, sir, she said' depending on the change in the possessive pronouns. Who is 'she of Aulis'? The answer, Iphigeneia, the daughter of Agamemnon, would be obvious enough were it not for the title of D.'s watercolour (now in the

Tate), which coincides (though accidentally) with George Moore's *Aphrodite in Aulis*. For the substitution of Aphrodite for Iphigeneia, see above, comment on *Ana*. p.56.

Or may I never keep company: the lavender-seller speaks of the first of her lovers, the 'inceptor' (one who has taken a full degree in a medieval university: the verb is still in use at Cambridge; and cf. 'commence' and 'commencement'). 'dunce' and 'maudlin' both carry a double meaning, the former suggesting Duns Scotus, the thirteenth-century Scottish Franciscan philosopher, and the latter covering both the college and the normal sense of the adjective. **seraph:** used here of one who delighted, as did the Schoolmen, to distinguish and sub-distinguish; so St Bonaventure is known as the seraphic doctor, and Duns Scotus as the *subtle* doctor.

did black deth: William of Occam, another Franciscan scholastic (the third, if he is here referred to, for both Duns Scotus and Bonaventure were Franciscans) is believed to have died in the Black Death that ravaged Europe in the middle of the fourteenth century.

in oriel'd halls: both in the literal sense of halls with oriel **129** windows, and with an eye to Oriel College, chosen by D. because it was founded by Edward II (Edward of Carnarvon) or rather by his almoner Adam de Brome. See p.211 n.5.

in a cure o' Christ and shorn to sign it: cure in the sense of cure of souls, and shorn in that of tonsured. The same passage from Piers Plowman (Prologue 88) 'Bischopes and bachelers, Bothe maistres and doctours, That han cure under Criste and crownyng in tokne', is borrowed for the dedication of the *K.M.*

The rest of this page is an elaboration of the question with which it starts: does he sit, 'degreed and silked', and teach to an admiring audience? In the **the budged owls** Milton's (Comus v. 707) 'budge doctors of the stoick furr' reappear. D., I think, intended to share Milton's meaning of 'pompous', but at the same time had in mind the 'budge-bachelors' (gowned and with hoods of budge-fur) who took part in the Lord Mayor's procession. These were poor men and would pull their forelocks, 'like remunerated errand boys' when given an alms: as the 'budged owls' would do in token of their grateful admiration. 'thalamos' in the sense of 'bridal chamber.' The dance of the liberal arts leads to the music of the spheres; natural science leads to philosophy and philosophy leads to theology, whose handmaid she is.

Averroes, the twelfth-century Arab philosopher, for all the debt the Schoolmen owed him for their knowledge of Aristotle, will hardly dare to show a leg here; for Rome (*caelian consistory*) will be guided by Paris and Oxford (*Seine* and *Isis*).

Mother is requisite to son: in the sense, often stressed by D., that the incarnation depended on the Virgin's acceptance of the angelic message. 'theosis' is explained by note 4.

they come – and they go, captain. The girl leaves her 'cock-clerk' and returns to the London churches, leaving them immediately for her next paramour, the 'freestone mason'.

130   **At Sepulchre's** picks up from 'In Pellipar's' at the head of p.128. ('Smoothfield' = Smithfield.) This reminds the girl of the masonry of another gate ('rag' is perhaps still used for some types of coarse, hard, stone: and 'tile' for the clay from which tiles are made), and this again reminds her of her mason. He told her that the work was Roman; and she had learnt enough from her clerk to know what Roma spelt backwards meant. The nones of July is the 7th. 'Mystery', i.e. the mystery of his craft, as the word is used of the printer's craft, but with a capital initial here, to indicate the almost religious reverence that attaches to Rome, *Roma aurea*. 'Mason's paper hat': the square hat, made from a cunningly folded sheet of paper, worn by E.G., as in his well-known self-portrait. He copied it, I believe, from Italian masons.

the Hammerer: Thor, son of Odin, 'my exasperated son' in another draft, 'who handles my hammer'. 'the Arx of Julius': there were some who believed that Caesar built a fort on the site of the Tower. 'Gomery': Welsh, and from a stock-raising county.

from the right side: *a latere dextro*, the title of one of D.'s **130**
grandest drawings. Water issuing from the right-hand side is an
image that he found particularly moving, It came to him from
several sources: from the *Dream of the Rood*, v. 20, where blood
issues from the right: from the representation of the wound
caused by the spear of Longinus, whence issued blood and water
(the spear which dealt the dolorous stroke), traditionally shown
on the right side; from Ezekiel's water issuing from the right
hand of the Temple; and from the blessing before High Mass,
at which (in Paschal time) is (i.e. was) sung 'Vidi aquam
egredientem de templo a latere dextro, alleluia: et omnes ad
quos pervenit aqua ista, salvi facti sunt, et dicent, alleluia' –
'I saw water coming forth from the temple, on the right side,
alleluia: and all to whom this water came, were saved, and
shall say, alleluia.' The image recurs on page 139, where
right is again italicised. That chapter of Ezekiel, 47 (paralleled
by the 'pure river of water of life', of Apocalypse 22, and many
other biblical water-images) was ever vivid in the poet's mind.
Thus, in a letter of April 1964, written just after he had moved
from Northwick Lodge to Monksdene in Harrow, he includes
a little map of his new surroundings. A small lake is shown,
around which he has written, 'Ecce in ripa torrentis ligna multa
nimis ex utraque parte' ('Behold, at the bank of the river were
very many trees on the one side and the other'). To this is
appended a note, 'quote from Ezekiel 47. Not much of a *torrens*
I may say but a rather stagnant 18th cent lake'.

the blessed guardian head: ' "Gwynfryn yn Llundain",
the White Mount in London, was familiar in Welsh tradition
as the mound by the river where the marvellous head of Bran
the Blessed was inhumed to secure the land against invasion
(and, I suppose, failure of crops), the place of the cist that
Arthur opened because he would allow nothing to secure the land
but his own prowess' ('The Myth of Arthur' in *Epoch and
Artist*, pp. 222–3). The story is told in the Mabinogion,'Branwen,
daughter of Llyr', from which is drawn the passage that serves
as a prelude to *I.P.*, 'Evil betide me if I do not open the door . . .'

Bran's head is used in Dai's Boast (*In Parenthesis*, p.81), 'I saw the blessed head set under / that kept the narrow seas inviolate'.

131 In 'once in especial' we meet again the Wyatt reference with which *I.P.* opens, the N.C.O.'s sarcasm, 'I'll stalk within y'r chamber' – 'they flee from me that sometime did me seek . . .'

And again, once in especial: it might be possible to take this as the introduction of a third lover, a man who (p.133) had been a soldier; but it is much easier to connect this incident with the mason. That she has him in mind all the time is apparent from the repetition of 'Roma aurea Roma' on the next page, and from her speaking on p.147 of 'the tale I regaled my mason with' and on p.160 of 'these freestone masons'.

the day of the British Elen that found the Wood: a ms. note reads, '*Corrigendum to page* 131: Owing to the fact that on August 18th, the feast of St Helen, the Collect, the Gradual and other prayers of her mass commemorate her association with the Cross, I state on p.131 that her feast is also the Feast of the Finding of the Cross. This is erroneous, May 3rd and September 14th being the dates when that event is specially celebrated, the latter date being the original one.'

her own Cornhill, because Ceres (Demeter) was a corn-goddess. **de Arcubus:** so called, says Stow (p.227) because 'the first in this city was built on arches of stone'.

132 **crawlers:** in the rude, modern sense.

the lode already over the fen: in Chaucer's time all to the north of the wall between Bishopsgate and Cripplegate (the northern section of the wall) was the Moor, crossed by the Walbrook, marshy and waste. Later, it was drained. A lode is a watercourse in fenny country, but this will hardly fit the context. Here (as on p.135) the lode must be the lodestar, the North Star, which is already visible over the fen of Islington. The modern borough of Islington is pretty well due north of Newgate.

the whitest of the Wanderers: of the planets, Venus; and we may accept the girl's exaggeration of the legendary birth of Aeneas, whose mother was Venus. 'her fish day': Friday was Venus-day to the Romans. Note 4: the first verse of the song ends: 'A cowslip's grace is her nominative case, And she's of the feminine gender.'

Sanfairyann: Great War soldiers' French. **of my mob:** 133 the Buffs, we might say, with a little of what D. calls 'pre-application' – the Royal East Kents, raised in the sixteenth century as one of the 'independent companies' serving in the Netherlands against the Spanish.

note: the medallion is illustrated in A. R. Burn's *The Romans* 134 *in Britain*. One purpose of the note might be overlooked, to explain that the mason is looking towards the Fleet Bridge, by Ludgate, because it was there that the emperor, it is suggested, entered the city.

nigromantics: (note the elegance of 'nig' [necro] – 'romance') 135 prompted by Morgan le Fay, but with an eye also to what is referred to on the next page, the belief that astronomers, astrologers, mathematicians, and navigators were all versed in the black arts. **the ample shape:** i.e. the all-embracing character of the Redemption. **the second indelible mark:** i.e. when she was confirmed by the bishop of her diocese (the Ordinary), for it is held that the three sacraments of Baptism, Confirmation and Holy Orders imprint an indelible character, mark, or seal upon the soul.

Papeys-in-Wall: the church of St Augustine in the Wall (cf. the mention of Augustine below), so called 'for that it stood adjoining to the wall of the city, and otherwise called St Augustin's Papey, or the poor . . . the same church was allowed to the brethren of the Papey, the house of poor priests, whereof I have spoken in Aldgate Ward' (Stow, p.145). **lily i' the shipman's card:** the conventional fleur-de-lys marking the north on the compass rose. **Lode:** the seaman's only constant was the North Star: it is not, however, precisely at the Pole, and is itself circumpolar in motion. It was therefore important to know its relation to the Pole at any particular hour of the night, and it was for this that the regimen or rule of the North Star was needed. In the sixteenth century Polaris had a

polar distance of about 3 1/4 degrees. This had to be allowed for
when the navigator was determining his latitude by its altitude.
In Homer's day it was too far from the pole to be of any use.
(See Waters, pp. 43–7). D.'s note is something of an exaggeration, for there were other manuals of navigation, and before
them there were the rutters (*routiers*) pilot-books or sailing
directions.

As him, the skipper of the Margaron: the lavender-
seller's third lover. 'I had named the two vessels "The Margaron" and "The Troy Queen" in honour of Princess Margaret
and our reigning monarch' (D., Sept. 1974: he had said the
same to D.M.C. in 1953; He adds a note to the former remark:
'a similar allusion in I.P. page 66 "come with sweet princes by
malignant interests deprived" shows that though I.P. was
virtually finished by 1934 – I completed it in Sidmouth after
Nov. 1936 [the abdication of Edward VIII]. It also shows how
upset I was at the time. It would take a hell of a lot of detective
work to get that one. And now [Sept. 1974] of him too we can
only say *Dona ei requiem sempiternam.*') 'entranced': 'entrance,
the bow of a vessel, or form of the fore-body under the load-
water line': so, the more delicate and elegant the design of the
vessel, the harder it will be to direct her steering.

136   *Helyon:* the full title of the engraving which is reproduced
(much smaller than the original) facing p.213, is 'he frees the
waters of Helyon'. It was the last engraving D. made, and the
block bears the marks of the engraver's exasperation. According
to John of Hess, the unicorn sweetened the waters, by dipping
his horn into it, that the other animals might drink.

the conjuror-doctors . . . Deva: the master of the Margaron
had palmed off on some Cambridge scientist (as it might be Dr
Dee) a piece of ivory (a narwhal's tusk) as genuine ('ine' to rime
with 'wine') unicorn's horn: these Cambridge men mix true
science ('draughts of Cam') with the magic of sibylline Dee
(both river and man). The word-tangle is given further brilliance
by the references to Deva or Dee on pp. 67 and 69.

As take . . . vergil: explanation, I fear, will annoy all but the few who do not know that Anaximander of Miletus (born 610 B.C.) was one of the early Ionian philosophers, that Anaximander sounds somewhat like hexameter, and that Vergil wrote in hexameters. Appropriately to this context, Anaximander was an astronomer and is said to have discovered the obliquity of the ecliptic (the sun's apparent passage through the stars) and determined the equinoxes. Merlin's association with Vergil, both being regarded as magicians, is in keeping with the medieval view of the latter; and the use of lower-case initials is an elegant touch. 'As take' and *as him* = 'the sort of person who, for example, gives such and such a recipe, or works out horoscopes and makes up different sorts of coloured water as remedies'. 'The curia, up stream', the court at Westminster.

A very John-on-Patmos for uncovering: like St John on the island of Patmos, writing his apocalypse (uncovering) or Revelation. 'rombus': rhomb, magic circle. The description of Britannia comes from Dee's reported use of the term 'British Empire'.

But, he were had: 'he' is John Dee or a similar person, deceived by the narwhal-tusk.

Or him from Aleppo come: the girl moves on to her next 137 lover, the master of the *Mary*. *Macbeth*, i.3 (whence – not that there are not many other places where D. would have seen the phrase – comes 'the shipman's card' of p.135): 'Her husband's to Aleppo gone, master of the Tiger' says the First Witch, and then curses him, '. . . Though his bark cannot be lost, Yet it shall be tempest-tost'.

Wot a tiger! when D. wrote this he must have had in mind, in addition to *Macbeth*, a meeting with Christopher Dawson, on the sea-front at Sidmouth, in 1935. D. was with a friend who had not met Dawson before. They conversed for a few minutes, and as D. and his friend walked away, the latter, impressed in that short time by the extent of Dawson's learning, said to D., 'My God! what a tiger!' D., in consequence, and some of his friends, would often speak of 'Tiger Dawson'.

Overdue a nine month: from here to p.149 we have a

137 description of the troubles of the *Mary*, which includes a couple of digressions, as told to the girl by the master, and re-told by her. 'lost bottomry': loss of the ship pledged as security for a loan, so that both borrowers and lenders are as much dependent on charity as any homeless cat or dog. The idiom of 'pledge', 'repayment', 'redemption', given point by 'nine months' and the coming reference to the Annunciation, shows great delicacy in its combination of meanings.

The ship, however, was **not a loss,** but made port **very early, on the second day of the week.** 'Here I used bits of each of the four evangelist accounts of the hour of the Resurrection, and the ship comes to port on the morning of the feast of the Annunciation, (March 25) so the mass of Gabriel containing the *Ave* has already been said. The dry wood is becoming lissom and things in general are beginning to look up.' (To D.M.C. March 1953.) D. hints at the Resurrection by using 'the second day of the week' for 'Monday', as the four evangelists speak of 'the first day of the week'. They all speak, too, of the dawn. The ship was *Mary*, and it was Mary of Magdala and another Mary, with Joanna or Salome, who first found the empty tomb.

Rotherhithe mate and her Limehouse skipper: 'Shallow Brown' again – 'with a Yankee mate and a lime-juice skipper'. Cf. p.182, 'vine-juice skipper', and p.53, 'Who d'you think is Master of her' (from the same song).

woolded: a much favoured word. To woold is, for the landsman, to mend a broken spar by lashing to it a wooden splint. 'Why, I'd wager' says Peter in the K.M., p.13, / my good woman's aged mother / but scarce ris from / dire fevered bed / would, if needs be / learn 'em to woold a fished spar / firm enough to serve sufficient'.

138 **dressed for Breaker's Yard:** as opposed to 'dressed over all' or ceremonially.

from the right side: see above, on p.130. The point is stressed by 'about midships'. Her list may be 'to her lade-board' because the heart is popularly regarded as being on the left of the body, and the *Mary* is hulled seven times (the seven swords that pierced the heart of Mary). Or should we say: 'from the right side' – the water came from the right side, of course, because the water in Ezekiel came *a latere dextro*; but 'her list were heavy to her lade-board' not because of the supposed position of the heart, but because (as D. says in his note) the port side was the 'lading side', and she bore a precious load, like the 'galley laden Up to the highest board'. The conceit will not bear too literal-minded a scrutiny.

The description of the storm continues until the middle **140** of page 143, and it is only the occasional word that presents any difficulty. **red-tawnies:** of the clouds (I would not note this, had I not seen it glossed 'of the sailors'). *vancurrers:* no coinage but lavender-ese for vancourier, forerunner, herald. Again ('vaunt couriers') from the storm scene in *Lear*. 'scend': 'the carrying or driving impulse of a sea or wave'. 'fretted and veronica'd': the interlacing (marrying) of foam from each bow (which flow together midships) is seen as a veronica, or vernicle – originally a representation of the face of Christ as on the miraculous napkin with which Veronica wiped his brow, and later an emblem of this nature worn in a person's cap. The Pardoner in the Canterbury Tales (Prologue 685) 'A vernycle hadde he sowed upon his cappe'.

gilted . . . bends . . . paly: heraldic terms, used, I think, to soften the transition to the boldness of the next simile. 'white as the Housel of spume': 'of' = by the agency of – white as the consecrated Host because of the foam. This is carried into the metaphor that follows. **The tilted heavers** (the rearing waves) are the stone of her altar; **immenser** is the comparative of the adjective 'immense'; *hovers* is a noun (a variation of 'heavers'). So: even more immense waves curl over the ship, forming a dark apse for her. The image goes back to Homer (e.g. Iliad 4. 425–6), the crest of the wave rearing up as it curls over; so, too, the Homeric adjective katêrephês, used of a wave that arches over from above, and of a cave – like D.'s 'apse'. Such was the wave that shattered the boat of Odysseus (5.366–7). In 'immenser' there is also an echo of 'mensa', the table or altar. D. saw later that he was mistaken in referring to Hopkins.

141   **sleep with father Ulysses:** D. cannot but have had in mind the enigmatic prophecy in Odyssey xi. 134–7 that peaceful death would come to Odysseus 'far from the sea' or 'from out of the sea'.

margaron'd relics: re-echoing the *Tempest*, from p.113, 'who knell the bell, who thread the pearls that were Ned Mizzen's eyes'.

the full rant of the Roarer: the Hammerer of p.130. Here again we have *The Spanish Ladies* song ('From Ushant to Scilly is thirty-five leagues): 'We'll rant and we'll roar like true British sailors . . .; and following this we are back with the storm scene of *Lear* (pp. 68, 97).

For certain this Barke was Tempest-tost: interjected by the Master – see the introductory note above.

FIVE on 'em: and so, from the *Dream of the Rood*, on p.190. I saw a wondrous tree rising aloft, encompassed with light, the brightest of crosses. All that sign was overlaid with gold (*Eall thaet beacen waes Begoten mid golde*); fair jewels were set at the surface of the earth; so, too, there were five upon the crossbeam (*swylce thaer fife waerọn Uppe on tham eaxlegespanne*): from R. K. Gordon's translation, in the *Everyman* edition: the five jewels for the five wounds of Christ. In **starring the wide steer-board . . . yard,** D. has adopted one of the most ancient Christian symbols, the mast and yards imaging the cross, and combined it with the omen of the 'St Elmo's Fire', itself a manifestation of the 'Great Twin Brethren', brothers of David's Trojan *margaron*, Helen. Since Castor and Pollux were guardians of mariners, and since Helen 'beyond all doubt' (so H. J. Rose, a severe judge of evidence, *Handbook of Greek Mythology*, p.230) 'seems to be an ancient tree-goddess', pagan and Christian image are happily brought together.

142   Although the mariners are comforted by the 'twin sign' and are assured thereby that they '*cannot* be lost', more dangers await them. **Vengeance of white great birds** shows that D. is

still thinking of the *Ancient Mariner*. 'Undergirdings': passing a cable under the vessel and binding it tightly to hold her together. 'neapings': to be 'neaped' is 'to be left aground on the height of a spring tide'. 'fire': from the song 'There's fire down below'.

With **suasion by melody** the master of the Mary, as reported by the Lady of the Pool, passes to the wonders he saw: the sirens. These were often represented when the ship, with mast and yard forming a cross, was used as a Christian image. Odysseus would be shown, bound to the mast, to preserve him from the bewitchment of the song of the sirens. See the essay 'Odysseus at the Mast' in Hugo Rahner's *Greek Myths and Christian Mystery*, pp. 328–86. **Twice as natural . . . Living:** 'as large as life and twice as natural'. 'foam-white': as white as Venus rising from the foam of the sea (Aphrodite anadyomene), Venus who gave her name to what we call Friday (not without a thought, suggested by Friday, of Venus as patron of fishermen – see Rose, *Handbook of Greek Mythology*, p.122). 'wetter' than Susanna of Daniel 13.

Absolon: the gilt-tressed Absalom of the ballade attributed 143 to Chaucer was with D. for many years, certainly since the 1914 war; and it is apparent from a still enigmatic passage in the *K.M.*, p.26, that he intended to make him the centre of one of the themes of that poem. In that passage the gold of the hair against the darkness of the tree is likened to the gleam of mistletoe, which opens the door to the country of the Golden Bough.

prose: in the liturgical sense of a 'sequence', a hymn, sometimes in no regular metre, which occasionally precedes the Gospel. The *Dies Irae* is such. 'set to . . . mode': reminiscent of the plainsong metaphor of p.63, as 'a near thing' is of Wellington's 'close run thing'.

O, they was real: the skipper has been saying that what the captain of the *Mary* saw was a mirage: but mirages do not sing nor toss to their listeners 'kist posies'. 'transaccidented': as opposed to transubstantiated. By sirens' witchery it is the 'accidents' of the spindrift that are changed, not the substance.

It was her first lover, her 'aurioled' (or 'orieled') clerk, who taught her how to reason, and the difference between substance and accident, so that, with this to help her native wit, derived from her mother, she can affirm with certainty that 'All that is comprised under mermaid is no mirage'.

primerole . . . violet: 'Do you like the bit on p.143 the primerole an'/the primerole an'/etc. I'm fond of that passage from O they was real/to (144) man at the wheel' (D., March 1953, referring then to 'Maiden in the mor lay' as in note 1 to the next page.)

144   **he did meddle me with this Bountiful Mother:** i.e. with his Alma Mater, his college: with his own mother: and with his mother country – so that he called her 'Angela'. And so the poet is enabled to elevate the lavender-seller into the figure of Britannia. In the pasage that follows on p.145 she mimes that transfiguration, with the appropriate symbols: the ivory comb in the hair, the trident, the anchor, the lion (don't twist the lion's tail!), the ring. The ring 'were gave us long since by a' ancient fisher': not that it is actually the papal 'ring of the Fisherman'; there is, however, a natural connection in the mind, and D. must have noticed in Stow a quotation from Stow's precursor, Fitzstephen (p.84): 'in the seals of the popes, until the time of Pope Leo, on the one side was St Peter fishing, with a key over, reached as it were by the hand of God out of heaven, about it this verse, "Tu pro me navem liquisti, suscipe clavem" (You left your ship for me: take, then, the key). And on the other side was a city, and this inscription on it, "Aurea Roma".' Cf. p.107.

145   **No Aegis?:** originally proper to Zeus, a shield of goatskin, terrible to behold, which struck terror into the ranks of fighting men; later lent to, and then associated with, Athene, and shown as tasselled with snakes, the Gorgon's head in the centre. It is a short step from Athene to Britannia. The girl proceeds to improvise an aegis from 'halliard-hemp'.

146   The aegis is to be adjusted to cover her breasts, destined to nourish seamen, and her shift is to be arranged decorously. (The correct date for the 'gannet's bath' entry in the A.S.

Chronicle is, I think, 975.) So: **146**

> Then, too, the bold-hearted Oslac was driven from the land,
> Over the tossing waves where the gannet bathes.
> The grey-haired hero, wise and sage in counsel,
> Was driven into exile over the turmoil of the waves.

(G. N. Garmonsway's translation, in the *Everyman* edition.)

No helm? Fortuna or Tyche was represented with a rudder – a point picked up by D. in connection with Llywelyn ('our last native prince'): see comment on p.110. Britannia may stand, too, as ruler and rudder. 'Mantling', both in the sense of the mantle she wears, and in the heraldic sense, will serve for decorum. 'Maudlin gilt streamers': 'Maudlin' is an adjective (the capital initial to introduce a memory of Mary Magdalen), 'streamers' a verb. The Magdalen-like gold of her hair streams out, or streams out into, a tangled order. 'sweet Loy': of his Prioress Chaucer says (as D. does, metaphorically, of Eb. Bradshaw) that 'Hire gretteste ooth was but by Seinte Loy' (Prologue, v. 120). (Loy = Eloi, or Eligius.)

Finally, a wreath for her hair. *A bunch of blue ribbons:* D. uses the same song in his Art-and-Sacrament, Utile-and-gratuitous argument, and in *Use and Sign*. 'Oh dear, what can the matter be . . . Johnny's so long at the fair. He promised to buy me a bunch of blue ribbons, To tie up my bonny brown hair'.

and let the Tilbury gulls . . . mode's Dorian: let the gulls proclaim Britannia as Neptune's spouse and queen of the seas. 'Dorian', i.e. let the music be solemn and stirring, as in *Paradise Lost* I. 549ff.

> Anon they move
> In perfect *Phalanx* to the *Dorian* mood
> Of Flutes and soft Recorders; such as rais'd
> To highth of noblest temper Hero's old
> Arming to Battel.

Cf. *Ana.* p.143, note 3.

For we live before her time: see introductory note to 'Middle-Sea and Lear-Sea'. Here we have the same pre-application, for the Lady of the Pool and the skipper to whom she is speaking live long before the time of the Britannia we know, with helmet, trident and shield.

147   After the 'Britannia' and 'mermaid' or 'siren' digressions, the girl returns to the story told her by the master of the *Mary*. They have a brush with pirates off the Barbary coast of North Africa: Moslems, who hate IMAGE (the capitals because, to D., image and sign are of the essence of Christianity – hence his amusement at Borrow's 'man in black' on the subject of 'a good bodily image'). 'by the board', overboard.

Then an attack from a Venetian vessel, commanded by a 'vandal' (vandal – for nothing is chosen at random – because of the North African connection) 'of a baptised Christian Jew'. 'Wicings', to rime with Dickens, and cf. *Ana.* p.199. By a fortunate shot the clerk blows up the enemy's powder magazine, and so reverses the *Tempest's* (Act 1, sc. 1) 'All lost! to prayers, to prayers! all lost!'. 'uncommon actual' as opposed to potential (her orieled clerk had taught her something about act and potency.)

no matter where his commas come: by removing the commas, the gunner makes it possible to interpret 'To prayers all is won' in a number of different ways. The real point, however, is, I believe, the contrast between the optimism of the clerk and the distress of the gunner, broken on the deck. The former, in his delight at his unwonted success, wishes all to offer a prayer of thanksgiving. The latter cries out what may be read as an echo of the clerk's exclamation, but may equally well mean, 'To prayers: all is one.' In other words, prayers or no prayers, all is now over, all is one. With that (with either interpretation) there can only be agreement – 'they've nowt but *concedo*'. And we might add that, from the clerk's point of view *concedo* also means 'concede' in the sense of 'surrender'.

God's arlot: 'harlot' used, as originally, as a masculine noun, as Chaucer's Summoner (Prologue 647) 'was a gentil harlot and a kynde'. 'God's arlot', because it is addressed to the clerk who (and this suggests that the gunner is recovering his spirits) has just, he now understands, given the enemy an argument they cannot answer. He has literally 'redistributed their middle'.

God's dumb hound: as though the clerk were a Dominican **148**
(*Domini canis*) – dumb, alluding to Aquinas as 'the dumb ox
who will one day fill the whole world with his lowing'. The
gunner is saying that men of his profession will now have to learn
from the schoolmen. 'Lombard': Peter Lombard (c.1100–1160),
the 'Master of the Sentences' (sentences from Augustine and
other Fathers, with accompanying objections and answers)
who taught in, and became bishop of, Paris. 'the Scot' is Duns
Scotus, whom we have met before.

rutters: early pilot books and sailing directions (*routiers*).
'rhumbs': on early charts rhumbs or direction lines were drawn,
known as the 'rhumbs of the winds', and these appeared on the
compass-rose. Here the four cardinal points are indicated, with
four more for N.E., S.E., N.W., S.W. A rhumb (or loxodrome,
for it is in fact a spiral on the surface of the globe) is now defined
as a line which cuts all the meridians at the same angle, and we
speak of a 'rhumb-line course' as opposed to a 'great circle
course' (the shortest distance between two points). 'Wadman',
gunner, for he tamps home the wad.

to dare and display: (Alfonso Spagone) – 'watching his
daring display. When I went for some nuts and a programme, the
dirty dog stole her away . . .' The 'lilies' of France loom up at
Ushant and gild (golden lilies on a white ground) the thirty-
five leagues between Ushant and Scilly. 'jack-o-lantern sea-
marks', of the Cornish wreckers – and Caliban plotted murder.
'chops': chops of the Channel, as on p.101.

We turn to a description of the crew of the *Mary*. First,
briefly, the doctor (who voyages in his Muslim book because
much of the medieval medicine came through the Arabs), the
priest, and the mate.

is it in itself a good? there are still survivors from the **149**
twenties and thirties who will smile as they recognise the
Dominican behind this.

Trastamara was a medieval county occupying what is now
the north-western part of Galicia: hence, the many points and

headlands either side of Cape Finisterre.

Then comes the Welsh boatswain, from Milford Haven, who 'for each circumstance finds antique comparison'. He is an echo, but much less serious, of the Dai who intones the great boast in *In Parenthesis*, pp. 79–84. He speaks 'as though' he had sailed with the Argives to Troy, as though he had taken part in Caesar's invasion of Britain, had been present when Brutus sailed up the Thames and founded Troy Novaunt, as though he had been shipmates with Jonah. Finally (pp. 150–4) he runs

150 through a number of Welsh legendary voyages. **Maddoxes, Owenses, Griffins and Company** is a confusion of Madoc, son of Owain Gwynnedd, said to have sailed to South America in the twelfth century, and the Norse voyages to North America (see note 4, p.150).

Readers will remember the controversy in 1965 and later about the so-called 'Vinland Map'. See *The Strange Case of the Vinland Map*, by Helen Wallis and others, reprinted from the *Geographical Journal*, vol. 140, Part 2, June 1974.

bulled oar: or 'bolled', i.e. rounded, like a paddle.

151 **double-ended nave:** like the Homeric adjective for a ship, *amphielissa*, which probably or possibly means 'curved at both ends'. 'ensign to a jack-staff': because the ensign is flown from the stern, the smaller 'jack' from the jack-staff at the bow. 'modrern': so spelt, because it is only the English who do not pronounce the 'r' in such words as 'modern', pattern', or, indeed, in 'iron' etc.

152 **the Troit** and **note 4:** the subject, too, of D.'s *The Hunt*, in *The Sleeping Lord*, pp. 65–9, D.'s recording of which may be heard on an 'Argo' record (PLP 1093). 'elf-sheen': the 'sheen' is both for the suggestion of glimmer or glitter, and for the Irish Sí or fairy.

the marvel thorn of Orcop: the thorn bush on Orcop Hill which is said to (indeed, does – see p.206) flower at Christmas. 'Pernels': the capital initial disguises the unusual and obsolete 'pernel', loose or wanton woman, concubine, effeminate man. The O.E.D. quotes More, who sarcastically refers to Tyndale as a 'good tender pernell', and, from another sixteenth-century source, 'Master Campion, being the Pope's tender pernell, accounteth a little racking of himselfe . . . to be crueltie'.

Gildas, the sixth-century Romano-British author of the *De excidio et conquestu Britanniae* (ed. Hugh Williamson, with trans., 2 vols., 1899–1901), which covers a period of history that is essential to D.'s picture of Britain. 'The historical information which it gives', says Stenton, 'is quite incidental to its real purpose of recalling the British rulers of its author's day to repentance. But it gives a coherent impression of a possible sequence of events.'

Geoffrey of Monmouth: there are a number of references to him in *Epoch and Artist*. Tedious, conceited and bombastic though Geoffrey is, D. is always grateful to him for being a half-way house to Malory, or (he might prefer to say) a half-way house back from Malory to Romano-Celtic Britain. Geoffrey is only too readily available in an 'Everyman' translation. He finally succeeded in becoming Bishop of St Asaph's, but died three years later without ever having visited his see. 'Semprington sister': a Gilbertine nun, of the order founded by St Gilbert of Sempringham in the twelfth century – appropriately, the only purely English order.

Quo warrantoes: a way of saying 'on what authority do you **153** make these statements'. (There is no surety, she adds, because destructive critics will go too far.) The writ *Quo warranto* (by what authority do you claim this right or exercise this privilege?) was a favourite weapon used by the Plantagenets against Irish and Welsh rulers. Rose the dish seller confuses Maid Marian and Mary the Virgin: but what odds, she says, by Martha of Bethany – both lays (the ballad of Robin Hood and Mary's *Magnificat*) are directed against those who are 'sitting pretty', the rich and great ('Deposuit potentes de sede, et exaltavit humiles', He hath put down the mighty from their seats, and exalted them of low degree): nice exegesis, indeed.

untoward: an adjective, qualifying 'out-mere' (the open **154**

sea, which is perverse) and placed where it is to rime with *brim-ward* in the first line, O.E. 'brim' being a different word from 'brim' = edge, and meaning 'sea'. With 'out-mere' cf. the Vikings' 'out-north' and 'land-north' for north-west and north-east, 'out-south' and 'land-south' for south-west and south-east, as explained by Professor Taylor in *The Haven-finding Art*, p.8.

A **white hound** is associated with Celtic rulers. Is not the Prince of Wales (as Duke of Cornwall) still given a white greyhound?

That Caesar flew the arms of Gruffydd, **were too much,** but, like St John Chrysostom, the Welshman was golden-tongued.

155 We leave the Welshman's tales and return to the troubles of the *Mary*. **The cook scalded:** as in Chaucer's *Knight's Tale*, 2020, 'The cook yscalded, for all his longe ladel'. 'fouls and fairs', again from the witches' scene in *Macbeth*, I.3. The 'filthy airs' (which entail a change in 'accidents') are the work of, are woven by (*weft and warped*) 'glamour' in its original meaning of enchantment: and the reason for this is that a Scotsman from north of the Forth (*Bodotria*) was taken on as second mate. 'Gup Scot' is the opening of Skelton's diatribe against the Scots. 'Gup', exclamatory, like 'Giddup!', 'Get out!'.

more sotted than the Welshery of grammarie: D. takes advantage of the two cognate forms, *grammar* and *gramarye*, the former meaning (here) education, and the latter being an obsolete word revived, appropriately, by Scott, meaning magic. The girl apparently confuses *grammar* with *glamour* (see above) and says, rightly, that the Scots are even more devoted to education and to the magical than are the Welsh. We meet the same word, 'a stir of gramarye', in a Welsh context in *The Sleeping Lord*, p.95, where it is followed by another Scottish word, *ferly* (marvel), and another hint of substance and accident.

156 **Malabarbers** (the Malabar coast of India) . . . **Elfred:** The Anglo-Saxon Chronicle (tr. G. N. Garmonsway) under the year 883: 'And pope Marinus sent the *lignum Domini* to king

Alfred; and the same year Sigehelm and Athelstan took to
Rome, and also to India to St Thomas and St Bartholomew,
the alms which king Alfred had vowed to send thither when they
besieged the host in London'. G. quotes from Dickins and Ross's
edition of *The Dream of the Rood*, 'It is just conceivable that the
Brussels Cross (now in the sacristy of the Cathedral of S. Michel
and Ste Gudule) preserves the fragment of the True Cross sent
to Alfred by Pope Marinus . . . It may also be suggested that the
occasion for the revision of the poem was the gift of a piece of the
True Cross to Alfred.' The Rood, Alfred, the navy: what better
for our poet ?

Narvesund: 'In the *Ynglingatal Saga* [tenth-century] the
Straits of Gibraltar are called Norvasund, but I cant find the
bit about the first Viking who sailed through them. I cant *think*
where I read it.' (D., April 1960.)

Spartel Head: at the southern entrance to the Gibraltar
Strait. This final recorded voyage (Herodotus iv.42) is the occasion for a return to the highest seriousness. 'the Two Lands':
the Upper and Lower Kingdoms of Egypt. 'the winepress': see
the Preface, pp. 30–1, for the significance to D. of this type of
image.

upon a' ass's pony: no poet but D. could sanctify the 157
blasphemy of comparing Christ's entry into Jerusalem to
Yankee Doodle. 'the bishop's curia': the Sanhedrin. 'the Justic-
iar's mote-hall': the tribunal of Pilate. '*and*' and '*column*':
'again, just for emphasis [the scourging at the Pillar]. An important emphasis carried on with captain being spelt cap-tin.'
(D. to D.M.C. Jan. 1953.)

stel'yard . . . man-geld: D. delights in carrying on the
traditional medieval metaphor of the literal 'weighing' of the
ransom to be paid. D. laments the 'Eclipse of a Hymn' in *E. &
A.*, pp. 260–1 – the *Vexilla Regis*, whence he took the *statera*,
steelyard. (Were it the business of a commentator to praise rather
than attempt to explain, what words would he find for this interlacing of images drawn from the nursery rhyme, the waste land,
and the life-giving power of water ?)

158   **And other such prospectors:** the archaeologists' 'prospectors' in the sense of those who spy out the land in advance, fore-
runners. It is for these, too, that 'that shower that does all fruit
engender moisted the droughts': for these, and for the 'many
yet to come'. For all these we say *dona eis requiem*. But the prayer
is specially for those who travel the seas, 'precursors at the
steer-trees', and those, to come, who will use the new-fangled
backstaff to measure the altitude of the sun, and so determine
their latitude and their rhumb-line course.

159   D. slightly disguises the *Doctor mirabilis* (Roger Bacon) in his
admirable. 'scab-shin', says the O.E.D., was applied specially
to the (barefooted) friars. 'Nominalist': the controversy
between nominalists and realists raged throughout the height
of the middle ages. The nominalists denied the real existence
of universals, which, they held, were no more than a name or,
at most, a mental concept. D.'s statement that 'in common
opinion, if you were a Franciscan you were a Nominalist' is
a little strong. Both Bonaventure and Duns Scotus were 'mod-
erate realists', with the Dominican Aquinas.

    haw: as in 'keel-haw', yard, shipyard.

    Ovid's book: presumably the *Ars amatoria*. 'Knower';
gnostic, for Albigensianism was a form of gnosticism. 'significa-
tions on walls': as Daniel interpreted 'Mane, Thecel, Phares' for
Baltasar. 'ceromancer', chiromancer, palm-reader. 'mot': a form
of ('mort' or 'mott', girl; 'obsolete by 1915', says Partridge,
'except in Ireland, where it has, since late 19th cent (if not earlier) been used in low society, but not necessarily pejoratively.'

    My fine Lady of the Pool: the homeliness of the origin of
the title of this section is an added gratification.

160   **signed me:** with the sign of the Cross.

    But by what lode's regimen: not literally but metaphori-
cally – how could you find your way through all these puzzling
tales ('queer runes')? 'lode's regimen': as before, the 'rule of the
north star'. 'Jacob's staff': an improved form of the cross-staff.
'Hood's cross-staff is of great importance in the chain of developments that led up to the modern sextant. It was perhaps the

first nautical instrument devised to measure the sun's altitude by indirect observation' (Waters, p.189; see also pp. 53–5).

queer runes: here, queer tales, expressions, idiom; but 'rune' carries for D. a great weight of meaning; see comment on p.225, 'Who made the runes would read them'.

tow-haired Jute: 'Jute' because he is from Kent: 'Jutish Kent is distinguished by customs which, like its material culture, point to an early connection between its inhabitants and the men of the Rhineland' (Stenton, p.10). And so 'tow-haired', an adjective, much favoured in drafts that deal with continental invaders. 'I-tie-wise', popularised in the second World War, as 'from base to apex' ('arse over tip') was in the first. 'pontiff', i.e. pontifex, bridge-builder.

Rhodopis: note that the next line in *The Princess* is the line made familiar by D., 'Cloelia, Cornelia, with the Palmyrene . . .'. She is said to have built a pyramid with the profits from her trade; it was the same as that of the Lady of the Pool, but with a richer clientele. Ovid speaks of her, so that the 'Ovid's book' of p.159 may have included the *Heroides*.

Here we leave the sea-faring tales, and return to the celebration of the feast of the Holy Cross in London Churches: first, at St Peter-upon-Cornhill (n.3.) **Wildgoose Lane;** it is the 'goose' (providing feathers for the arrows) which suggested 'Fletcher'; he, too, was a Welshman ('Wellin', like 'Fluellen', for Llywelyn). Stow (pp. 209–10), writing of the hall of the Hanseatic merchants in Thames Street, says: 'They hired one house next adjoining to their old hall . . . a great house with a large wharf on the Thames, and the way thereunto was called Windgoose, or Wildgoose Lane, which is now called Windgoose alley, for that the same alley is for the most part built on by the stilyard merchants' i.e. the 'merchants of Almaine'. **161**

Fletcher reckoned to have seen Old King Cole being baptised (hence 'in a candidate's vesture'). Stow, again (p.174): 'There remaineth in this church (St Peter-upon-Cornhill) a tablet whereon it is written . . . that King Lucius founded the same church . . . Jocelin of Furness writeth . . . that Eluanus, the second archbishop, built a library to the same adjoining, and converted many of the Druids, learned men in the Pagan law, to Christianity'.

skimble-skamble: W.J.K. reminds me that in view of the tall tales told by Fletcher and, earlier (p.153) by the Welsh bosun, it is worth looking at the passage from which 'skimble-skamble' is taken (I Henry IV, 3.1.147–54). Hotspur is speaking of Owen Glendower, and shares the Lady of the Pool's view of such 'Welshery':

> I cannot choose: sometimes he angers me
> With telling me of the moldwarp and the ant,
> Of the dreamer Merlin and his prophecies,
> And of a dragon, and a finless fish,
> A clip-wing'd griffin, and a moulten raven,
> A couching lion, and a ramping cat,
> And such a deal of skimble-skamble stuff
> As puts me from my faith.

The same scene (see on *Ana.* p.225) was quite possibly in the poet's mind later.

fair-garnished percher: the Paschal candle of note 1. 'percher', partly because it is set up on high, and partly because it is a symbol of the Holy Spirit, represented as a dove. There is a magnificent treatment of this rite in Rahner, pp. 80–4.

Next, All Hallows Church, by the Tower. 'Upon this hill (Tower Hill) is always readily prepared, at the charges of city, a large scaffold and gallows of timber for the execution of such traitors and transgressors as are delivered out of the Tower, or otherwise, to the sheriffs of London by writ, there to be executed' (Stow, p.118). The molls pray to Christ and his mother ('Stabat Mater Dolorosa') for the unfortunates. 'The molls I had in mind were the various Sukey Tawdries of the Beggar's Opera.' (D. Sept 1974). 'At 'Hallows' . . . 'all hallow'd be', the change from noun to verb, as so often, enclosing the sequence.

162   **and no candle to light you to bed:** preceding, in the

children's 'Oranges and Lemons' the 'chopper to chop off your head'. 'apse-end': see on 'apsidal houses', *Ana.*p.49.'mind-days': the month's mind' is a vigorous survival in Ireland. It is a happy day, or a day of hope (of Paradise) which is marked with a 'white stone'. D., I suspect, took the phrase from Martial, who crops up more than once in unpublished material.

Finally (still on page 162) Crutched Friars and Holy Trinity, Aldgate.

Uncreated Trinity . . . created fays: the transition from p.162 to 163 comes awkwardly, for we should read, 'the three created fays do play under (underneath), worked extra antique (carved long, long, ago) in the creature of stone which is under'. 'creature of stone' parallels the liturgy's 'creature of water' ('that innocent creature' of *Ana.* p.161). 'adytum', the shrine which is 'over' (above). 'Where under', as one word, under which.

The **fathering figures** of legend both protect and fertilise **163** the city, its gardens and its livestock. They are 'strong binders', reinforcing the London brick and mortar. 'stereobate', solid mass of masonry.

tyrannoi come in keels: the Greek word for absolute **164** rulers is appropriate, for Gildas uses 'tyranni' of the British rulers, after the departure of the Romans. Procopius, too, says that 'Brettania' remained, after the withdrawal, subject to 'tyrannoi' (*Vandal War*, 2.38).

quondam king: we need a comma after 'king' for the meaning is that the legends say of one other such quondam king, that he will be king again.

Sejunction Day: separation day, the Last Judgment, when the sheep are separated from the goats. Should 'these' (the ancient heroes, the 'strong binders') not hold firm, then our English living-space (cf. *Lebensraum*) won for Angles in this island of Albion, whose capital was in legend founded by the Trojan Brutus, will collapse.

All London churches and chapels are now brought together again in adoration of the Cross, as on *Ana.* p.127. **when he sings out:** 'he', the celebrant, singing the Preface proper to the Feast, a cockney ('His cock's egg tongue'). 'the Vulgar lingua', the Latin of the Vulgate. Why 'like any *Trojan* licentious' (licentiate)? Because he is by descent one of the original inhabitants, not a Norman, like Geoffrey of Monmouth, and so he emphasises

165 his Trojan ancestry. 'hot herring pies': the truly traditional Cornish pasty, so I am assured by a matelot from those parts, contains a herring, with the head and tail projecting from the pastry.

carry out Chloris: we carry out summer because the official date for the end of summer is said to be Sept. 12th, the feast that is being celebrated. 'Chloris' is used in a similar sense on p.190.

166 The first half of the page is the good-bye to the captain who came ashore at the head of p.124, and the girl goes back to calling her lavender. *bell'd clout of Martin:* both the cloak of St Martin, bell-shaped, which he shared with the poor man, and the clout or clapper of the church's bell.

livid flower: i.e. purplish, and the unusual word for that colour may have been used with a thought of the bruised Christ; or, again, with a memory of the line in the *Vexilla Regis*, 'Ornata regis purpura', adorned with the purple of the king.

167 The *consolatrix afflictorum* pities the 'poor boatswain's boy', kidnapped, no doubt on the North African coast. **Jack** in 'jack bucket', giving diminutive force. **Note 1:** Stow (see comment on *Ana.* p.135) has a different explanation for 'Papey'. D. might have added that Monica was the mother of Augustine (that the Lady of the Pool should be named Helen goes without saying). 'bollocky', the ruder alternative in the song 'Barnacle Bill the sailor'.

Mistress of Lodemanage: as before (comment on p.110) Our Lady as Stella Maris, guide of mariners. 'Lady Lea' and n., cf. *Ana.* p.113. **Eight Bells:** the crucifixion took place before eight bells in the afternoon watch (1600 hrs), it is true, but we would expect here to read 'six bells', 1500 hrs. Cf. p.96, 'What bells is that?'. **Belin's drink** is here the Sea of Galilee.

168 **Gogmagog:** behind, or in addition to, the many forms

taken by Gog and Magog, lie the leaders of the forces of evil **168**
in Ezekiel 38 and Revelation 20. 'Trelleborg [the Swedish port]
sea-kings' looks to Vikings.

m' living flower: the vowel-repetition (from 'livid' on p.166)
is characteristically deliberate.

VI

KEEL, RAM, STAUROS

In this section we have no change of scene, and no change in the type of character presented; but there is a great change in time, for, although the opening runs on immediately from *The Lady of the Pool*, it is soon apparent that the point in time from which the poem is written is much the same as that of the voyage in search of tin described in *Middle-Sea and Lear-Sea*. From that point the poet can look forward to fifteenth-century London (with which this section starts), to the empire of Rome, and to the exaltation of the greatest Christian symbol, the Stauros or Cross. This is seen as the mainmast of the vessel which is a symbol of the Church and of man's voyage to his appointed end under the guidance of the vine-juice skipper (Christ) and his vicar – the vessel whose safety depends also upon the strength and solidity of the keel upon which she is built. Hugo Rahner treats at length of this symbolism; and our poet was much moved by a passage in the *Octavius* of Minucius Felix, the second-century (probably) Roman advocate, a convert to Christianity, who was one of its earliest apologists. D. may not, I think, have understood that, for our purpose, the point of that passage (*Octavius*, 29.6–8) has to be somewhat diverted; but the last sentence is too good to be given away: 'Ita signo crucis aut ratio naturalis innititur aut vestra religio formatur' – 'So the whole system of nature rests upon the sign of the cross; or it is by that sign that your religion is shaped.'

René Guénon's *Le symbolisme de la croix* (1931, with later editions) will take a western reader into the deeper waters of a broader ocean.

As *Middle-Sea and Lear-Sea* ended with a 'berthing to schedule' with 'the old Pelasgian' conning her, so does this section. The first and third parts of *Keel, Ram, Stauros* are,

170   accordingly, elaborations of the themes of the Good Friday
hymns which moved the poet so intensely, *Vexilla Regis*, and
Crux fidelis. *Ram* is a very different matter, of which more below.

Such phrases as 'fluidity' or 'flexibility of temporal scheme'
may be convenient for expressing the poet's handling of time,
but they may be dangerous if they mask the clarity of his own
vision, when he moves in 'that wholly indefinable age of mixed
legend, history and genuine mythe'. He uses the phrase quoted,
which has already appeared in the introductory note to *Middle-
Sea and Lear-Sea*, when speaking of Shakespeare's brilliance
in shifting the Fool, at the moment he wanted and for the purpose he wanted, into the age of Merlin, and attributing to
him what Merlin was many years later to say. D. had the same
idea in mind, he says, when he wrote at the beginning of *Keel,
Ram, Stauros*, 'did he hear them say / when will you pay me ?'

From p.170 to 'the trembling tree' on p.173 we are concerned
with the master of the vessel, who is evidently preparing to
sail for his home port in the Mediterranean, and with his
comments on those who are enriched by sea-traffic at the expense
of the men who face the dangers. The words 'the trembling
tree' lead to the first change of theme, the laying down of the
keel, the 'central arbor' 'on which our salvation sways', on
which the whole construction of the ship is based, including
(p.175) mast and rigging. At the foot of p.175 we turn to the
mast, and almost immediately (line 4 of p.176) the timber suggests
the timber of the Roman military engines. This is, typographically,
a turning easy to miss. It is a by-road which comes to a dead end
at the middle of p.178. 'Ram' and 'ram': the poet adopts the
former as a personification of the latter, having taken it from the
two-horned ram of Daniel's vision. In Daniel (ch. viii) the ram
represents Medo-Persia, in D.'s writings Rome. What the
Ram stood for for D., and what it stood in opposition to, is seen
most clearly (apart from this passage) in *The Tutelar of the
Place* (*S.L.*, pp. 59–64). Thus (p.63) in the prayer to the 'Queen
of the differentiated sites': 'in all times of *imperium* save us
when the *mercatores* come . . . When they escheat to the Ram /

in the Ram's curia / the seisin where the naiad sings / above **170**
where the forked rod bends / or where the dark outcrop / tells
on the hidden seam / pray for the green valley.' In the same
passage we read of 'the Ram's magnates', 'the Ram's book of
Death', 'the exorbitance of the Ram', 'the house of the engines
that fabricate the ingenuities of the Ram'. On Trajan's column
we can see the Ram's head, on a pole, like the legionary signum
of the First Legion, *Minerva*.

This execration of the Ram, cold and sarcastic rather than,
as in *The Tutelar*, impassioned, is followed, after the gap on
p.178, by the praise of the 'vertical'd', as opposed to the
'horizontal'd' (p.176) beam – the Stauros, which ends on p.180
with 'Agios Stauros / *stans*'. There is then a brief return to the
'recumbent' tree, the keel. Finally (pp. 181–2) the ship sails,
and the 'old padrone' berths her 'to schedule'.

he: the same 'typical' he, but of this one we may say with
certainty (cf. note 3, p.172) that he is Greek. Although he goes
ashore at Billingsgate, between the Tower and London Bridge,
into a fifteenth-century London, it soon becomes apparent
that he stands outside the times which are described. 'Frigg-
day's': *Friday's* (Freyja's day, the day of the Scandinavian
goddess of love, replacing the Roman *dies Veneris*, or Frigga's
day, the day of the wife of Odin) – fish day (as Friday used to be),
hence *ichthyophagous*, fish-eating.

Is that why . . .: Yes, because this is a Greek vessel, and,
like the skipper of the vessel that sailed to Mount's Bay for tin,
he will take back Cockney slang ('back-cant', combining 'cant'
in the sense of dialect, idiom, slang, with 'back-slang', itself
close to the Londoner's riming-slang). The phrase was prompted, too, by the substitution of Scandinavian (later English)
names for days of the week. The lines that precede what D.
lifted from Dryden suggest that back-cant is designed to
suggest Bacchant: 'Boundless and mad, disordered rhyme was
seen; / Disguised Apollo changed to Harlequin.'

when will you pay me: the 'oranges and lemons' question,
answered ('I do not know') by 'the big bell of Bow', pushes

the date back to at least the fourth century B.C. This is clear from what we read at the foot of the page (sailing in our *Mori Marusam*) combined with the reference to Pytheas in note 1 to p.171. It raises, however, the further question, ever present in the poet's mind, 'but when *is* when?' Writing, as quoted earlier about the prophecy of Merlin, D. continues: '. . . part of the thing I express in another place page 170 (Keel Ram & Stauros)': he then quotes this passage, ending *Mori Marusam*, 'see note on page 171'. The following, unpublished, is a corresponding passage:

> 'Must this be played again by Clio's whim?
> History, they say, repeats herself but
> never in the expected accidents.
> Is Julius not yet fallen,
> his mantle muffling his face
> In the Senate House?
> How or when?
> Ah! but when is when?'

171 **in Cronos-meer:** (with D.'s note) did Pytheas wrongly conclude that the (supposedly) Celtic word was linguistically the same as the Latin *mare mortuum*? Pytheas was reported to have circumnavigated Britain, and although the ancients did not believe him, modern scholars (including the late Professor E. G. R. Taylor) find his story consistent and credible. (See *The Haven-finding Art*, pp. 43–6.) 'Goidel': Goidelic Celt, i.e. Irish or Scots, as opposed to Brythonic.

has he been on the spree etc.: these questions are asked as though Pytheas and our skipper were the same person; for we may well regard the latter as typical of the adventurous navigator, which is what the former undoubtedly was. And if the Pythean-skipper has been consorting with the Welsh, he will indeed be a slippery customer – for **Keltoi on land are twisters enough**! The kernel of these lines is the shrine of Nodens at Lydney in Gloucestershire (for which see, conveniently, Collingwood & Myres, pp. 264–6). 'Less than thirty miles away (from Bath) across the Severn, Nodens, the hunter-god of the

Forest of Dean, who survived in later mythology as Nuada of
the Silver Hand, king of the Tuatha de Danaan, and later still
as King Lear, had to wait for his splendid temple, with its
hostelry and baths and precinct, until the pagan revival
initiated by Julian the Apostate [in about A.D. 364], though, no
doubt, his hill-top above Lydney had always been sacred ground'.

What D. seized on here was the opportunity to bring together
classical and Celtic cults. He writes (4 Sept, 1974) of 'cult
figures of a prehistoric Celtic pantheon – and especially associated with the sea, estuaries, storm & weather, & equated with
Nodens of the Silver hand, with Lud, Llyr, Nuadens of the
Severn estuary, who had a special shrine at Lydney and had
fire-rites (cf. the Vestal Sisters and Brigit) and quite lateish
in the Roman occupation of Britain was given a stone-built
temple and, as so often was the practice, was worshipped alongside a typical classical Cult-figure – Minerva in this case,
I think, &, what always amuses me, under the Roman order, the
fire was still kept alive, but they brought coal from the Forest
of Dean in place of wood – more efficient & utile & less wasteful
of wood. Again I meander . . .'

chinas: mates ('china plate', riming with 'mate').

beyond the Pillars: it could mean in the Mediterranean, or
on the Atlantic side of the Gibraltar Strait, or even down the
west coast of Africa.

clencher-build: clencher, clincher, clinker-built, as opposed
to carvel: an appropriate method for this tough 'johnny-cake'.
Stow, pp. 124–5, (in a passage that bears on the image D. uses
on p.173) speaks of 'ship nails called rough and clench, to wit,
rough nails with broad round heads, and clenched on the other
side with square plates of iron' – see below on 'inverted vaults'.

bends: wales, horizontal timbers running the length of 172
the vessel. This is one of many shipwrights' terms (see pages
174–5) which D. uses with great care for accuracy, and with
great respect for the niceties of the craft. Their precise meaning
may well be unfamiliar to the landsman, but the nautical sense
of all of them is given in the dictionaries.

172 **He's drained it again:** as on p.97, where exactly the same type of hard-drinking, 'knarred', experienced master is in command. 'It's wonder the owners stand for' his drinking.

lading so precious: the carol mentioned in the note runs,

> There comes a galley laden
> Up to the highest board,
> She bears a heavenly burden,
> The Father's eterne Word.
>
> She saileth on in silence,
> Her freight of value vast,
> With Charity for mainsail
> And Holy Ghost for mast.

Contingent risk: all who take the risk – a contingent and not an absolute risk – are in the financial swim; and when the seamen 'embrace the sea-stript dead', where will the investors be? They will be off with the 'coverage', the insurance money, on a 'proper siren's cruise'. 'Sirens' most appropriately, as being seducers who lead sailors to their death.

adieu to y'r: *Spanish ladies* again: 'Farewell and adieu to you, Spanish ladies, Farewell and adieu to you, ladies of Spain', the 'Ushant to Scilly' song.

Pluto's Thalassocracies (dominion over the seas): 'Pluto' for capitalism – the *mercatores* of The Tutelar. At the time this was being written the term 'pluto-democracy' had been popularised, largely by Mussolini.

their bleedin' miracle: as in Poe's *Helen*. 'the thousand ships': cf. 'she of Aulis' etc. p.128. We need a break here, for 'Caulk it, m' anarchs' is addressed to the near-mutinous grumblers of the crew. 'Caulk it': nautical for 'put a sock in it' (so, too, 'cork it') with the added bite of an obvious obscene usage. 'anarchs': mutineers, but not without a memory of *Paradise Lost*, ii.988, 'the Anarch old'. 'ichthyoid': although there is the obvious literal meaning that the master has his eye on the grumblers, a cold, fishy eye, there is also emphasis on his position in the ship of salvation and as vicar of him whose symbol

is the fish. If it were objected that this man is something of a
reprobate, a hard master, a boozer and a fornicator, and so hardly
a fit deputy for the Redeemer, D. might well answer that this is
an instance of the theologians' teaching that it is 'the office
and not the man' that counts.

the old ichthys: as in the preceding line, and elsewhere, e.g. 173
pp. 74, 125, where see comment.

pelasgian: as 'pelagios' of the corresponding man, on p.96 –
oceanic, and also of the original stock. Cf. *marinus* at the end of
this section, and 'us marines', p.105. In both those places the
notion of a fighting man on board ship is also intended.

disciplina: before the mast, with the crew, he is a strict
disciplinarian. After the mast, in the officers' quarters, and in
the centre of command, watch (note, admire, take notice of)
his nautical science – *disciplina*, discipline in the sense of
learning, science, practical knowledge of a trade or art –
Fluellen's 'by Cheshu, he will maintain his argument as well
as any military man in the world, in the disciplines of the pris-
tine wars of the Romans'.

By ending this picture of the master with the words **abaft the
trembling tree,** the poet is enabled to return to the mast,
stauros. 'ridging the straked, dark inverted vaults': in *Rite and
Foretime* we met the image of church as ship. Here we have a
brilliant inversion. We look down into the darkness of the vessel
and see ship as church. There is a passage in Stow (pp. 124–5),
part of which was quoted above in connection with 'clencher'.
He is speaking not of a church, but of a nave-like hall; and D.
must have noted the mention of shipwrights, which reinforces
his use of the image. 'It seemeth that the builders of the hall of
this house were shipwrights, and not house carpenters; for the
frame thereof (being but low) is raised of certain principal posts
of main timber, fixed deep in the ground, without any groundsell,
boarded close round on the inside, having none other wall from
the ground to the roof, those boards not exceeding the length
of a clap board, about an inch thick, every board ledging over
other as in a ship or galley [i.e. 'clinker-built'] nailed with ship

nails called rough and clench . . . The roof of this hall is also wrought of the like board, and nailed with rough and clench, and seemeth as it were a galley, the keel turned upwards.'

As salvation depends upon the cross, so all rests upon the keel: design ('base-line' etc.) tonnage (an expression of cubic content), draught, cost of berthing dues, insurance, cargo, **and, policy.** Since *tormenta* are engines of war, catapults, that line refers to another sense of 'policy', Hitler's policy of 'guns before butter'. Finally, as spiritual, so physical salvation depends on this timber, and on the care and accuracy of the jointings associated with it. 'tholing': enduring. D. probably took the word (noting the resemblance to the nautical 'thole', the noun) from Chaucer's *Friar's Tale*, v. 1546, 'So muche wo as I have with yow tholed!'

Tree-nailed: to be pronounced, I would say, 'trenelled'. A tree-nail is a cylindrical pin of hard wood. (D. had in North-wick Lodge a seventeenth-century manual of ship-building.)

175 From the ship herself to the sails and rigging. **a poet's gale:** a friend asked what was meant (*Ana.* p.99) by 'a soldier's wind'. Explaining this, I said that it was sometimes called a 'farmer's wind', and was on the point of saying that it might well be called a 'poet's wind' – and D., no practical seaman nor navigator, also, I am glad to see, thought the phrase appropriate.

altus and hoist: standing and running rigging leads to the anchor and its gear: 'altus' up, aloft, secured at the cathead, or lowered by the bower-cable to the bottom, 'fundus', the sea-bed. The pronunciation awl-tus is as the R.N. pronunciation awl-titude.

And the thewed bodies: from the vessel herself and her rigging to the crew, but immediately back to the vessel – for in spite of the borrowing of Coleridge's 'the many men so beauti-ful' we must, surely, punctuate after 'true-hearted men'. It is the ship that is so beautiful 'between perpendiculars and over-all', i.e. when she is seen broadside on. **'Between perpendicu-lars and overall** refer to the measurement of length of a ship, the former being taken from the stemhead to a point perpendicularly

above the rudder head; the latter is between extremities. There 175
is a further measurement which is *water-line* length, which is
self-explanatory.For various reasons length between perpendicu-
lars is a trifle archaic now (with balanced rudders, skegs &c.).'
(I quote from M.W.R.)

That we should punctuate as suggested above is confirmed by
some lines from an upublished ms., in which D. uses the same
terms. (Peter is speaking of the master of a fishing-boat on the
Sea of Galilee): 'In short he must know the bias of her between
perpendiculars and over all, no less than were he Master of an ocean-
going nave . . .' The absence of any pointing after 'true-hearted
men' is explained by D.'s unwillingness to break up Coleridge's
phrase and his habit of using the indentation of a line as (generally) an indication that it runs on from, and completes the sense
of, the preceding line.

Timber of foundation . . . arbour lands: an anticipation
of a theme to be introduced into the *Kensington Mass*, but left
incomplete, 'That great lignum arbor una nobilis within the
inmost *nemeton* [secret, hidden, grove] of this wild Ephraim
holt' (K.M. p.16). 'ringed': marked by the forester for cutting.

The return to the timber of the keel suggests other uses for
such magnificent sticks: the maypole first. With London and its
churches in mind, D. was undoubtedly thinking here of St
Andrew Undershaft and the maypole that used to be set up
'in the midst of the street, before the south side of the said
church: which shaft when it was set on end and fixed in the
ground, was higher than the church steeple . . . this shaft was
not raised at any time since evil May-day (so called of an insur-
rection made by apprentices and other young persons against
aliens in the year 1517); but the said shaft was laid along over
the doors, and under the pentises of one row of houses and alley
gate, called of the shaft Shaft alley . . . It was there, I say, hung
on iron hooks many years till' in consequence of a sermon
preached against it by 'one Sir Stephen, curate', of whom
Stow has more to say that can be quoted here, 'the neighbours
and tenants, over whose doors the said shaft had lain, after

they had well dined, to make themselves strong, gathered more help, and with great labour raising the shaft from the hooks, whereon it had rested two-and-thirty years, they sawed it in pieces, every man taking for his share so much as had lain over his door and stall, the length of his house . . . thus was this idol (as he, poore man, tearmed it) mangled and after burned.' (Stow, pp. 130–1). D., writing in September 1974, without his books, had an indistinct memory of that story, but it must have been fresh in his mind when he was working on *The Anathemata*.

176   **gibbet:** another awkward turn of the page – for the trophies taken in war. So Aeneas (Aeneid xi. 5–11) fastens to a huge oak-trunk the arms he has stripped from the Etruscan Mezentius; 'A locus classicus', says Conington, 'for the construction of a trophy.'

Shafts of timber are similarly used (vv. 83–4) in the funeral procession of Pallas. – A gibbet, too, for malefactors. In D.'s note to *ad vincula*, he might have added that the Arval brethren were the Fratres Arvales, i.e. of the fields.

Or horizontal'd? This is the turning (see introductory note to this section) that a hasty reader might miss. Had it not been necessary to include the footnotes, we would have had a space, as we have before 'Or vertical'd' on p.179.

The keel is horizontal, the maypole and gibbet are vertical. Reverting to the horizontal, the timber becomes the weapon of the Ram, blessed by the priest. 'He can gloss text and context': i.e. he has no difficulty in applying his text to a very different context. 'Asperged'? certainly: that is why the 'pallid boy' has his 'bucket', with holy water. 'to wear down the proud': as in the *Magnificat*, *dispersit superbos*, and, even more – with a sort of visual paronomasia – Vergil's *debellare* ('war down') *superbos*.

177   **Ossifraga:** bone-shatterers, as we spoke in the Second War, for example, of 'anti-personnel' mines or missiles. 'lammer-geyer', (lamb-snatcher), the largest European bird of prey, picking-off the young recruits. 'preponderant': the 'pre', as often, intensive. The huge machine then described is no ex-aggeration; see Stuart Jones, pp. 215ff. 'the immaculate

tribuni', like the 'brass-hat swells' of *In Parenthesis*. We might, perhaps, think of these as Brigade staff-officers. 'Under-*optio*': the *optio* was one of the three assistants to the centurion; he appears in *The Fatigue* as roughly corresponding to a platoon sergeant. The layer from London, naturally enough, slides into cockney. 'agnomina': names proper to one individual, as *Cunctator* to Fabius, *Africanus* to Scipio: and so these excellent nicknames, like 'Big Bertha' and 'Jack Johnson' (the latter applied to a shell) of the first war. 'Marmor's other flail': because Marmor (Mars) first has a flail as an agricultural god; 'Bellona's left:' the 'straight left' of the goddess of war. 'right dook': duke, Victorian slang for fist, as in 'Put up your dooks'. The Royal Artillery, moreover, have the honourable position of 'the right of the line'. *Lysistrata* No. 1 is the play by Aristophanes in which the women of Greece force the men to abandon the war.

D. delights in these lists of things expressed in administrative jargon: and uses one with 'maximum impact,' 'penetrative power' and, indeed, 'rebound', at the end of *The Fatigue*, (S.L. pp. 39–41).

After the engines of war, we return to the **vertical'd** tree: 178 as it might be set up for a torch-goddess (Demeter), or as the *asheraim*, wooden cult-objects. The king Josiah, in the seventh century, ordered the removal of 'all the cult-objects that had been made for Baal, Asherah and the whole array of heaven.' (2 Kings 23.4).

to vermilion and incise is from the condemnation of the worship of idols in Wisdom xiii. 13–14, the chapter which speaks of the wooden image in the bows of the wooden vessel. Here it is *erect* as a fertility symbol, for the corn, the catch of fish (in wattled pots or weirs), the cattle, the lover and his lass.

Now it is the cross itself, and later on this page, the crucifix. 179 **invention morning:** the feast of the Finding of the Holy Cross, May 3rd. Do the fastidious, the beautiful, kiss the crucifix, along with the dowdy and the pious ('and, brow-bright Pietas herself') just where the leper ('swaithed incurable') has crept in and kissed it? Do they put a patina upon it, wear it away ('adzed beauties': the lovely adze-work of the wooden carving) by salutes that are sometimes fond (ineffective) and sometimes efficacious ?

Knowing the changing fasti: does the cross know the different feast-days, for sometimes it will be palled (as all images in the church are swathed in purple from Passion Sunday until Easter) or stripped, as the altar is stripped to the bare stone on Good Friday. (Here, I think, what applies to the altar is attached to the cross.) 'Polyhymnia': the muse of song. Will the cross see her coming and going, diurnally for the day hours of the Divine Office, and at night, for the night hours, Matins and Lauds – Matins, in particular, for it is divided into nocturns.

So, too, when **the maimed king pays a call,** to pray for an heir.

Twice a century – perhaps; there is a crisis, a nine-days wonder, and the mob flock to church to pray for 'counter-wonders', but normally, **day by day,** the prayers and praises of only the few are to be heard. The courtesans *Phryne* and *Lais*: one comes in regularly, maybe, and the other to say a quick decade of the rosary. People put up candles among the flowers. There is a ms. extension or development of this scene, the courtesans slipping into the church, where we read:

'But as the preacher's tirade continued, Kaellech, sharp of ear as of eye, was sharper still of memory; and she recalled another figure, a fourth, who, when the large church was like to be most empty and his reverence known to be away, came soft-footed to that same spiked harrow [as in the wood-engraving 'The Bride' and the water-colour drawing 'A latere dextro'] where Phryne and Biddy and Thais had come (singly of course) to say their swift decades or swiftly put up a votive flame and swift away into the gathering fall of Eblana's [Dublin's] night'. – This movement culminates in the veneration of the Cross (Agios Stauros, Holy Cross), on Good Friday, and on the feast

180 of which the Lady of the Pool spoke earlier. **stans:** *Stat crux dum volvitur orbis,* the cross stands while the world revolves.

After the break we return, for a few lines, to the keel, as we look down into the bilges. **tabernacles:** first in the shipwright's sense of the socket into which the mast is fitted, but also with a thought of the tabernacle which contains the consecrated host on the altar, of the Jewish tabernacle, too. **Lignum for the life of us:** echoing, too, Eb. Bradshaw's lignum vitae.

Cheerily, cheerily: after the sailor shanty, 'Oh Nancy 181 Dawson, I-Oh . . . Chee-lee men. She robb'd the Bosun, I-Oh . . . Chee-lee men. That was a caution, I-Oh . . . Chee-lee men. Oh Hauly, I-Oh . . . Chee-lee men'. (Appropriately, a halliards shanty).

Finally, we pass on to the ship's master, about to end his passage home. The 'aphlaston' (latin *aplustre*, but this is a Greek vessel) is the upward-curving, decorated poop. 'to apse his leaning nave': here and in the concluding lines, the allegory is clear. 'the still ship's cat': as drawn, so elegantly and with such sympathy, though in a different posture, in D.'s Tristan and Iseult water-colours.

While retaining, and emphasising, the mixed nature of the 182 man, D. raises him to the grandeur of representing the Re-deemer, the vine-juice skipper: **calix** reinforcing the image, as does the liturgical 'asperging'; 'to mingle' (mix with) 'the dead of the wake' there is also ('the wake of the dead') a *dona eis requiem*. 'Diocesan', in much more than the modern sense, in that of one who manages, guides, orders, provides for, safeguards.

Compare with this the ending of *Middle-Sea and Lear-Sea*, p.108.

The Christian adoption of the ship-symbol (used in a way that differs somewhat from D.'s) is most strikingly presented by Clement of Alexandria, in the 12th chapter of his *Protrepticus*; and for an inspiringly 'anagogic' pre-Christian use, see Professor Burnet's *Early Greek Philosophy* (4th edn. 1930), pp. 293–4, the 'world-ship' of the Pythagoreans, with the dodeca-hedron for 'hull' and the central fire for 'keel'. So, too, we can add a Platonic tinge to our interpretation of D.

VII
MABINOG'S LITURGY

'I suppose for myself personally, I have most liking for Section
VII Mabinog's Liturgy, but that may be as Malory says "that
was but favour of makers" (or in this case of a maker) but
Gwenhwyfar at Midnight Mass, within the screen, for she was
wife of the Bear of the Island – in her linea of Eblana flax,
tunica in the Roman manner folds of her splendid garments –
Its cold in West Chancels & the chanting of the Evangle +
In illo tempore, exiit edictum a Caesare Augusto . . . & then
from page 213–215 the three witches 'as three clerks inclining' –
may be I have a liking for that part because I found it so appal-
lingly difficult to fit in what I needed to say.' (D., Sept. 1974.)

And it is easy enough for the reader to understand why the
poet had a special liking for this section: all that is most dear
to him is here – the solemn determination in historical time of
the Incarnation, the blossoming of the Rood, sibylline figures,
Helen, Gwenhwyfar, and outshining them both the Lady and
Queen and mystery manifold, And very Regent of the untroub-
led sky, Rome – not the Roman Ram, but aurea Roma; and
finally the anticipation of the bread and wine and timeless
offering in the upper room and on the Hill, with which the
poem will end.

In the last section we were moving in a somewhat indetermin-
ate age: the exact joinering of the ship-building or repairing
belongs to post-Tudor times; the *Ram* sequence to imperial
Rome; the 'old padrone' and his crew to Greece of the fifth
century B.C. Here we have great precision in the statement
of time. We open with an approximation to the date of the
Passion, and are given much detail connected with the preceding years. This takes us to the break on p.188, at '*Stabat*
by the Blossom'd Stem'.

185   The times then become exact. First, the Annunciation; then, p.189, with the 'Cherry-tree carol', Mary's pregnancy; then (pp. 189–90) the Nativity and Epiphany. We then return, more precisely, to the date of the Passion. This allows the introduction of the anticipation of spring by the 'Blossoming Rood', which, though it is yet so early in the year is already bursting into leaf and flower. There is a similar introduction to Calvary in *The Fatigue*, where the grimness of the immolation is preceded by the lyrical 'Arbor axed' poem: '. . . see what sheen the lopped boughs / Now lift high / . . . Fronde, flore, germine'.

The title is explained in notes to pp. 200 and 215: it means the liturgy of an infant, or the liturgy based on the story of an infant. The word 'Mabinogion' is familiar to all as the name for a collection of Welsh stories which, in the form we have them, date from the second half of the eleventh century; but it has a curious history, best explained by Gwyn Jones and Thomas Jones, whose translation has replaced that of Lady Charlotte Guest, in their introduction:

'No one doubts that much of the subject matter of these stories is very old indeed, coeval maybe with the dawn of the Celtic world. But paradoxically the title 'Mabinogion' by which the stories are collectively known, is a modern one. It was used by Lady Charlotte Guest as the title of her translations from the Red Book of Hergest and of the *Hanes Taliesin* (first found in a sixteenth-century copy). She understood it to be the plural of *mabinogi*, to which in common with Welsh scholars of her time she attributed an incorrect meaning. But the word *mabynnogyon* occurs once only in the manuscripts, and it as certain as such things can be that it is a scribal error of a common enough kind. In any case, the term *mabinogi* can apply only to the Four Branches of *Pwyll*, *Branwen*, *Manawydan* and *Math*, and not to the other contents of the White Book or the Red. Thus Lady Guest's title was really a misnomer at two removes; but it has proved so convenient (rather like the Icelandic *Edda*), and is now so well established in use, that it would be the sheerest pedantry to replace it with a clumsier if more correct alternative.'

After the break near the top of p.190, where the poet, or the **185** reader as observer, can see 'One, two . . . three . . . five' flowers (or gems) on 'that old baulk', he asks first Chloris (that is, spring) why the tree flowers, for she should know: or Flora should know. And when they have no answer, the sibyl is asked; she, too, cannot help. Perhaps, then, Calypso ? or Persephone ? or Nestor ? (But on him, see below.) Martha, the sister of Mary of Magdala, is called: and her concern for her household tasks reminds us of the old dog (whom we met earlier, on p.79), of the 'How else ?' argument in *Rite and Foretime*, and, bringing us to the very heart of the theme, the *Corpus Christi carol* (p.192).

At the head of p.193 we naturally progress to the two midnight scenes, at Bethlehem and in the Garden of Gethsamene. It is the former that is mentioned on the next page, 194, and this introduces, with 'Brow of Helen!' what must be the most magnificent even of David's glorifications of Womankind – first Helen, then the Lady of Heaven, then Guenever. The last is seen at the Christmas midnight Mass (p.195). The description of her ceremonial clothing provides an easy transition into a description of the last ocean journey in the poem, that of the 'cruising old *wicing*' who brought back the ivory that adorns her 'high-laced buskins' (pp. 198–201). Guenever's fine linen leads to the linen of the altar-stone, and this again to the bread, wine and water of the sacrifice (pp. 203–5).

Legends of Christmas night follow: old wives' tales suggest the nine witches of Gloucester and the three witches (p.206) of Macbeth, and the many sibyl-like prophetesses of Wales. They ask, 'What says his mabinogi ?', and the answer is given on pp. 207–9, and, from the foot of p.209 to 'bray a *Gloria*' on p.215, the 'three malkins' are speaking to one another.

After a digression (p.216) which is concerned with a very much later Christmas, one known to the poet by hearsay, the Christmas in the trenches in 1915, this particular midnight mass at the court of the Romano-British ruler is described in more detail (pp. 216–20) and after *Laetentur caeli* on p.220 there is a natural and appropriate shift to the Christmas masses at

185 St Mary Major and St Anastasia in Rome.

Two centuries . . . Nile bank: this gives a date round about
A.D.15. *note 1:* 'the great Marcellus', Marcus Claudius Marcellus, whose character was after D.'s own heart. In a eulogy
of Marcellus, Mommsen writes, 'His life was consecrated to the
two divinities, to whom he erected the splendid double temple
at the Capene Gate – to Honour and to Valour'. He appears in
the parade of the future heroes of Rome which Aeneas sees in the
sixth Aeneid:

> 'aspice, ut insignis spoliis Marcellus opimis
> ingreditur victorque viros supereminet omnis'

– see, overtopping all warriors in battle's triumph, splendid
strides Marcellus with slaughtered captain's trophy. The *spolia
opima* were the arms and armour of an enemy commander
killed in single combat by a Roman general. Marcellus was the
only Roman consul to win this prize, and the last Roman to do
so. It was Marcellus, too, who, with the great Fabius, checked
Hannibal after Cannae. The correct date for Clastidium is 222, I
think, not 223.

torque-wearers: both from the torque, for arm or neck,
as a typically Celtic ornament, and because the *torques* was a
decoration awarded to centurions and lower ranks: we might
regard the 'torque' here as a 'rooty medal' or rather M.M. or
D.C.M. Cf. *The Tribune's Visitation (S.L.* p.46)

> and you good Cockney bred
> born well in sound of the geese-cry
> and with the Corona up, I see
>   and of the First Grade.
> Where won? or was it an issue, sergeant?
> On the German *limes*, sir.
> And y'r bar?
> On the German *limes*, sir, North Sector.
> And the two torques?
> On the same *limes*, sir, South Sub-Sector, in front of
> Fosse 60, sir, the other . . .

The dates on this page – the 'Dying Gaul', the attack launched by the Cimbri across the Alps and checked by Marius, the Celtic rankers in Egypt, and the arrival of the Celts in Britain, all point to a date round about A.D. 15–20. In the last paragraph we are given the exact date, which D. is here taking as the date of the Passion, A.D. 30. (Arminius also serves as a bogey-man in another (ms.) context, where we read of a Roman Nanny, '. . . mind you, she served three generations of us, to my knowledge – she found employment in our menage at that time when "I'll fetch Arminius to you" was sufficient to sober any Roman child, and any Roman grown-up too'.)

fourteen years since the recovery of the Eagles: not the eagles lost at the disaster of Carrhae in B.C. 53. These were recovered, not by force of arms but by diplomacy, in B.C. 20. (From one of the many mentions of this by Roman poets, Horace, Odes 1.2.22, D. took the 'grave Persians' of the *S.L.* p.48.) Here D. is alluding to the defeat inflicted by the German Arminius on the Romans under Varus in A.D.9 ('Vare, Vare, redde legiones'): the massacre in the Teutoburg Forest. This was avenged by Germanicus in A.D. 14 and 16, so that 'fourteen years since the recovery' again gives the date of 30. This campaign was in D.'s mind when he wrote *The Dream of Private Clitus* (in the *S.L.* pp. 15–23 . . . 'These big, fair-hued square-heads had hung on our exposed flank for five days . . .') Tiberius was first granted the *tribunicia potestas* in 6 B.C. (some confusion here in D.'s dating), and was proclaimed Emperor (and so Pontifex Maximus) in A.D. 14. He retired to Capri in 26; add four years and we have 30.

defensor: used (see note 2) with the title of the British sovereigns, *fidei defensor*, in mind. There is sarcasm in the mimicking of Christian titles and phrases: *defensor*, pontificate, *soter* (saviour, as of Christ), from the City to the World, which last is a characteristic variation on the *Urbi et Orbi, to* the City and the World, of the papal blessing from the balcony of St Peter's.

Sejanus: no better symbol for the ruthless power-politician with his S.S. (the Praetorian Guard concentrated in a single

186

barracks), secret police, treason trials and endless plottings which led (when the Emperor Tiberius discovered his conspiracy) to the Tiber by 'way of the Mamertine' prison. Behind 'Co-ordinator of groupings' lies the ugly word which we find in The Sleeping Lord, p.63, the Nazis' *Gleichschaltung*, 'co-ordination', 'In all times of *Gleichschaltung*, in the days of the central economies . . .' – see Alan Bullock's *Hitler*, 1962 (reprinted 1975), pp. 270–1, for what *Gleichschaltung* 'meant in practice'. We may note that a draft of this passage reads 'co-ordinator of police-groupings'. Here the ominous German *Gruppe* is not far away.

187   **his weather-eye on the Diaspora:** this is an artificial way of saying that the Diaspora, the great dispersal of the Jews after the capture of Jerusalem by Titus in 70, is still to come. There is an allusion, too, to the Jews who, under Alexander and the Ptolemies, had spread through Asia Minor and into Egypt (Sejanus's father was Prefect of Egypt) and to Rome (see p.186 n.2). 'His weather eye', because it was to the East he was looking, and it was from the East that the wind blew which was to bring new life to the West.

Mamertine: the Mamertine prison, where Sejanus was imprisoned before being thrown into the Tiber.

Ariel mountain . . . Flail-floor Hill: as on p.233, and in *The Kensington Mass*, p.16, 'the Royal Seat on Flail-floor Hill site, Jebus height above the conduit, the West-most rise of twin-hilled Hierosolyma'. 'Ariel' ('lion of God'), is used by Isaiah (29.1) for Jerusalem: 'Woe to Ariel, to Ariel, the city where David dwelt'. D. discusses the pronunciation, and prefers 'Arry-ell' to 'Airy-ell'. 'Flail-floor' from David's building of the Temple (1 Chronicles 21.18) 'on the threshing-floor of Ornan the Jebusite'.

articulated instrument: the hinged flail, and the jointed Cross.

late frost for sharp spines: the late frost hardening the thorns of the Crown of thorns. So, John 18.18, 'the servants . . . had made a fire of coals; for it was cold', which will re-appear

in *The Kensington Mass*, p.12. *Gilead brake:* Jeremiah laments
(8.22, and cf. 46.11) 'Is there no balm in Gilead?', the fertile,
wooded, belt of the eastern (Transjordan) hills. *wood into his
bread:* Jeremiah again, (11.19). 'Mittamus lignum in panem
eius': so the Vulgate, following the Greek, and so the Douay
version ('put wood on his bread'). The A.V. and R.S.V. have
'Let us destroy the tree with the fruit'.

eighteen days: counting, as the Romans did, both the day **188**
from which, and the day to which, we are counting. With the
close of the first paragraph of this page, we pass to the date of
Annunciation. A 'germinal March', for it was in that month
that Mary conceived; and a 'terminal day', for it marked the
term, the 'appointed time'; and there was **no drought**, because
it is of that year that we say 'Benedictus *fructus* ventris tui',
Blessed is the *fruit* of thy womb.

his Leda: 'Only the utmost skill and the nicest delicacy, **189**
combined with an absolute purity of mind and intention, could
make it possible to skate so beautifully over the thin ice of
blasphemy.' The *talaria* are the winged sandals worn by Hermes
or Mercury: and here a reader of Hugo Rahner will be led into
entrancing elaborations of this theme, when (pp. 196ff) he
speaks of the tendency in the early days of Christianity to
assert an identity between Hermes and the Logos. '*Mercurius
Verbum esse traditur* – it is said that Mercury is the Word.'
'In this we are at one with you', he quotes from Justin, *Apologia*
1.22, 'in that we both regard the Logos, whom you call Hermes,
as the messenger of God.' D.'s messenger, it is true, is
Gabriel, but by presenting the archangel as Hermes he opens
the door to Rahner's speculations.

It is as Mercury, too, that Gabriel appears in one of D.'s
best known watercolours, 'The Annunciation in a Welsh hill
setting'.

the hamadryad: the wood-nymph or spirit of the cherry-
tree in the 'Cherry-tree carol' which D. quotes in his note. 'As
Joseph was a-walking' is not, in fact, the carol he means, which
starts 'Joseph was an old man'. As Joseph and Mary walk in the

orchard, Mary says 'Pluck me one cherry, Joseph, For I am
with child'.

> O then bespoke Joseph
> With answer most unkind,
> 'Let him pluck thee a cherry
> That brought thee now with child'.

> O then bespoke the baby
> Within his mother's womb,
> 'Bow down then the tallest tree
> For my mother to have some'.

Joseph understands that he 'has done Mary wrong', and Mary
plucks a cherry 'as red as any blood'. (See the *Oxford Book of
Carols*.)

The second paragraph moves to the time of Christmas. **in
Pales brighted yard:** we noted D.'s kindly memory of Macaulay earlier, on p.86 (in connection with the battle of Lake
Regillus). From Christmas to the Epiphany (**the Showing**).
'Arya-van': (to put it in lamentably prosaic terms) when the
three kings (a) halted their Indo-European caravan at Bethlehem
(b) when the three kings, representing the van of Indo-European
cult and culture halted – which was *our van*. With 'advanced
details' compare the 'rearguard' of p.50.

190   **the young sun . . . Ram's:** this memory of the beginning of
Chaucer's Prologue recurs in a letter of Nov. 1973. D. is writing
of the Calendar in the Sarum Missal: 'It reminds one of
Chaucer's prologue ". . . and the yonge sonne hath in the Ram
his halve cours yronne" – for the zodiacal periods in which each
festival occurs are noted.'

In this year: i.e. A.D. 30 again, the time of year being 'lent'
in the sense of 'spring', but the cruel opening of spring ('shrill' –
'March winds'). We now have an elaboration of one of D.'s
favourite images, the blossoming of the wood of the Cross.
Behind this lies the *Dream of the Rood* (see comment above,
on p.141) and the Good Friday hymn, *Crux Fidelis*, which D.
uses in the poem that precedes *The Fatigue* in *The Sleeping*

Lord. ('See what sheen the lopped boughs / Now lift high /
. . . Fronde, flore, germine'). The girls in the orchard can see
one bud, two . . . five! 'Five' as the five jewels on the transom
of the Rood, because of the five wounds of Christ. So, even more
clearly, in a MS. draft of a different piece:

> I see the tumulus and the
> claved wood laid trim
> this same black rock
> this same Moriah hill-site – and
> 'cross wady, the provided anathema
>> I see five fresh briary roses
>> bright the strong members
> and the spiked briary-bush
> forces the meek head askew.

(Caiaphas is speaking; he is looking back to the sacrifice of
Abraham and, unknowingly, expounding its pre-significance.)

They ask Chloris first, taken as flower-goddess or nymph.
'Did you, Chloris (or, below, Flora) have any hand in these
blossoms on this tree?' *Chlôris*, with its connection with the
Greek adjective *chloros* – the light yellowish green of early
leaves – suits the context.

Flora, who formed the 'maidens contrived of flowers',
should know. **variant:** in the uncommon sense of inconstant,
changeable; and the mind runs back to *varium et mutabile.*
Note 2: add to this D.'s own *Petra im Rosenhag* (reproduced in
the Penguin D.J. booklet). 'galloon': trim with braid, adorn.
'this arbour': both arbour and *arbor.*

If Flora cannot help, surely the Sibyl can – and Calypso
(see note 3) may well serve as a Sibyl. Calypso sits moping
after the departure of Odysseus 'on the back balcony that gives
toward the sea' – which is also the scene of D.'s *Manawyddan's
Glass Door* (reproduced in the same booklet).

dendrite beauties is explained in the note; but there is an-   **191**
other sense in which Calypso saw the beauty (fitness for purpose) of timbers – for she chose the trees for Odysseus's boat,
and gave him the tools with which to make it.

little Persephone: she would love to pluck, for it was as she was tempted to pluck the flower of surpassing beauty that the earth yawned, and Pluto snatched her away.

192   **old Nestor:** why Nestor? Nestor was old (he had already, at Troy, lived through three generations of men), and wise: but was he blind? or, as W.F.B. asks, is 'bad blind' a misprint for 'bat-blind'? Is he confused with Teiresias, blind and a seer?

he lives to collate phenomena: may be taken straight-forwardly to mean that he has nothing left to do but to take note of concrete facts, compare and record them; and this could have a connection with his 'badness': he is bad, because positivist. (See *Epoch and Artist*, p.14: but in fairness, read Caird, as well as D. on Caird.) In any case, **prop his lids** is another reminiscence of the Mabinogion. In the Culhwch and Olwen story Ysbaddaden Chirf Giant calls (see, for example, p.112 of the Jones translation) for the 'forks' to prop his eyelids.

Returning to **Nestor:** a passage from Clement of Alexandria (*Protrepticus* 12), quoted by Hugo Rahner (p.45), suggests that it *was* Teiresias whom D. had in mind: 'Come thou also to me, old man. Leave Thebes, throw away thy prophecy and Bacchic service, and let thyself be led to the truth. See, I give thee *the wood of the cross* to lean upon.' In this case, 'bad blind' may well be correct; Teiresias was bad, and was punished by blindness, because, according to one of the varying stories, he told men things they should not know. There is a slender link, too, in the Odyssey, Book 10, with Circe (and so Calypso?) and (v. 494) with Persephone, who has just been mentioned.

Martha: the name is an ingenious transition to the immediate context of the Passion: and her busy-ness with her household tasks allows the introduction of the dog (who, again, provides a link with earlier mythology), and so the *Corpus Christi carol* and so the sacrifice.

193   **the week of metamorphosis:** i.e. the week of the Pass-over. The time is near midnight of the night Thursday-Friday. For *a second time* Christ girds himself and goes out into the Garden of Gethsemane, and so, after his arrest, 'within doors'.

D.'s notes sufficiently explain the scene in the Praetorium. 'nor now far-duces star-night': nor is this a night on which a star leads the 'dukes' (as D. elsewhere calls the Three Kings) to Bethlehem. 'Hill-*pastores*' is linked to 'far-*duces*' by the Latin ending in each.

Note 3: D. places a question-mark after 'Paul's', because the phrase is from Hebrews (13.20).

Again a nicely-joinered transition. The contrast between the Christ of Good Friday and the Christ of Bethlehem turns our attention back to Bethlehem, and so to Mary. As D. preferred this section, of all eight, so in this section he must have preferred the passage that starts with **Brow of Helen,** and **194** moves on to Gwenhwyfar at midnight Mass. For the reader it has, too, the attraction of great simplicity; it is purely descriptive, and D. provides any annotation that is required. A few trifles may be added. **green or devastating grey:** alluding to Athene's epithet *glaukôpis*; the precise meaning of this is uncertain, but some take it to mean 'grey-eyed', some 'gleaming-eyed' and some 'with eyes of steely grey' – and Athene was one of the three goddesses 'on Ida mountain' when Paris gave the golden apple to Aphrodite.

our own Gwenhwyfar: we owe this splendidly elaborated **195** comparison to the Mabinogion, p.157 of the Jones (Everyman) translation – 'the least lovely of them, lovelier was she than Gwenhwyfar, Arthur's wife, when she was ever loveliest, Christmas day or Easter day at Mass.' What is more, the sentence comes in one of the 'Three Romances', and in that one of the three (*The Lady of the Fountain*) which is the furthest removed from the Celtic origins and the closest in language and feeling to Malory. (**The Offering** is from Lady Charlotte.)

synaxis, or **syneleusis:** in the early Church, the general meeting 'of the whole local church' before the Eucharist. See Dix, pp. 17ff.

the offertory-light: the single candle, lit at the Offertory, survives in the Dominican rite, though not in the Tridentine. D. was familiar with the practice, which E.G. maintained in the chapel at Pigotts. 'fine-abb'd Eblana' (Dublin) flax: cf. p.100, and *The Kensington Mass*, p.9, 'Three-fold, fine abbed fair cloths of Eblana flax'. 'and under again the defeasible and defected image': i.e. under the linen the queen's own body – defeasible, because corruptible; defected, because no human thing is perfect. We are said to be made in the image of God. He alone 'imagined' us i.e. made us, in his image, ornated us (gave us such beauty as is proper to man) and set Gwenhwyfar's 'favours' (her beauty) fast, forming her beauty of flesh, flesh which is braced sternal and vertebral (at breast-bone and backbone) and so bound to her graced bones.

196   **consort of a regulus:** it is as well to remember that this Gwenhwyfar is also Geoffrey of Monmouth's Guenevere, i.e. to think of her as Roman rather than Malory-Arthurian. 'He (Arthur) took unto him a wife', says Geoffrey, 'of a noble Roman family, Guenevere, who, brought up in the household of Duke Cador, did surpass in beauty all the other dames of the island' (IX.9). Her Welshness, or Britishness, is stressed later.

   North-Humber barley-corn: D. may well have associated Guenevere and barley with Northumberland, for Malory was much in his mind when he stayed at Rock, near Alnwick, in Northumberland (cf. such paintings as *The Chapel Perilous*) and Bamburgh Castle was not far away, which was reputed to be the Joyous Garde to which Lancelot took the queen.

197   **the crescent whiteness:** of Gwenhwyfar's forehead.

   silver to the gilt: that so hackneyed a metaphor for maturity of years can be used so perfectly is, to my mind, astonishing. 'judgmatic': the bonfires of autumn are 'judgmatic', are judicious, of sound judgment, both because they decide what shall be burnt as worthless and because, by rounding-off the year, they are (if the word be not too pompous) eschatological, and so resemble the *dies illa*, the 'in-favilla' day of Judgment.

   Since the time is Christmas, those autumn fires are well in the past; still more so are the midsummer, St John's Eve, bonfires; and it would be as absurd to speak of gathering knots of may as it would be to regard the mature queen as a virgin.

knots of may: most of us know, from childhood, the corruption 'nuts in may'; 'knots of may' are nosegays or breast-knots of hawthorn, white or red.

Within this arc: 'this arc' is the 'crescent' of her forehead, as distant (because of her great dignity) as Venus, the whitest of the planets; and yet as near (because of her splendid clarity); as singular (because unique).

Selene . . . Helene: D. overlooks the quantity of the middle vowel in each word, long in the former, short in the latter, and the position of the stress accent. We should, then, pronounce 'Sell'-en-ee . . . Hell'-en-ee'. *stress and drag* (the influence of the moon on the tides), cf. p.57, 'the fiery stress / *und* icy counter-drag'.

The note makes it clear (though the turn of the page disguises it) that 'the stress and drag' means that it was the loves of Lancelot and Guenever that caused the final collapse of the Round Table and the death of Arthur, for D. reminds us that there is *also* the 'more basic and more political theme'. So the poet brings together in Guenever both the possibly historic and the certainly romantic.

clavicled torus: 'torus' is carefully chosen, as being the **198** lowest moulding at the base of a column – in this instance, formed by her collar-bones.

The **poised neck** is the neck of the deer, 'found' but not yet 'viewed', so limber is it to turn, so quick. Arthur's gillies are not quick enough, but the anchorite in the forest, quiet in his hut, sights it, for an instant, as he finishes a decade (ten 'Hail Mary's) of his rosary and before he starts the 'Gloria Patri et Filio' which divides one decade from another.

Downward from this terminal: i.e. from the 'clavicled torus' and the 'wide shoulders beneath'. What flows downward from this we are not told until the last paragraph of p.201 **199** or rather the last word of p.202. After telling us that it flows down over the 'buskins' but stops short at the ivory of the 'eyelet-rings' and 'thong-tags', the poet digresses, and we have an account of the voyage of the 'cruising old *wicing*' who brought back the ivory, the 'rare dexter tooth of the living bull narwhal'. The latitude of the Arctic circle is 66½ N, of the Faroes 62.10 N. The narwhal's bluff nose was meeting the south-west wind head-on ('nose-ender'). Running free, with the south-west wind on his starboard side, the mariner must have been on a course east of north-east: which is correct for Norway. 'the North Drift': the Gulf Stream, continuing into the North Atlantic current, which sets north-easterly.

200   **to Noroway o'er his faem:** cf. p.111. 'from Schleswig over the foam'. 'The Yggdrasil for mast': as though, by sailing to Norway, he were substituting the tree of Scandinavian legend that holds the cosmos together (see p.225, 'Nine nights on the windy tree' and note 1), for the Christian 'Stauros'. 'moot': like 'thing', assembly, place of assembly.

where he latins his oghams: as the name (Demetia) is romanised, so will the Roman influence affect language, creed, and culture, including lettering. 'to get some Passion into his Infancy'; will he express *mabinogion* (tale of infancy, and so tale of Christ's nativity) in Latin, and so, by learning first of the Nativity proceed to the Passion? This he will do when he reads ('runes', learns the mystery of) the 'Lesson of the Cross' (the Passion), as it is sung in all the Christian churches. For 'By the Mabon' see note 5 of the preceding page.

201   **the white bangors:** the wattled fence or enclosure is an image very close to David's heart. A drawing, dating from his early childhood, includes a wattled fence, and such an enclosure re-appears in his 'Welsh Annunciation' picture. One of his nieces remembers her grandfather, D.'s father, telling her that D., aged about 7, when asked to draw an 'imaginary' picture of a wolf whose escape from a zoo had been reported in the press, again drew a wattled enclosure for the animal. The words 'bangor' and 'wattle' occur many times in his poetry and other writings, always with the sense of the marking off, and protecting, of something that is sacred or precious.

Thus, writing in 1954 of a visit to Wales over fifty years earlier, when he must have been about nine or ten, he says: 'In a few

days I was to meet my grandfather, John Jones, Plastrwr . . . **201**
He was seated near the little stone oratory of St Trillo on the
sea-shore above the wattled sea-weir that was in those days still
in use in Rhos . . . That wall of wattles and boulders set like a
sheep-pen in the sea-channel, in the *camla*, impressed me from
my first sight of it and so did St Trillo's chapel with its well of
fresh water springing so near the sea-margin.' (*Epoch & Artist*,
p.27). Again, in 1960, in a message sent to apologise for being
unable to attend in person and receive an honorary degree from
the University of Wales (University College, Bangor) he writes,
'But the name Bangor evokes a more universal warfare [than
'the unequal and tangled warfare of the princes of Gwynedd'],
and it is indeed appropriate that the University which has for
one of its mottoes *Optima Musa Veritas* or *Goreu Awen Gwirio-
ned*, should have as one of its four centres the place where St
Deiniol's ascetics sought the Perennial Truth within the lime-
washed, wattled *bangor* some fourteen hundred years ago.' To
this he appends a pencilled note: '*bangor* as a common noun
means a wattle & the place-names Bangor derive from those
chaps enclosing their communities with wattled fences. Only
three such place-names have survived in Wales & one in Ireland.'

The 'sea-wattles' appear in *The Anathemata*, p.178. *The
Tutelar of the Place* is full of wattles, 'the wattles of illusion'
(S.L., p.64), 'marching their wattles' (p.59), 'wattled tref'
(p.61), 'lupa's bite without our wattles' (p.61), 'wattles of mist'
(p.63) – and other examples could be found. In one of the last
letters he wrote (dated 25 Oct. 1974) there is a particularly
touching allusion: speaking of the phrase *scipwisan gesceapenne*,
he says, 'I agree wholly with a little Moses in the wattle *basawd*
in the form 'ship-shape' it lifts up a bodily image [note 'the man
in black' again] strange how one finds delight in some single
simple few words that define and hold up a visible and evocative
thing'. As with wattles, so with lime-wash; and the two are
often combined. To the examples quoted we may add 'the
points of flame / tended with care / within the lime-washed
bangor' of *The Kensington Mass*, p.8. Wattles are to be found,

too, in the unpublished MSS. Thus we read: '. . . in which case, come by the Maunche in a coracle (this you will find tethered, pitched & sound under Isoud's sea-fence, where the white wattles groin the Armorican fret, southward of Pagus Constantinus)' – a sentence which may be read with the allusion to both the Iseults on *Ana*. page 98, ('to blanch main and Ushant').

With **Or, was he a liar?** the digression ends. The question is put more elaborately in the paragraph that follows, which reminds us of the narwhal-tusk passed off as the horn of the unicorn we met in *The Lady of the Pool*, p.136.

Downward then continues from 'Downward from this terminal' on p.198. D., we note, has no words to contain the beauty of Gwenhwyfar's face ('whatever strong enchantment
202 lay between forehead and chin'). the 'lacerna' (last line of p.202) covers the whole of the column-like figure. 'laticlaves': the broad purple or crimson-purple stripe proper to the patrician, dyed with kermes. 'firestone': the 'asbestos' of p.196. For *Habitating* read *Habiting*.

203 **Ischyros and all his Basils:** as one might say 'Great Caesar!' (*Ischyros*, as in the Good Friday liturgy, strong; and Basil from *Basileus*, king.)

British wild-woods: the fur lining and trimming of her lacerna came from her native woods. In a ms. draft of a different piece there is a most charming expansion of the theme of a garment (the cloak of a Roman general, made for him by his wife, a British lady of high birth) for which the 'British wild-woods' have been searched: a centurion is looking down at the body of his fallen commander.

He 'continued to gaze carefully at every detail in the fallen Commander's pierced figure. One long, steady, glance observed in the thrown-back pallium the broken stitches of the interlining that laid bare the markings of the Lady Elena's skilfully sewn-in pelts of wild-cat. He even had a guess at where, from its markings, one at least of these had graced the thick wood-ways of a particular area of Britain – from round about Viroconium [Wroxeter] . . .' The wild-cats had been trapped for their pelts,

said the Lady Elena; 'much as I love the quick-limbed denizens
(of flaming fury are they, and unknown to fear when men would
corner them), the most perfected leaping beauties of our dense
woodlands . . .)'

The metaphor of column for the queen's figure is continued in
the architectural use of *abacus*, the native gold of her hair being
as the abacus that supports the architrave. The queen's ceremonial dress leads to the ceremonial dressing of the altar-stone.
'the palled cup': D. refers in the note to the Carthusian practice
of covering the chalice, outside the action of the Mass, with part
of the 'corporal'; the 'pall' is normally a square veil; 'the open
dish' (which is the same as 'the shallow dish') the paten, the
circular, slightly concave saucer on which the host rests.

from the reserve-granaria: a reminder that this is a time
of invasions and devastation. Saxons are burning the harvests
on the east coast. 'the white sign': the host; i.e. Irish raiders, too,
are destroying the corn from which the host is made, and for
three years the rain has blackened the standing crop.

the three waiting munera: offerings, first, the bread (of
Ceres).

Of Liber: the second offering, the wine, perhaps from over **204**
the Channel. The wine is mixed (made confluent) with the
water which Britain's water-nymphs never cease to bring
from the virgin rock (*parthenogenic*). D.'s syntax is, deliberately,
defective in this sentence. He is saying that the nymphs bring
the water from the rock, either flowing fast down the high
valleys, or meandering, and that these streams (or the nymphs
themselves) 'sign the whole anatomy of Britain'. We should have,
before 'sign' either a relative ('which') or possibly 'to' (in such
a way as to sign); but it is evident that D. did not wish to
separate 'sallowed (willow-bordered) way' from 'sign', and so
allowed himself the anacolouthon.

sign with his valid sign: mark, both in the literal sense of
marking by the water-courses, and in the sense of 'impress'
with the fundamental and powerful (valid) sign of water. 'Valid',
we may note, too, is used in the theological sense of the 'valid

matter' of the sacrament. Cf. *Ana.* p.236 and n.

The water is carried out to where the sea-nymphs bring in the **shoal-gift** for fishermen: and this is Him (Christ) in sign – the ichthys sign.

the proud column: Gwenhwyfar, standing (as was the older practice, and as the columnar figure of Charles de Gaulle used to stand, at the very front, alone, in the little Catholic church in a Buckinghamshire village, in days of other pressures) leans towards the altar as the consecration approaches.

Magian . . . Apollinian: not to be taken too seriously. D. adopted the adjectives, because 'Magian' fitted the middle-eastern origin of our cult (cf. p.230) and 'Apollinian' the Greek and Latin of our cult-language. Nothing, however, could be further from D.'s absolutist view of culture, religion, and truth then Spengler's relativist view: nor did D. read Nietzsche.

205   **By whom also this column was:** i.e. by whom Gwenhwyfar was created. **in the Two Lands:** the Upper Kingdom and the Lower Kingdom of Egypt.

Had not all eyes been turned to the elevated body of Christ, those present would have paid to Gwenhwyfar the worship (latria) which is proper to God alone. D. must have wondered whether he could carry off successfully so fantastic an exaggeration of praise; and it is only his own sense of worship and the obliquity with which the praise is offered that enable him to do so.

to add to the taint: i.e. to add to the heresy of the British Pelagius, who denied original sin, the further heresy of regarding a human being as a fit object of worship. To do this would be an even more eccentric (deviating from the central norm) reading of the New Mandate, the Maundy of Maundy Thursday: 'Mandatum novum do vobis: ut diligatis invicem, sicut dilexi vos' – 'A new commandment I give unto you, That ye love one another; as I have loved you' (John 13.34). We may also take the 'new mandate' in a more general way, to mean the New Testament or Covenant.

206   **berm:** a ledge or shelf, between a ditch (fosse) and rampart.

Part of Masefield's *Box of Delights*, where the boy of whom the story is written is shown the Roman legionaries on patrol in a country harried by wolves (though the Wolves are the Britons) is so alike in feeling and spirit and sense of history and of wonder, that to read it is greatly to increase the pleasure of reading D. himself. 'Pannage-run': pig-pasture.

animals-all: D. could not have written this without E.G.'s well-known engraving, both the large version and the small, in mind.

grannies' tales: the transition through grannies to the witches of Macbeth ('that do and do and do/north of the Bodotria') paves the way to the Welsh witches, who enter at the foot of p.209. 'Agger Antonini'; the Antonine Wall from Forth to Clyde.

transaccidentation: used appropriately of transformations 207 effected by sorcery, in a context (the Mass) of transubstantiation. Even these witches are saying their 'Hail Mary' unreversed (cf. the wizards' reversed Paternoster), for they, like the ox and the ass and the wolves, know that this is Christmas night, and that the 'poor babe' will be seen again as God (theophany) in Calvary, and, indeed, in the glory of his Resurrection: the 'war-soiled harness' being one of the poet's most favoured borrowings, from Langland, who describes Christ as jousting in Jerusalem, 'In his helm and in his haubergeon, *humana natura*' (P.18.23). That 'fragile haubergeon, humana natura' re-appears in the poem 'Cloelia, Cornelia'; and the often repeated metaphor of the armed knight, Roman warrior or legionary, will soon re-appear (at the head of *Ana.* p.210). Even though it is commonly said that the 'mates' of these witches are of the 'bathosphere' (the underworld) – an allusion to their commerce with incubi from Hell – yet do these creatures recognise the dignity of Mary.

his mabinogi . . . his Boast: the tale of his infancy, contrasted with the boast of his maturity, expressed in terms of the Celtic, classical and Judaeo-Christian tradition. 'that which the whole world cannot hold': from the Mass of the Birthday of

Our Lady, September 8, 'Quem totus non capit orbis, in tua se clausit viscera, factus homo', 'he whom the whole world cannot hold enclosed himself within thy womb, being made man'. *Alpha es et O:* not only the boast of Apocalypse 1.8 (I am Alpha and Omega, the beginning and the end), but its repetition in the carol *In dulci jubilo;* and so, too, *parvule* and 'lapped in hay' ('*O Jesu parvule* . . . he my love my wonder lies *in prae-saepio*'). 'Atheling': prince of the blood royal. 'Shepherd of Greekland', because, although the pastoral metaphor is Judaic, it is also Greek, and the 'Good Shepherd' (see *Ana.* p.91 and n.) comes to us through Greece. 'Harrower of Annwn' . . . '*dux et pontifex*': these are the boasts which will be fulfilled in 'Sher-thursdaye and Venus Day', *Ana.* p.224. The Celtic basis of the titles lies in two of the *Mabinogion* stories, Pwyll, Prince of Dyfed (descent into hell) and Peredur (freeing of the waters, 'Chief Physician'). Cf. notes to the following page, 208. 'ponti-fex', both priest and bridge-builder (between the human and the divine).

208   **legiones . . . alae:** Roman military terms are always used with accuracy (so here, the auxiliary troops and the flanking *alae*). Stuart Jones, Parker and Graham Webster are the books we need. The verse from Matthew is 'Thinkest thou that I cannot now pray to my Father, and he shall presently give me more than twelve legions of angels?'. D. applies Matthew's words to the second coming of Christ; hence the 'dies magna et amara valde' (that tremendous day) when the moon falls from her path in the heavens, when history is no more. At the same time, he has in mind the occasion on which Christ spoke the words, at his arrest in the Garden. It is then that only the muses of the Spondaulium are needed, for the sacrifice of the lamb. This short digression leads back, at the head of the next page, 209, to the Mass from which we started.

209   **Lares:** originally field spirits or *numina,* and so of sowing (*consitivi*). Is 'consitivi' correct? D. (writing in May 1960) refers to *Consiva* as a title of Ops (Plenty) and *Consivius* (the sower) as a title of Janus. Or should we read 'consivii'? Christ

is seen as both sower and harvest. 'under Marmor's sign': in **209**
the month of March, with an allusion, as often, to the development
of the agricultural Mars into the war–god (Marmor
miles).'

out from the mother: the reference to the note on *Ana.*
p.230 shows that D. is drawing an analogy between Mary and
Demeter (with Persephone, too, for both are corn-goddesses –
and so 'coronate of Persephone' = forming the ears of corn
under her daughter Persephone); here, too, the priesthood of
Melchisedek and Christ are brought together, the former prefiguring the latter.

Exact Archon: ruler, and so judge (cf. Triptolemus in the
note to p.230) – judge, because we are still concerned with *dies
illa.* **Astraea:** a name that some give to the constellation Virgo,
and identify with Dikê or Justice.

And who kneels suppliant as yet? He alone is rightly
called Mercy: but Mary intercedes between God and man
('kneels suppliant'), in particular for the souls in Purgatory
(hence the 'influence with regard to the fourth land' in note 4).
Marchioness of the Three Lands: of earth, sea, and heaven.
At the same time we are reminded of the 'three lands' that were
laid waste by the 'dolorous stroke' (Morte Darthur, Bk.2.16),
for Christ, and his mother, are the restorers of man's estate,
ravaged by the Fall. This 'seems' as 'much for a creature' as,
at a lower level, D.'s praise of Gwenhwyfar seems much for
human beauty. D.'s note 4 is not very explicit or exact – 'and
the influence theology predicates to the Mother of God with
regard to the fourth land'. The reference must obviously be to
Purgatory. Theology? Piety, rather? A draft of the note is more
explicit – after referring to Villon D. adds: ' – there is also
Purgatory'.

Whose grave eyes are said to be influential: a ms. note
reads:

> '*L'Allegro:* With store of Ladies whose bright eies
>   Rain influence and judge the prise.'

The break at the foot of p.209 marks off the appearance of the Welsh witches, speaking among themselves, for which we have been prepared by the 'heath-hags' and 'many sisters of Afagddu' on p.206.

One of these witches is speaking of Mary. 'grave', as used later (*Ana.* p.230) of 'dear and grave Demeter' conveys the highest degree of praise the poet can bestow. She is 'influential' because she is listened to in Paradise when she intercedes.

Is the poet – a question that often raises itself, and here most particularly – as successful in incorporating Welsh tradition, legend, and language as he is in doing the same for the classical world? His own Welsh creations are eminently successful: the witches here, for example, and the various Celts in his Roman pieces ('73 Crixus, in 'The Fatigue'). Not so long after the publication of *The Anathemata*, when the assimilation of Celtic material was much in D.'s mind, he was asking the same question himself:

'About the Welsh influence in my stuff – we'll talk about that next time. I see now that the use of 'Welsh' or Brittonic allusions in the mythological & legendary sense does not work very well because of the lack of any feeling for the stuff on the part of almost everybody – & so without bloody boring notes & explanation I don't know what the answer is. Classical allusions are still, as yet, *more or less* understood, but I suppose that won't be true much longer either. Then there's the phonological Welsh element & that I suppose works even less . . .'

Despondent though D. must have been when he wrote the above – and still more despondent about the problem of trying to make the Welsh *word* stimulate the reader's mind appropriately – he nevertheless never abandoned the attempt, upon which, indeed, in his later years he concentrated more and more. I, for one, would be chary of questioning the poet's judgment, and would prefer to advise myself as I would advise a reader who lacked any classical knowledge.

210 **guerdon-grove:** Paradise, where the reward is won. But 'guerdon' looks back also to the garden of the arrest, where the price was paid. The legions (again a glance at the same scene) of the Saviour God ('Theos Soter') exchange their corselets ('Loricas') for their heavenly clothing.

To return to Marged and Mal Fay: we have here a dialogue. The first witch speaks of Mary in heaven. The 'war-band' is also the *turba* in Aquinas's *Pange Lingua*, 'cibum turbae duodenae se dat suis manibus', 'with his own hands, he gives himself as food to the band of twelve'. Mal Fay intervenes with a reminder of the punishment of the wicked, echoed by Marged.

One of them then recalls the Annunciation, six days (but might not D. have written 'eight'?) before the Kalends of April: the time being determined as March 25, and the place (see notes) as Nazareth in Galilee. 'commot' (Welsh *cymwd*), a sub-division of a cantred, or 'Hundred'.

mixed gentes in the tetrarchate: 'Galilee of the gentiles' of Isaiah 9.1, to which Matthew refers (4.15), the point being that Christ has come to all the *gentes*, and that Galilee was a region of mixed nationalities. This, so far as the surviving mss. can provide a text on which to base the inference, was to be one of the themes of *The Kensington Mass*; the ms. sheets, reproduced in the *K.M.*, illustrate D.'s method of working. 'the Lake of Wonders', i.e. the Sea of Galilee, in the tertrarchate of Herod Antipas.

Who rose up: Mary's visit to her cousin Elizabeth. 'over the marches twice', crossing from Galilee to Samaria, and from Samaria to Judaea. the 'archelaos' (ruler), i.e. Herod Antipas, son of Herod the Great (who rebuilt the Temple), ethnarch of Judaea until he was dismissed by Augustus in A.D. 6.

As with 'The Lady of the Pool', we are allowed some licence 211 with historical time. We have moved from the particular Christmas at which Gwenhwyfar attended midnight Mass to Christmas in general (preceded by the birth of the Baptist); so that when one of the girls asks the other (in the second paragraph of p.211) whence she obtained her learning, we can have allusions to Christ Church meadows, to Magdalen Bridge and the deer in the park, to Oriel, and to the confluence of

Cherwell and Thames (Isis); so, too, the scholastic 'appetite' in 'very appetitive, ar'n't we', used of an inclination towards intellectual knowledge, an exercise of the will, and 'infused' knowledge (near-angelic, divinely poured into the soul).

the Conditor . . . the Thunderer: the founder of Rome, by whom she means Augustus, confusing him with Romulus, who was the son of Mars (*Mars Gradivus*, the Strider – cf. *Ana.* pp. 86–7). The Julian gens claimed descent both from Mars, to whom Ilia or Rhea Silvia bore Romulus and Remus, and from Venus (Gwener), who bore Aeneas to Anchises. Through Venus, too, the line went back to Venus's father, Jupiter (the Thunderer), whose vicar the emperor may be taken to be. 'Greats': the final examination at Oxford for Honours in Literae Humaniores. 'Isis abers', i.e. is confluent with; but it would appear that the girl confuses the Cherwell, which joins the Thames at Oxford, with the Isis, which is a name for the Thames at and above Oxford; unless, indeed, she means that at Oxford Isis and Thames are one. 'gromatici': for the *groma*, see on *Ana.* p.85. 'fitz Nut': see note 1 to the next page, 213.

The continuation of the conversation is straightforward, the only apparent difficulty being (as in *The Lady of the Pool*) the peculiarities of the speech (you need a certain sort of Welsh girl to read this part to you).

213   **Imago Mundi etc.:** the cosmographical treatise of the twelfth-century Honorius of Autun; the fifth-century Augustinian Prosper of Aquitaine; the encyclopaedic work of Isidore of Seville in the sixth-seventh centuries; and the fifth century Martianus Capella, whose *De nuptiis philologiae et Mercurii* ('the sweet nuptials of Philologia') introducing the seven 'liberal arts' (Grammar, Dialectics, Rhetoric, Geometry, Arithmetic, Astronomy and Harmony), was popular for hundreds of years. 'Maridunum': Carmarthen.

Time is already big: an ingenious amalgam of the fourth ('Messianic') eclogue with Scripture. Thus 'iam redit et Virgo, redeunt Saturnia regna' reappears in 'the maiden, Equity' and 'the chthonic old Sower', and 'his new orient' starts from Luke's (1.78) 'dayspring from on high'.

The witches continue their praise of Mary, with uncommon theological exactitude.

his tunic . . . Treventum (a slip for Treveri or Treviri?):   **214** the Holy Coat of Trier; the church of Argenteuil also claims possession of the original 'coat without seam' (John 19.23). The legend of this garment provides the framework of Maurice Baring's *The Coat without Seam:* far removed from *The Anathemata,* and yet, by its awareness of man's condition, one more piece to add to the knowledge on which a reader's delight in the poem is based.

gladius transfixed? Whose psyche . . . : the sword that will   **215** pierce Mary's heart, Luke 2.35: *et tuam ipsius animam* (D.'s 'psyche') *pertransibit gladius,* a sword shall pierce through thy own soul also. It is from the Mass for the feast of the Seven Sorrows of Mary that D. took 'coeli regina et mundi domina' (p. 209 n.4).

the old gray ass may bray a Gloria: i.e. there are acts which benefit the doer *ex opere operato.*

The poet speaks again in his own person at 'If much of this   **216** is fancy-fed'. **columned Purbeck:** 'marble' from Purbeck in Dorset, much favoured in the middle ages for church interiors. This is an intricate sentence. The white owls can be the learned, who will find more true wisdom in the humble stable than in their marbled halls. At the same time, the owls are seeking their Lady Wisdom, who is Athene. This, says the poet, and the legends of which he has already spoken, may well be allegory, but the 'fraternisation' in the trenches on Christmas Day, 1915, is fact.

Of this D. writes in a MS. note: 'The famous fraternisation of Xmas 1914 was, to my own knowledge, repeated in a lesser degree at Xmas 1915; I cannot recall anything of the sort for Xmas '16 or '17. Official disapproval combined with a decidedly civilian but less civilized attitude seems to have prevented any further repetition of these instinctive gestures normal to front-

line soldiers. The allusions are to such names as Gretchen
Trench, the Pope's Nose and the Neb, salient features for the
German and British front line in the Richebourg sector in 1915.'

After the break at **Because of the Child** we return to the
Christmas Mass at the court of a Romano-British princeling,
in more general terms.

the second official: the deacon, who will sing the gospel.

217   **Note 1:** on this see Gregory Dix, p.413. The deacon sings
from *his Liber Mandatorum*, because the book of the Gospels
has taken the place of the 'secular instrument'.

note 3: the complexities of Rhiannon, the Caluminated Wife,
Modron etc., are briefly disentangled in the introduction to the
Jones translation of the Mabinogion, pp. xiv–xvi.

219   **She that makes the gillies of Bride:** the same theme, the
Christianising of Brigid's handmaids ('gillies') or 'Vestals'
recurs in *The Kensington Mass*, p.8.

whose spouses we are all: i.e. the soul (as the Church) is
'female to God'. 'naiad-signed': baptised, signed by the sign –
water – of the water-nymphs.

Just where . . . : the palimpsest, with the Messianic Eclogue
faintly to be seen under the Roman capitals of Luke's Gospel (of
which D. gives a beautifully elaborated version in the next
paragraph) is an admirable physical symbol of the transition
from myth to mystery.

Aramaean brut: chronicle (*brut*, originally a British chronicle, starting with 'Brutus' and the coming of the 'Trojans' to
England, now modern Welsh) of the Aramaic-speaking people
of Palestine. 'the wolf-watch': the shepherds of Luke 2.8–17.
These are also the 'poor men from the villein-trev'. The 'amnesty' is the 'Peace on earth to men of good will', 'In terris pax
hominibus bonae voluntatis'. 'Voluntatis' is the last word of
the gospel for midnight Mass, and it has been preceded by 'et
subito facta est cum Angelo multitudo militiae caelestis', 'and
suddenly there was with the Angel a multitude of the heavenly
host' ('the messenger . . . the bright-mailed war-band of full

complement'); and after 'voluntatis' the deacon takes the book to the celebrant, who kisses it.

The Wyclif Bible's version of the angelic phrase gave special delight to our poet: 'and sodeynli there was made with the aungel a multitude of heuenli knyghthod', which sorts well with the later jousting in Jerusalem, wearing the fragile haubergeon of our human nature.

This is the night: first, in still Romanised Britain, with the schoolmaster teaching his Irish pupils their Latin. Cf. 'the Goidelic vowels' of the *Kensington Mass*, p.7, and the nudging altar-boys in any Irish Catholic Church, or English, for that matter. Next, the second, dawn, Mass at St Anastasia's in Rome ('fetching early Hemera [day] from her bed'). **220**

aid-fires: See Frazer on Christmas fires at the solstice 'to help the labouring sun of mid-winter to rekindle his seemingly expiring light.' **221**

She (head of p.221) is Day (rosy-fingered Dawn). D. adopts, but reverses, Milton's image, with the added touch of converting Milton's adjective 'gaudy' into a verb. The Dawn must do no less to honour Mary than the poor rustics. Is it their carol we hear, or the clear-voiced cantors in St Anastasia's singing *Lux fulgebit hodie*, to-day the light shall shine?

from the wide-pomoerium'd Urbs: the pomoerium is here, again, the real or imagined circle that encloses the city of Rome. We can see that, to D., the Pleiad (note the change from plural to singular) may be an archetype of the ordered city, the individual stars being ordered in the group. What, then, is as ultramundane to the Pleiades as to Rome? It can only, I think, be the cosmic light which will shine to-day. The cantors sing 'from the wide-pomoerium'd Urbs' and that of which they sing is 'ultramundane'.

On the *pomoerium* (which we met on *Ana.* p.127) see Stuart Jones, p.14. Here again it is the ritual that commended itself to the poet. 'The founder of the city then marked out the limits of the templum ['the foursquare space standing at the central point'] with a bronze ploughshare drawn by a white bull and

221   heifer, the latter on the inside.' So in Aeneid 5.755 'Aeneas urbem designat aratro', marks out the city with a plough, where Conington quotes Servius' description of the ceremony. It was by jumping in scorn over the *urvus* (furrow) and *fossa*, the hollow whence the soil had been turned, that Remus so infuriated Romulus. D. would have met the *pomoerium* in Spengler, too, (1.185), where the note (and text) emphasise the sacredness of the precinct.

Warde Fowler, who in an incidental remark refers to the *murus* and the *pomoerium* as the physical and spiritual defence of the city, writes delightfully of the *pomoerium* as 'a boundary line between the sacred and the profane, as that of the farm,' in his *Religious Experience of the Roman People* (pp. 213ff.), a book which allows the reader to understand the solid historical foundation of D.'s love for the 'tutelar'.

Mabinog's Liturgy ends briefly and cheerfully with the third Mass for Christmas morning at the Basilica of St Mary Major: the tune of the carol echoes the short-lived gaiety of the cockneys in France in 1914 who saluted the 'happy morning', and the most 'stella'd night' echoes 'his' 'stille nacht' – for both sides an 'amnesty'. I cannot turn the blank leaves between the end of this section and the opening of the last, without that feeling of excited anticipation which fills the short interval between the end of the third movement of a tremendous symphony and the opening of the last: when the listener knows that the climax is now *here*.

VIII
SHERTHURSDAYE AND VENUS DAY

This last section is the consummation of the poem, as the **224**
sacrifice on Calvary was the consummation of what was
announced to Mary by Gabriel – when 'his Leda said to his
messenger (his bright *talaria* on) *fiat mihi*' (p.189) – and of what
was the inevitable consequence of the oblation (the *oblatio
immolanda*) in the upper room of p.51. This is the appointed
time and place – 'this appointed night (Sherthursdaye bright)' –
continuing into the Friday, so often insisted on by the poet as
giving factual reality in history to what is foreshadowed or
hinted at or glimpsed in myth.

Sherthursdaye and Venus Day differs from the seven preceding
sections in that it is almost without action or conversation. In all
the others some happening is described, often with much detail,
or some person other than the poet himself serves as his mouth-
piece. Here the only action is the indistinctly marked alternation
between the Last Supper and the hill of Calvary, and everything that is said is said by D. himself; and since his method
of writing depends upon his re-handling of material acquired
from his own reading and of what he has already written himself – for, while no poet is more original, none, either, except
Vergil, makes so much use of what he borrows from others or
from himself – the text is extremely dense and tight-packed.

The date and time of year: Peter Levi's text in Westminster Cathedral on 13 December 1974, at the Solemn Requiem
for David Jones, was most happily chosen: Exodus 12.5, 'Erit
autem agnus absque macula, masculus, anniculus', 'Your lamb
shall be without blemish, a male of the first year.' And it is with
the Paschal Lamb that we are now concerned. 'You shall keep
it until the fourteenth day of the same month', the month of
Nisan, the first in the Jewish calendar. The first day of Nisan

224 coincided with the day after the appearance of the new moon after the spring equinox (taken as our March 21), so that the fourteenth of Nisan was the day of the spring full moon, the first full moon of the year. 'It seems fairly certain', says the *Jerusalem Bible*, 'that in this particular year the Passover Supper was celebrated on the evening of the Friday (or Preparation Day)' – the paraskeuê. Christ's Last Supper, which the Synoptics put on the day before, i.e. on the Thursday evening, must therefore be explained in one of two ways: either a whole section of the Jewish people thus anticipated the rite, or (and this is preferable) Christ anticipated it on his own initiative. In this second hypothesis, Jesus, unable to celebrate the Passover on the Friday (though, indeed, he celebrated it in his own person on the cross), instituted his new rite in the course of a supper which, in consequence, became endowed with the characteristics of the old Passover. Nisan 14th (the day of the Passover supper) fell on a Friday in 30 and 33 A.D.: interpreters therefore take one of these years as the date of Christ's death according as they assign his baptism to 28 or 29 and reckon a longer or shorter public ministry.' That last sentence explains the occasional discrepancies in D.'s determination of time. Generally, we have seen, he takes the year 30 as the year of Christ's death.

Rahner speaks of this Jewish reckoning as being 'transposed into Hellenic time-reckoning', according to which (and here lies the opportunity for David's imagery) Christ 'died on the day of Venus, lay in his grave on the day of Saturn and arose from the dead on the day of Helios. Jesus arose on the middle day of the month whose beginning fell in the Roman Martius which, be it noted, was in the Roman empire also the first month of the year. He arose on the day on which, in the waxing light of Helios as he began to move towards his summer zenith, his sister Selene, irradiated by his light, stood before her brother and bridegroom.'

He that was her son: *Mabinog's Liturgy* has given us, again with the most precise dating, the Annunciation, the birth of

Christ and the Epiphany. In *Rite and Fore-time* the mention of 224
the priest's singing 'high' and 'low' (p.51) allowed a neat
transition (through 'as one who speaks . . . gathered in a high
room') to the upper room and the institution of the Eucharist
on Maundy Thursday; similarly in *Mabinog's Liturgy* the
mention of Helen allowed the reference to Mary as 'more
lovely than our own Gwenhwyfar' at the Christmas midnight
Mass, which again allowed the move to the dawn Mass at St
Anastasia and the third Mass at St Mary Major in Rome. Now
the move is from Rome to Jerusalem, and the transition is
effected, again by a natural sequence of thought, through the
transformation of the son into the lover: a concept (based on
the identification of Mary with the whole Church as Christ's
beloved) as bold as the analogy of Leda and the swan which
was used for the virgin and the Holy Spirit.

signed with the quest-sign . . . ford: the image of the
quest and the journey has run through the whole poem: here it
marks the beginning of the quest with Christ's baptism at the
hands of John the Baptist in the Jordan, and the appearance of
the dove which authenticated him as the appointed person.

Bough-bearer, harrower: the two are well associated, for
the golden bough was Aeneas's token for entry into Hades, and
the harrowing or harrying or invasion of Hell by Christ (see
D.'s note on this page) to release the souls of the just who died
before the Redemption is an article of the creed which is seldom
given the emphasis it receives from D. Whether the golden
bough was Vergil's invention (in the Sixth Aeneid) or whether
he took over the Teutonic symbol of life in death (the fresh
white and green of the mistletoe in winter's darkness), it gave
Frazer, from whom D. drew much material, repugnant though
Frazer's theory was to him, the starting point for that massive
and beautiful book. Much of D.'s imagery is to be found,
treated with comparative brevity, in Jessie Weston's *From
Ritual to Romance* (see *Ana.* p.226 n.1), published in 1920 and
read by him at about the same time as Eliot's *The Waste Land*,
in the early or mid-twenties. The descent into Hell is essential

224 to D.'s theme, for it makes 'credal' (note 2) the efficacy, by pre-application (see the opening lines of *Rite and Fore-time*) of the pre-Christian sign-making.

It is very probable that when D. wrote of the Bough, he also had in mind 'the Branch' as a Messianic title: so Jeremiah 23.5, 'I will raise unto David a righteous Branch, and a King shall reign and prosper', and Zechariah 3.8, 6.12, 'I will bring forth my servant the BRANCH', 'Behold the man whose name is the BRANCH'. The Zechariah verses are noted on the back of a MS. sheet. The Vulgate's *germen* for 'branch' would commend itself to the poet, as would the name it uses for the man ('Oriens', the day-spring), an alternative preferred by the Douay translators ('the Orient is his name').

torrent-drinker: Psalm 109 (Vulgate). A 'king and priest' psalm. The torrent may be regarded as an ordeal, and this fits in with the theme of quest: cf. D.'s engraving (or is it a drawing?) of a storm-tossed ark with the words 'Forsitan pertransisset anima nostra aquam intolerabilem', 'Then the proud waters had gone over our soul', Psalm 122.5. It is of special interest, as we shall see later in this section, that it is Psalm 109 which contains the verse 'Thou art a priest for ever after the order of Melchisedek'.

restitutor: restorer, the word having for the poet both a scriptural and a Roman (Ennius and Vergil, cf. p.238) flavour. One of many examples of the scriptural use of the word is Acts 3.21, 'Christ . . . whom heaven shall hold until the time when all things are restored'.

gristle and his mother-wit: to stress the true humanity of Christ. 'beautiful in his shirt': Isaias 63.1 (not 7). To keep in line with 'gristle and mother-wit', D. has neglected the formality of *stola*; 'glorious in his apparel' is the A.V. rendering of the Vulgate 'iste formosus in stola sua'. *beautiful* (or beautiful-in-his-shirt) is a noun ('her beautiful one is white and ruddy') for it is of the bridegroom that the words 'white and ruddy' are used in the Song of Songs.

At night . . . Skull Mountain: first, on the Thursday

evening at the 'lit board' in the Upper Room; later the same night, over the brook Kedron, in the Garden of Gethsemane; and on the Friday, on Calvary, 'the place of a skull', or in Hebrew, says John, Golgotha. Cf. *Lle'r Benglog* in *The Fatigue* (*S.L.* p.38).

Marquis . . . Four Lands: 'marquis', warden of the frontier, of the march, had a special appeal to D. as a title – the Welsh March and marcher lords, 'Rollant li marchis', warden of the march of Brittany. Hence the play in 'demarking' and the title 'Warden' in the next line. *the Four Lands:* 'A river flowed out of Eden to water the garden, and there it divided and became four rivers.' The tree of life in Eden, with the four waters flowing from it, was seen as an image of the Cross and the waters of salvation (see Rahner, pp. 61–5). To this we may add that 'the mysterious character of boundaries (which usually follow rivers and streams) enhances the significance of combats fought at fords, which are a recurrent feature of Celtic story' (Rees, *Celtic Heritage*, p.94).

The introduction of 'waters', as marking safe from unsafe, good from bad, allows the passage (for D. never tolerates abruptness in transition) to her (i.e. the virgin's) **salined deeps.** Here we have the unborn child in the womb. It is thence he has come (line 3); there he lay like those who are buried with their limbs 'in-folded', for nine dark months. **22**

He frees the waters, not only as Redeemer when he has reached manhood (*grown in stature*) but also, literally when he has grown within the womb and the amniotic fluid is released (the 'rupture of the fore-waters') before birth: to my mind, an astonishing spiritualising of the physical.

where she ark'd him: 'ark'd', not only because she sheltered him, but with a more special reference to Mary's title of *foederis arca*, ark of the covenant; cf. p.235, 'her federal waters ark'd him'.

'he frees the waters', in spite of the full-point, leads into **the windy tree,** since it was on the tree or cross that the 'waters were freed' and the quest fulfilled: and, as with Odin, Christ, as

225   God, was offering himself to his Father, also God and one with
him. We may note, too, that the tree Yggdrasil, on which Odin
hung, held the cosmos together by its roots, and beneath it
flowed the fountain of all fertility.

Who made the runes would read them: an embroidery
on 'himself to himself'. Habbakuk 2.2, 'Write the vision, and
make it plain upon tables, that he may run that readeth it'. The
prophet has been complaining that, although the Jews have
sinned (hence 'wounded with *our* spears') it is through the
savage Chaldaeans that they are being punished. The Lord
answers that the prophet must make it plain to all (so that he
who runs may read) that the 'vision will be fulfilled at the
appointed time'. In the Advent liturgy this is applied to the
Messiah, and so in Hebrews 10.37, 'he that shall come will
come, and will not tarry' – and the whole of *The Anathemata* is
a building up to the appointed time, person, and place. The
elaboration into 'who made the runes' was suggested by the
fact that the invention of the runic alphabet was attributed to
Odin; and on Calvary the God who inaugurated the vision (the
coming of the Messiah) is also he who realises it in person (or
'reads' the runes). So, in this and similar contexts 'rune' is used
as suggesting 'mystery'. Although the Redemption is often seen
in D.'s work as a payment, a ransom, a 'man-geld', 'our spears'
is the only allusion to individual sin.

Her Peredur: the great complexity, and antiquity, of the
myths surrounding the restoration of the waste land (deliberately
simplified by D. in the note) are conveniently summarised by
Jessie Weston in the chapter entitled 'The task of the hero'.
Whatever the distant origins of the story of the maimed king,
the lance, the dish or cup, we now have them in the Christianised
form of the Grail story. Here D. adds a further Christian touch
by assimilating Peredur's (Perceval's) sheltered life with his
mother, before he sees Gawain and others of Arthur's knights,
with Christ's life in Nazareth before his ministry. In spite of
D.'s rejection of any parallel between the sufferings of the
soldiers in *In Parenthesis* and Christ's sufferings, he could not

resist the substitution in his note of 'military persons', (the *milites* of the text) for 'knights'.

Earlier ('skimble-skamble', *Ana.* p.161) we met I Henry IV.3.1, and here we have an adaptation of a later line (194) from the same scene, where Glendower says, 'My daughter weeps; she will not part with you: She'll be a soldier too: she'll to the wars'.

suitor: keeping alive the 'espousal' theme – and so with 'margaron' (pearl) gainer, which (see page 56 and note 1) recalls the pre-Christian cult-figure of Helen, and the governing metaphor of the Middle English *Pearl*.

Tryst-keeper: observing the 'appointed time'; the 'twelve-month-and-a-day' pointing to the nature of the tryst, for at the start of the quest for the Grail, as told by Malory, Gawain, the first, vows 'I shall laboure in the queste of the Sankgreall, and that I shall holde me oute a twelve-month and a day or more if needs be' (Book 13, ch.7). Cf. also *The Unquiet Grave*. **226**

There is a more particular sense in which D. uses 'tryst-keeper', for which he was indebted to Maurice de la Taille. Christ is keeping the tryst on Calvary. He is carrying out – or rather, a devoted victim, he is allowing to be carried out – that to which he had pledged himself irrevocably at the Last Supper. What the poet retained throughout his life, from his first reading of de la T., was the explanation of the three-fold relationship which unites the Last Supper, Calvary and the Mass.

De la Taille's thesis is fully expounded in his massive *Mysterium Fidei* (1921, second edition 1924). This is written in Latin, a language that fits the exact technicalities of the argument. *The Mystery of Faith, an Outline*, appeared in English in 1930 in two forms: a shorter form (37 pages) and a longer which, in addition to the 'outline' contained many pages of 'elucidations'. *Mysterium Fidei* was the centre of heated controversy. In the last year of his life, D. was writing, in this connection: 'I can never forget the occasion (at Ditchling Common in 1921) . . . I innocently mentioned that I had read an article outlining de la Taille's thing & found it most illuminating.

226 Vincent [Fr Vincent McNabb, O.P.] looked at me and said that
the whole proposition of the great French Jesuit was fraught
with grave danger and was in fact heretical. As I was about
twenty-four [twenty-five or twenty-six, in fact] years of age &
only recently had become a Catholic, I could not with decency
argue the toss with the elderly and much esteemed O.P. except
to say that to me it appeared to open windows.' What those
windows opened onto is suggested at the head of this commentary. He could, in the first place, look back to man's first
ritual acts: 'Even those who lived in times of long ago, among
shadows and figures, had to unite themselves by desire to this
divine flesh, and to eat in spirit of this heavenly bread' (*Outline*,
p.32). We can understand how D. would accept and elaborate
the paragraphs quoted earlier from de la T., at the beginning
of the comments on 'Rite and Fore-time': the 'outward rite',
the 'material gift', the 'formalities of an outward act'.

Secondly, D. was entranced by the neatness of de la T.'s
explanation of the triple relationship mentioned above (repugnant though that explanation was to some theologians of that
day); and finally, he could use a phrase he quotes from de la T.
(*Epoch and Artist*, p.179), 'He placed himself in the order of
signs', to reinforce his view of artefacture as sign-making, in
the sense in which Maritain, too, uses 'sign': 'Art . . . goes
beyond shapes and colours, sounds and words, taken in themselves and *as things* (although they must initially be so taken),
and takes them *also* as making known something other than
themselves, that is to say *as signs*. And the thing signified can
also, in its turn, be a sign, and the more the artefact is charged
with significance . . . the vaster and richer and higher will be
the possibility of delight and beauty' (*Art et scolastique*, revised
edition, 1927, pp. 92–3). This matter is treated at some length
in D.'s essay (which ends with the quotation from de la T.) *Art
and Sacrament*. It is part of, or the core of, his plea for the
'gratuitous' as opposed to the 'utile', and it extends to acts as
well as artefacts. Thus in *Use and Sign* (a radio talk printed in
1975, but written in 1962) he says: 'When Mary Maudlin

fractured the alabaster of nard over the feet of the hero of the **226**
Christian cult, the Sir Mordred at the dinner-party asked: "To
what purpose is this waste?" But the cult-hero himself said
"Let her alone, What she does is for a pre-signification of my
death, and wherever my saga is sung in the whole universal
world, this sign-making shall be sung also, for a memorial of
her.'

That enigmatic phrase 'he placed himself in the order of
signs' is used by D., as quoted above, to sum up his argument;
but although it has been re-quoted from D. more than once as
though it were perfectly clear, many readers must have been
as puzzled as I have been. For 'that he himself should serve
to figure something else, he, the Lord of glory, the ultimate
goal and term of everything – that is unbelievable' (de la T.).
This problem is discussed, and an explanation offered, in the
essay 'The Real Presence and its Sacramental Function' (*The
Mystery of Faith and Human Opinion Contrasted and Defined*,
pp. 201–23, in particular pp. 209–13): an argument which is
too close to summarise but which centres on the thesis that 'the
body formed in the womb of the Virgin Mary and carried upon
the Cross, the Body glorified in the heavens, is in the Eucharist
the sacrament of that mystical Body which is made up of Christ
and of us'. It is this conviction in the poet's mind, and filling
his whole being, which is the real key to the secret of his
intellectual and artistic power. See also *Myst. Fid.*, Elucidatio
XL.

his man's lorica: the emphasis is on *man's lorica* (breast-
plate, hauberk) to remind us of what D. borrowed from Langland (as noted more than once before) in his inscriptional poem
'Cloelia, Cornelia . . .', 'The pliant puella who alone wove his
fragile haubergeon: humana natura'; in a note to that poem D.
says, 'humana natura refers to a passage in Langland where he
says that just as a bloke puts on his mail haubergeon to fight
in a tournament, so Our Lord put on human nature to "ioust
in Ihreusalem . . . with fals dome & deth".' (See above, on
p.207.)

226   **his caligae on:** the poet is always anxious to keep the correct atmospheric balance between mediterranean, Celtic and Teutonic; so that here the Latin *caliga* (soldier's boot) and *lorica* balance the Celtic of Peredur and the Scandinavian of *Odin* and *Thor's day* on the preceding page – to be followed by the Teutonic *mark-land* and *Volk* and the Latin *gladius*, camp, auguries etc. The three strands are here plaited in and out of the fabric. *two-edged*, as in *Apoc.* 1.16.

His dispositions . . . takes the auguries: with the semi-sacerdotal character of the Roman general in mind.

quarter-less: i.e. no quarter being given, and at the same time a reminder that Christ's body, unlike those of the two thieves, was not to be broken.

the mound: of Calvary; and so the metaphor of **mound-war.** There is, however, another substantive 'mound', now obsolete except in heraldry and when applied to the orb (often surmounted by a cross) held by a monarch, which represents the 'mound' or globe of the French *monde*, Latin *mundas*. (So, too, there is a double meaning in 'the mundane site', i.e. Rome, in 'The Wall', *The Sleeping Lord*, p.13.) This must also have been in the poet's mind, as adding the sense of 'world-war', and in a peculiarly apt way; for *mundus*, in the New Testament, is the world of sin, imperfection and evil, against which the battle was fought on Calvary. This is the 'hard war' of 'The Fatigue' (in *The Sleeping Lord*, p.32), where 'the division of the spoils' and 'with his hands stretched out' is developed and elaborated in the passage that starts on p.31 with 'And others of you to be detailed'. What is said there of 'those who handle the instruments / who *are* the instruments' brings out even more clearly D.'s notion (adopted from de la Taille) that at the Last Supper Christ bound himself ineluctably to what he was to suffer as a passive victim on Calvary.

This reference to 'mound-war', together with the corresponding lines in 'The Fatigue', reinforces the interpretation given below of 'Here at the spoil-dump' (*Ana.* p.231). The reference in each case to the division of the spoils makes it clear that what is to be divided is the fruit of Christ's victory on the Cross. However prodigal the cosmocrats may have been with their slaughter (and it is the cosmocrats who direct the instruments of the Passion) never have they provided so rich a spoil to be legitimately (i.e. in fulfilment of the covenant) divided. – Nor should we forget that *mundus* (world) in an earlier sense, means implements for gathering the harvest.

Is there, as some have urged, a reference to World War 2 ? The time and place of composition lend colour to the suggestion; but it is surely inconceivable that any parallel should be drawn between the iniquitous and fruitless slaughter of the war and the self-immolation on Calvary.

There are but children: 'There' corrected, possibly, in **227** later printings to 'These' ?

quiet apses and (ten lines later) **lighted apses** provide still two more examples of D.'s dwelling on a structure made by man that, in shape, material and purpose, was for him of more than earthly significance: 'apse' rivals the 'bangor' or 'limewashed wattled enclosure'.

With this page, 227, we move (through the 'children, weak') to the unbloody sacrifice of the Mass. Those who take part in that re-enactment of the sacrifice cannot tell what the bloody sacrifice (the 'mound-war') means. **where it's very still:** i.e. during the silent Canon of the Tridentine Mass. **The fracture-sound . . . under the sign of that creature** is annotated, but with it should be read p.69 'This is how Cronos reads the rubric, *frangit per medium*'. Anyone who has attended, or even more served, a Low Mass in a small chapel – as D. often did – will remember how audible is the sharp 'fracture' sound of the host as it is broken in half by the priest. We should attach 'the fracture sound' to 'For these', i.e. 'For these . . . (is audible, or effective) the fracture-sound'. **Under the sign of that creature:** the 'creature' is the made entity, the flour made by human hands. **comfortable,** in the sense of strengthening.

Within, with lights brighted . . . Two songs are fused here, the folk-song, *John Barleycorn*, to which D. refers in his note,

227   and the *Coventry Carol* ('O sisters too, how may we do, For to preserve this day'). So, too, are fused the themes of the pre-Christian corn-god slain cruelly (on which see Frazer) and the Christian sacrifice. Moreover, the *Coventry Carol*, being concerned with Herod's slaughter of the Innocents, re-emphasises the tryst to be kept by the child born in Bethlehem. As we turn to p.228, we are reminded of this; soon 'he must be broken off at knee'. As yet, however, *the signum* (the sign, which is the standing barley *and* the unbroken host *and* the upright figure of the Redeemer) **stands dressed – reg'mental:** soon it will suffer the brutality of Calvary (and of the scythe). The *agger* (rampart); the military term, used here for the mound of Calvary, introduces the complex notion (see the note 4) of the affinity of the Roman soldier's *sacramentum* and the Christian word *sacrament*. The etymology and application of the Greek *mysterion*, the Latin *mysterium* and *sacramentum* is a wide subject. Its ramifications may be guessed at in the following quotation from Professor E. O. James's *Sacrifice and Sacrament* (London, 1962, p.232):

'Etymologically, "sacrament" is an ambiguous term . . . In Roman law, the word *sacramentum* was used to describe a legal religious sanction in which a man placed his life and property in the hands of the supernatural powers who upheld justice and honoured solemn engagements and contracts. It then became an oath of allegiance taken by soldiers to their *imperator* sworn under a formula having a religious connotation. In the Early Church it was given a numinous and esoteric interpretation when the Latin *sacer* was brought into conjunction with the Greek *mysterion*. Thus, it became a convenient term for efficacious sacred signs or symbols which convey something "hidden" – a mysterious potency transmitted through material instruments as appointed channels of divine grace in a ritual observance. In this sense it acquired "all the richness of the significance of *mysterion*" [the quotation is from Dom Casel] and in the third century A.D. it was adopted by the Church for its appointed ordinances instituted by Christ as "effective signs" to impart certain specific benefits to those who participated in them.'

re-affirmed: affirmed again, because the *Mysterium Fidei*   228
is the new covenant, fulfilling and replacing the covenant made
with Abraham, of which D. will be speaking on p.230.

his stumbling Grenadiere: in conjunction with 'com-
munication-ways' – as it might be 'communication trenches' –
and preceded by 'reg'mental', suggests Part 3 (going up the
line) of *In Parenthesis*; and 'Grenadiere' may well be chosen
because the cap-badge of the R.W.F. is the bursting grenade,
symbol of the Fusiliers and the Grenadiers. The re-enactment
of the sacrifice of Calvary at every Mass in the course of history
is a re-affirmation of the new covenant. There are two sides to
every covenant: the Roman soldier takes the 'sacramentum',
the 'burdened infants' (burdened with the baggage and distress
of this world, as the soldiers going up the line were burdened)
also affirm the *mysterium* (or *sacramentum*) of faith.

As a paterfamilias . . . D. refers, in note 1, to Stuart Jones.
The quotation is from p.271, and the words quoted are attached
to the *paterfamilias*. These pages in Stuart Jones were of great
value to D., and are most rewarding for D.'s readers.

In this passage (down to 'from the boundary-time') we have   229
a double form of libation or pouring-out. We have already met
the libation poured out by the master of the vessel, as an
offering to secure or give thanks for safe haven, on pp. 97, 172,
182, the last giving us 'the vine-juice skipper' from *Shallow
Brown*. Here we have the further, Pauline, notion of the self-
emptying or *kenôsis*, Philippians 2.6–11. 'His state was divine,
yet he did not cling to his equality with God, but emptied
himself to assume the condition of a slave'. The Greek *heauton
ekenôsen* (himself he emptied) is not recognisable in the A.V.
'made himself of no reputation', but is retained in the Vulgate's
semetipsum exinanivit. It is from this passage in Philippians
that D. took the words which accompany the 'Capel crucifix',
painted, with an inscription, on the wall of a large room in the
monastery at Capel-y-ffin which was first used as a chapel and

229 later as E.G.'s stone-workshop. Of this Pauline passage the *Jerusalem Bible* notes: 'Vv. 6–11 are a hymn, though whether composed or only quoted by Paul is uncertain. Each stanza deals with one stage of the mystery of Christ: divine pre-existence, *kenôsis* in the Incarnation, his further *kenôsis* in death, his glorification, adoration by the cosmos, new title of Lord. This hymn is concerned solely with the historical Christ, in whose personality godhead and manhood are not divided.' The notion of *kenôsis* is contained, too, in *The Dream of the Rood's* 'Ongyrede Hine' (un-geared, stripped, 'emptied' Himself') said of Christ embracing the timber – see the inscription facing p.240. We may thus understand the recurrence in *The Anathemata* of the image of the pouring out, liberally, of something of great value.

Christ is compared to the Roman father who pours a libation to the *paterfamilias*, the genius of the family, he himself being a paterfamilias. In 'this place', which is Calvary, Christ is the Lar, the god of the family. He does the same, too, at the Mass ('under the roof-beam') where the household is gathered, 'in session'. It is a family of 'new-gens founders' for two reasons: first, because the church is a new, but universal, *gens* or clan, and secondly, because Christ's mission being to the *gentiles*, the use of *gens* reminds us that, while the Old Covenant was made with Abraham and the chosen people, the New Covenant is made with all *gentes*.

When we say that the libation is poured out both at Calvary and at the Mass, we are not overlooking the significance of 'inaugurally met'. This shows us that there is a third, and more direct, allusion to the 'first Mass', the first ('inaugural') meeting in the Upper Room.

Informed: in the sense of given form or being. At the very dawn of recorded history, near the beginning of the second millennium B.C., the 'boundary' when Abraham migrated from Ur to Canaan.

They say that, once-upon-a-time: Genesis 14, referred to in note 4, is essential to an understanding of this passage (to the foot of p. 230). That chapter describes the 'tribal war' (see p.230 n.1), the priesthood of Melchisedek, and the payment of tithes to Melchisedek by Abraham; and it is the pre-Levitical character of the priesthood of the former which is emphasised in Hebrews 7, and is put to such good use by D. as a reinforcement of the argument of *Rite and Fore-time* – the existence from the earliest times in man's ritual and artistic actions of the quality proper to the creature who is 'Reasonable as an Aungell'. Two points, moreover, have impressed commentators from the earliest time: that Melchisedek blessed Abraham, and blessing can be given only by the superior to the inferior; and secondly that Melchisedek's sacramental offering consisted (unusually) of bread and wine, even as Christ offered bread and wine.

D. seizes on the same point as did early Christian writers, some of whom, following the first-century Philo Judaeus, exalted Melchisedek to the position of a pre-incarnation of the Logos. Reflecting the language of the beginning of Hebrews 7, he attaches the Christian rite to pre-history. How close is the reflection, quotation will show: 'For this Melchisedek, king of Salem, priest of the most high God, who met Abraham returning from the slaughter of the kings, and blessed him: To whom also Abraham gave a tenth part of all; first being by interpretation King of righteousness, and after that also King of Salem, which is, King of Peace; Without father, without mother, without descent, having neither beginning of days, nor end of life; but made like unto the Son of God; abideth a priest continually.' D. repeats the Vulgate of these verses in *Rex Pacis*, and *sine genealogia* (without descent); we may note, too, that Isaiah (9.6) speaks of Christ in prophecy as *Princeps Pacis* (Prince of Peace). **gentle:** the nursery-rime 'gentle' is appropriate to Melchisedek, both because of his high position and because he was outside ('gentile') the clan of Abraham.

Our chrism'd Triptolemus: it is Christ himself of whom **230** this is said, as well as (see D.'s note 1) Melchisedek, for Christ was the Lord's anointed ('chrism'd'). At the foot of the page we are reminded that it was with Melchisedek that the 'new rite'

230 was inaugurated before the 'older rites' (of the Levitical priest-
hood) existed; and the new rite is 'here', both 'here' with
Melchisedek and 'here' in the Mass and 'here' in the Upper
Room and on Calvary.

Of this passage D. writes (19 January 1973): 'According to
our earliest documents what was done at the lighted board with
his chosen *turba* seated was by his command made to be repeated for an *anamnesis* of him. The ritual Oblation committed
him to the actual Immolation by the execution party on the
Friday. The Oblation itself, under the same species of Bread &
Wind had, two millennia back, been foretokened by the King
of Salem, *summus sacerdos tuus Melchisedec*. It is astounding
how this figure of vast importance is so very seldom mentioned
by theologians even though his rite was pre-Levitical. That was
what made me say in *The Ana.*, p.230, "Levites! the new rite
holds / is here / before your older rites begin".

'I meander as usual, but it is surely simply a matter that is
integral to the Xtian mythos that the Sacrifice of the Mass
could not be without the cult-man at the *mensa* handling certain
made things. The Xtian religion is committed to certain bodily
manual acts. It is not a matter of *mental God-directed thoughts
only*. You say that, "No artefacture, no Xtian Church" means,
in fact, "No artefacture, no *man*". But surely, as far as anything
I've ever written is in the nature of "asking questions" concerning the effect of obsession with "technocracy", the "utile", the
Dr. Caird thing [see *Epoch & Artist*, p.14], now ubiquitous,
tends to alienate the mind of the creator we call "man" from all
that has hitherto belonged to him as "man-the-artist", man
the "sign" of "sacrament-maker", & so be deprivative of the per-
ceptions & acts that belong to man as "poeta" – perhaps a kind
of sub-man.'

To return, however, to the text: 'Our chrism'd Triptolemus'
(anointed with the consecrated oil or chrism, and so Christianised: cf. the anointing of David, the young shepherd) is the
bringer of life-giving food. Cf. 'asperged and crux-signed
Brigantia' in *The Kensington Mass*, p.8, for the assumption into

the Christian Brigid of the pre-Celtic goddess. The story of **230**
Demeter and Persephone is most conveniently and delightfully
told in the Homeric Hymn to Demeter. (Here 'dear and grave
Demeter' is a beautiful translation of the Hymn's *semnên theon*).
The hymn describes how Persephone was snatched away by
Hades, how her mother Demeter searched for her and in her
wanderings was received into the household of Celeus, king of
Eleusis, and his wife Metaneira. The story ends with Demeter's
ordering that rites should in future be celebrated in her honour
at Eleusis, in her teaching to Triptolemus the arts of agricul-
ture, and in the restoration of Persephone for half the year.
(Hence D.'s reference on p.119 'when Proserpine unbinds the
Baltic in the spring'.)

It is interesting that D. should have taken hold of the idea of
Triptolemus as a judge of the dead, for there is only one mention of this in ancient literature – in Plato's Apology of Socrates.
Socrates asks his judges (41a), 'When a man reaches the
dominion of Hades and meets real instead of self-styled judges –
Minos and Rhadamanthus and Aeacus and Triptolemus –
. . . can we say that his change of home is for the worse?'. In
both cases, the giver of the bread of life is also a judge, for in
the Creed Christ will 'come to judge the living and the dead'.

There is a typical chiasmus, or cross-cross pattern in the
wording: 'quicken' goes with 'furrows', and 'judge' with 'dead';
and, at the same time, with the Resurrection in mind, 'quicken'
may be read with 'dead'.

Pausanias, the second century A.D. Greek traveller, writes
of Eleusis and the shrine of Triptolemus (I.39). Peter Levi
appends a note in his translation of Pausanias, as follows:

'Triptolemus was the young corn-god. The fundamental
myth of Eleusis was the descent and resurrection of the young
goddess of flowering things: Demeter was her mother, but also
simply the same goddess at another stage of her life. Personal
initiation into the secret ceremonies of Eleusis gave one happiness in the world of the dead. To understand the spirit of the
Eleusinian mysteries, one should not read the wild general books

230 about it, still less the detailed archaeological arguments, but the Homeric *Hymn to Demeter* and Aristophanes' *Frogs*. As late as 1801 Demeter was still worshipped at Eleusis; when her last cult-image, a two-ton kistophoros [basket- or chest-carrier] from the inner porch, was stolen by Professor E. D. Clarke of Cambridge, the villagers were terrified. An ox ran up, butted the statue repeatedly, and fled bellowing. The people prophesied the shipwreck of Clarke's ship; it occurred off Beachy Head, but the statue is now in Cambridge.'

The allusion to Demeter will naturally recall an earlier passage in *The Anathemata*, p.56, where D. speaks of the 'agelastos petra' at Eleusis (with which we may include 'Telphousa' from p.104). Although it is not immediately to the point, we may well, when we are concerned with the 'laughless rock' of Demeter, think also of her 'calling rock'. This is not at Eleusis, but at Megara, some ten miles away. Pausanias (I.43) writes: 'There is a rock near the Prytaneion (of Megara) which they call the Calling Rock, because when she was wandering in search of her daughter, Demeter, as you can believe, if you wish, called to her from here. Even to-day the Megarian women re-enact the story'.

I owe the following note to the kindness of Peter Levi, in a letter: 'The rock I call the "calling rock" . . . is not the same as the *agelastos petra;* as you say, one is at Megara & one at Eleusis. But stories get localized in many places, & similar monuments – for example sacred stones – in different places easily & often get rationalized into a single story. The phrase "calling stone" is the Greek word *Anaklêthris*, a unique word, related to *Anaklêsis*, which means a "calling" of the gods, a commemoration, & the sounding of a retreat. There are several other sacred stones in this area in Pausanias, but each is given a different kind of explanation.

'Telphousa and Delphi are forms of the same name, but the sanctuary of the Delphians was not at Telphousa. That is explained in the Homeric hymn to Apollo [see comment of *Ana.* p.102]. There were sacred stones everywhere in Greece,

& the *omphalos*, the navel or centre of the world at Delphi, was **230**
a stone. There were cults of Demeter wherever there was agriculture more or less; she is a very old goddess, & at one time the
local cults were independent of Eleusis, I suppose, but "Eleusinian Demeter" is a deliberate reference to the power & in-
flence & primacy of Elusis, & that also is old: we know too little
about Mycenean Eleusis to say how old.

'The story of the rock *Anaklêthris*, the "calling stone" (or
"recalling stone") as Pausanias gives it is also given in the
Etymologicum Magnum, under the word. Liddell & Scott
ignore the word, I don't know why. It is only a toponym, but
an interesting one. I wish David were alive to be told about
calling / recalling at the stone . . .'

'Recalling at the stone' is most apt in this connection, for D.
is saying two things on this page: that Demeter, by instituting
the arts of agriculture, gave us the 'germ of all arts'; and so,
secondly, gave us the power to do that which is normal to man
(*man's norm*) and that by which man is judged to be man (again
'man's norm'), the supremely poetic act of ritual oblation:
which takes place by another 'recalling' (*anamnesis*) at another
stone (the *mensa* or altar).

Apollodorus (I.5) says that the Agelastos Petra, the Laughless
Rock which was our starting-point, was so called because it was
upon that rock that Demeter sat when she came, unhappy, to
Eleusis, looking for her daughter. See Frazer's notes to his
version of Apollodorus in the Loeb series.

A good summary of what is known of the Eleusinian mysteries
is to be found in an appendix to the Loeb edition (G. W.
Butterworth) of Clement of Alexandria. Clement himself,
though or, indeed, because he presents the other side of the
medal, can be useful to the reader of D.'s work.

acceptable and valid: repeating, as at the opening of the
poem, the words of the Canon of the Mass, *ratam, rationabilem
acceptabilemque* – as does *munera*, the gifts, or offerings of wine
(Liber) and bread (Ceres). **Not desert-rites:** because the poet
is speaking of the Christian rite, not the rite of the nomad

'children of the wilderness' in the days of the patriarchs. It is the rite of the 'new covenant' that now prevails, a rite which was foreshadowed in the day of Abraham.

231   **Here / Where?**: where does the new rite hold? and when? In the first place it holds at the time and place in which the poem is now set – on Good Friday at Calvary. This is the **spoil-dump** (the place of the skull). It is at a **war's term**, because, as in the passage quoted more than once from Piers Plowman, Christ at Jerusalem is seen as a knight or a soldier engaged in fight with the forces of evil. The word 'spoil' may well have been suggested by what was known at Ditchling as the 'Spoil-bank crucifix'. The 'spoil' was the earth removed when a railway-cutting was made across Ditchling Common. This was built up into a bank on which E.G. set up a large wooden crucifix.

Not every year: it was in the year in which Abraham was blessed by Melchisedek that the spoil taken from the kings he defeated was made 'legitimate loot'. Here, and now, on Calvary, the *cosmocrats* (the Roman authorities: cf. p.187, where Sejanus is 'Prime Minister / cosmocrat') are prodigal in their slaughter, for they are slaughtering the supreme man, and he, the 'spoil', is shared among all men. (It is thus, though with some uncertainty) that I read this passage.

at the division of the spoils: in the wide sense, as in the paragraph above, but also in the more particular sense of the dividing of Christ's garments, itself an image of the sharing of the first-fruits of the Redemption. The land is wasted by the death of the king, until his resurrection; and the jackals meet to divide the spoils. **with his hands stretched out:** said both of the priest at the Mass (see note 2) and of Christ on the cross, who continues, because he holds out to the end, *usque ad mortem, mortem autem crucis*, unto death, even unto the death of the cross. (See also above, on 'mound-war'.)

The paragraph which starts **Failing /(finished?) West** is the very nadir of the sorrow of Good Friday. The fate of our Western cult and culture is threatened, is failing – is it finished?

Again the turn of the page, and the punctuation are a hindrance.   **232**
What is the food of the West appears to be failing, on this one
occasion ('once'). At this time ('Upon a time') Persephone's
torch (for torches were carried at the Eleusinian processions) is
extinguished, and Demeter's arch (also Eleusinian) is down.
Where, then, is corn and wine (see note: the source of *Ubi est
triticum* lies in the depths of liturgical lament for the death of
the Redeemer.)

Calling to mind: the backward look to the sacrifice is sufficiently explained in D.'s note, with the reference to Genesis.
'The wanderer-duke': Abraham, the nomad-leader, the man of
faith ('fidell'), father of the faithful, and 'alien' because he had
come from far away, from the upper valley of the Euphrates.

nemorensis, of the grove, because Abraham planted a grove
(see note), and because the hidden grove, the tree in the depths
of the darkness of the grove, the white of the mistletoe against
the dark, or the gold of Absalom's hair or the magic bough,
these are peculiarly dear to the poet. *Liknites* (a trisyllable): the
liknon was a wide basket used when winnowing corn. When the
feast of Dionysus was celebrated at Delphi, women brought
offerings to the newborn god, who was cradled in a winnowing-
basket.

Ishtar is the great mother-goddess of Babylonia, whose lover   **233**
was Adonis, the death and revival of the latter being another
foreshadowing of the Christian mystery. With 'poor Ishtar is
a-weeping' cf. the children's play-song 'Poor Jenny (or whatever the child's name is) stands a-weeping, a-weeping, a-weeping, All on a fine summer's day. Pray tell me why you're weeping . . . I'm weeping for a sweetheart etc'. **'lynchet'**, a strip of
land left unplowed (the word, I think, came from Collingwood
and Myres), and D. has in mind a narrow path in the bare, rocky,
country through which Abraham travelled (see p.232 n. 2).

That sacrificial journey took him, as did Christ's to **Ariel Hill**,
or Calvary. (See Isaiah 29.1; Ariel – 'Lion of God' – being
Jerusalem. D., in a letter to D.M.C., February 1953, prefers
the pronunciation 'Arry-ell'). What is said here of hills and

'help-heights' reminds us of 'on this hill' etc. of pp. 53–7.

His . . . oreogenesis: the cry is his, who is the author of all the making of mountains (oreogensis), and the cry come from his own mountain (*oros* rather than *oreos*) which he has chosen.

235   As the allusion to Ishtar on 233 suggested, D. cannot separate Mary from Calvary. The general hymn to Mary is clear enough, and the wording is explained either in D.'s notes on p.234 or by one phrase in the text explaining another (e.g. 'preclear and innocent creature' with *per creaturam aquae*). *at twelve years taught men:* i.e. at the Finding in the Temple. *her federal waters ark'd him* has already been beautifully elaborated on p.225, 'from her salined deeps'. (For *feoderis* in the note read *foederis*).

We return almost immediately from Mary to her Son, above all as the source of the life-giving waters, the Latin keeping constantly before us the words of the liturgy: and the praises of 'the preclear and innocent creature' giving added pathos to the cry, on p.237, *Sitio*, I thirst.

Hodni dell: the valley of the Honddu, so well known to D. from 1924 to 1926, is described at length by Giraldus Cambrensis (pp. 35ff. of the Everyman translation). 'Dingle' is not a local word – one would speak of the valley of the Honddu – it was imported to Capel-y-ffin by D. and one of his companions from Borrow's *Romany Rye*. 'The dingle' was a wooded cleft at the back of the monastery, down which ran a small stream. It was a branch of that stream which was dammed by an unkind neighbour (see p.238 and n.).

236   **his salpinx'd Diktat:** the *salpinx* as war-trumpet is as old as Homer. D. found that he had the last lines of p.22 of *The Sleeping Lord* 'handed to him on a plate' when he found Aristophanes' *salpingolonchypēnadai* ('lancer-whiskered trumpeters', *Frogs* 966). He made great use, too, of Ennius' 'At tuba terribili sonitu taratantara dixit' (see the *S.L.* pp. 42–3). So, too, in *The Narrows* we have 'No end nor cessation to the/convoking bucina-call/nor to the harsk-bray'd dictat/of the tuba's taratantara'; and, again on p.22 of the *S.L.*, 'a tart mouthed salpinx / brayed'.

Here the trumpet blows for *dies illa*, and the order it gives (the Diktat) is 'Uncover [as in *apocalyptein*, to uncover] everything'. We should connect 'As the many voices of them' with 'whose voice is', five lines earlier:.'whose voice is as the many voices of them', i.e. of all the waters that cry out.

Praefect of the strict conduits: the spelling of 'Praefect' suggests the *curator aquarum*, in charge of the Roman aqueducts – the 'strict conduits' being in contrast with the 'wild-brook'.

clamant waters: Ps.92.3–4, 'Elevaverunt flumina, Domine, elevaverunt flumina *vocem suam* etc', 'The floods have lifted up, O Lord, the floods have lifted up *their* voice.'

the Four Avons: Genesis 2.10, to which the note refers, **237** speaks of the four rivers of Eden. 'the axile stipe': 'axile', as in the last line of the poem, meaning that upon which the whole revolves; 'stipe', stem or trunk, (see below, on p.240) 'the dry node-height': 'dry', for the waters of life have not yet been released by the death of the victim; 'nodeheight', because it is on that height that all things are knotted, bound, together. **What unknown cloud then, is this?** Two answers may be given: first, there is an allusion to the cloud that covered the heavens at the moment of Christ's death; secondly, that Christ himself, as yet unknown save to a few, is as the cloud that heralds the coming of the longed-for rain. The wording of the phrase is designed to recall the medieval mystical treatise, *The Cloud of Unknowing*.

desiderate: cf. *The Kensington Mass*, p.9, 'the gentle-eyed quarry / desiderate of the water-brooks'. 'What will the naiads do now': again nursery rime and folksong – Robin. There is also an allusion to the emptiness of the font, which will not be filled until the 'preclear and innocent creature' (*Ana.* p.235 and n.8) is blessed on Holy Saturday.

Unus homo . . . builds up the water-theme to its climax **238** in the fulfilment of the quest. Years after the release of the waters mentioned in note 2, D. had a clear and sharp visual memory of the neatly cut sods which dammed the stream, stacked like the sand-bags of a trench parapet.

his cry before his mors-cry: Matthew 27.46 is Christ's final cry of desolation, 'Eli, Eli, lama sabachthani?, that is to say, My God, my God, why hast thou forsaken me?' which precedes his death-cry, *consummatum est* (John 19.30).

ninth hour: i.e. 3 p.m., as in the foreshadowing of this on p.96. 'What bells is that when the overcast clears on a Mars' Venus-Day?' and so, on the next page, 239, 'three hours since the median hour'.

239   **after tiffin:** not the only occasion on which D. compares the Roman authorities in Palestine to the British Raj in India; his legionaries are not so far from Kipling's private soldiers. 'The fact-man' is developed in *The Tribune's Visitation*. 'tiffany': the mosquito net, 'they' being the mosquitoes. For this sort of language but used by a different class of 'English' in a different context, and yet in juxtaposition with the poet's more elevated style, see the second paragraph of *From the Book of Balaam's Ass* in the *S.L.*, pp.97–8.

240   After the break at the foot of p.239, we are on the hill of Calvary, when, at the death of Christ, 'the veil of the temple was rent from the top to the bottom; and the earth did quake, and the rocks rent; And the graves were opened' (Matthew 27. 51–2). It is then that the great birds of prey fly overhead, and the **scree-fall** (the tumbling of the rocks) **answers the cawed madrigals.** The kites and crows plead that, as eaters of carrion, they, too, are cared for by him who cares for the fall of the sparrow; they, too, must gain their 'kindly' (both welcomed-and-welcoming, and suited to their kind) food.

rune-height: cf., also of Calvary, p.225, 'Who made the runes would read them' (with note) and Milton's (P.L.1.12)

and *Siloa's* Brook that flow'd

Fast by the Oracle of God

where 'Oracle' is used in the Jewish sense of the Holy of Holies, but coincides with D.'s sense of 'runes'.

mated corbie: see the ballad 'The Twa Corbies' (in the *Oxford Book of Ballads*): '. . . So we may mak' our dinner sweet'.

the raven's bill: so Job 38.41, 'Who provideth for the raven **240** his food? when his young ones cry unto God, they wander for lack of meat'; and Ps.147.9: 'the young ravens which cry'. So 'brinded Tib', the cat, needs to prey on the thrush.

The terror of this passage stops short of the rending of the flesh of the dead Christ, but the birds tear at the cross, the 'mortised arbor'.

There is another sense in which the gathering of the birds may be interpreted, and it may well be that when D. used the image he had in mind a paragraph (pp. 27–8) of de la Taille's *Outline*. He has been speaking of the completion in heaven, after the glorious resurrection, of the ecclesiastical Body of Christ, and of 'the eucharistic banquet given us by Christ as the sacramental figure of the heavenly banquet'; and continues, 'At all events, on the last day, wheresoever the Body of Christ shall be in the person of his inanimate members, there shall the eagles – the holy souls of paradise – also be gathered together from the four winds, to raise up that which had been struck down, and to build up in all its parts the finished and glorious Body of the Son of God, whose glory once more shall have swallowed up completely the very last traces of corruptibility and mortality (Matthew 24.28, Luke 17.37).' Both texts are very much to our point: 'Wherever the body is, there the eagles will be gathered together'. De la Taille's interpretation of the eagles (surely 'one of the windows he opened') harmonises with what D. himself does: it converts the misery and degradation of Calvary into the triumph of the consummation of the glorious Body of Christ, a triumph which D. points to when he speaks, at the foot of this page, of the cross as 'trophy-fronded / effluxed et fulgida'.

hydromel: properly honey or honey and water – used here of the blood of Christ (water and honey, as though water and blood, or water and wine) with which the cross is drenched. In the *Dream of the Rood*, vv.70–1, we have 'For a long space we [i.e. the three crosses] stood there in our place streaming with blood' – R. K. Gordon's translation in his 'Everyman'

240 *Anglo-Saxon·Poetry;* but see the editors for the alternative 'weeping' and the MS. reading. A draft of this passage reads, 'Shall he deny what's proper to the raven's bill, the hydromel that clots the crutched arbor', and note the clotted bloodmark on the tree in the picture *Vexilla Regis*, now in Kettle's Yard, Cambridge. If we may wander a little, D. was familiar with the line in Vergil's Fourth Eclogue, 'et durae quercus sudabunt roscida mella', 'and from the tough oaks honey-dew shall seep'.

trophy-fronded: like 'fulgida' and 'ornata regis purpura', this derives from the Good Friday liturgy, the *Vexilla Regis* for the first two and the 'Crux fidelis' for 'trophy-fronded': *nulla silva talem profert, fronde, flore, germine*, no wood bears your like, in leaf, or flower or bud. 'dry-stiped': 'stipe' (*stipes*, trunk), again from the *Vexilla*, 'electa digno stipite Tam sancta membra tangere', 'chosen to touch, with worthy stem, limbs so sacred'. D. puts side by side the dry, *infelix* (unhappy) wood and the glorious cross of the triumph over death. 'effluxed': radiant, the noun 'efflux' (that which flows out, emanates, radiates) being converted into a participle under the influence of the Latin *effulgere*, to shine forth.

lammergeyer: the largest European bird of prey. 'prevents:' as on *Ana.* p.87. So also in the Book of Common Prayer, 'Prevent us, O Lord, in all our doings', and T. S. Eliot, *East Coker*, 'the absolute paternal care / That will not leave us but prevents us everywhere'. D. translates the word in the next line 'Who goes before' i.e. goes before and ensures safe passage.

Vexilla Regis (note 1): D. loved this poem for a number of reasons (see Epoch and Artist, pp. 260–1); one that he mentions there, that it was written by a man 'of the dying Roman world, born and bred in Ostrogothic Italy, and living in Frankish Gaul', was connected with another that he does not mention: that its rhythm repeats the rhythm of a fragment (Ennius) that took him back to the spring-time of Rome – 'O magna templa caelitum conmixta stellis splendidis'.

241   In reading the first paragraph of this page, we must understand 'Endymion' after 'refused' – had Cynthia been on this

hill, would she have refused her love Endymion, for him whose
nuptials are celebrated in death. 'Jugatinus': in neither passage
(and these two are our only source for the god Jugatinus) does
Augustine speak of him as a god of hill-sites (as though from a
connection with *iugum*, ridge – hence 'Skull Ridge' – and also
yoke). On both occasions Augustine is ridiculing the multiplica-
tion of Roman deities.

On Ariel Hill . . . i.e. both on Calvary and in the Upper
room or 'cenacle', the 'white Beth-El' – see note 2, p.242 – which
is the second house of bread.

according to the disciplina [ordered ritual] **of this
peculiar people** returns to the opening, 'under modes and
patterns altogether theirs', because the rite at the institution
of the Eucharist followed the ritual of the Jewish Passover. –
And this covers and applies to all peoples that carry out ritual
observances, as, for example, the maypole dance (*dance by
garnished Baum*) or the sacrifice at the 'anointed stone'.

this peculiar people: i.e. the Jewish people, according to
whose custom the Passover was celebrated: from Deuteronomy
14.2, 'the Lord hath chosen thee to be a peculiar people unto
himself'. Since *peculiaris* (for the A.V. is translating the Vulgate
populum peculiarem) originates from *peculium*, property in cattle
(*pecus*, flock or herd), it is here a reminder of the metaphor of
the flock and shepherd which is used in *Rite and Fore-time*,
pp. 77–8 and p.65 (Of all those given him/he would lose none').

Here . . . his Body shows: the scene is still the cenacle ('the   **242**
upper cave of bread') The dog (who is again a memory of Argos,
the hound of Odysseus) sleeps at the entry to the cave of
Bethelehem – but that was much more than twenty years ago,
More than twenty years until the next 'here', in the high place
of crucifixion. There 'he', i.e. Christ both offerant and victim,
holds himself up (as the priest holds the 'stemmed dish' or
chalice), as he is held up and poured out wherever the Mass is
celebrated.

Ephrata: Bethlehem. 'But thou, Bethlehem Ephratah,
though thou be little among the thousands of Judah, yet out of

thee shall he come forth unto me that is to be ruler in Israel'
(Micah 5.2). As the first cave (of the birth of the child) was in
Bethlehem, so the second cave is the *upper* room in Jerusalem.

243   Does the old dog recognise in the child of Bethlehem the
Bread that will be consecrated for the Eucharist ? **But the fate
of death?** The question upon which the whole poem, and the
whole of the poet's faith, depend. The answer is given in the
final paragraphs. It is the only way by which we may be one
with 'this Wanderer', who, being bread, is life. We should read
'in his well-built *megaron*' with 'be coupled of this Wanderer',
i.e. we can be one with Christ in heaven (his megaron, palace,
royal hall) only by the monument of his own death. Here again
we should read 'whose only threnody is Jugatine' with 'this
Viander's', through the death of this provider of nourishment
('Viander') whose only death-lament is at the same time a bridal
song, a song of the bridal chamber (thalamus). **reeds then!/and
minstrelsy,** for the bride and bridegroom. **viatic:** of provision
for a journey, as in the 'journey-food' of p.61, the 'viatic meats'
of p.65.

   that fits the Gest: there is a similar ending to *In Parenthesis*,
'The geste says this . . .' The Old French *geste*, 'the high deeds
of a people or person', 'the memorable act' and so those who are
associated with such deeds, the family or race, was a word that
held great meaning for D. It meant the real, inevitable, enact-
ment of that which must be, and the expression of that enact-
ment in what he would call 'genuine myth'. So that *The Anathemata* celebrates the supreme *geste*.

   Nor bid Anubis haste: a most happy reminder of the birth
of Christ. Of this Milton says, in the *Hymn on the Morning of
Christ's Nativity*, which D.'s father would read to the family
every Christmas morning, 'The brutish gods of Nile as fast / Isis
and Orus, and the dog Anubis, haste'. D. reverses the notion,
retaining the ancient gods, for their purpose was to foreshadow
and make plain the body of the true lord.

   whelped but to discern a lord's body: Anubis was represented with the head of a jackal or dog: and there is a special

aptness in that here, at the end of the poem, we have a reminiscence of a Pauline phrase, 1 Cor. 11.29 ('For he that eateth and
drinketh unworthily, eateth and drinketh judgment to himself,
not discerning the Lord's body'), and so above, on the same
page, 'discern the Child'. See also comment on 'discern', *Ana.*
p.49. An unpublished draft of a similar passage provides a
fitting conclusion:

> '. . . he did well
>   to lift the jackal'd head
> for all must die to live
>   who would presume
> our dogma of the lifted Bread.
>   As I have elsewhere said
>   it was for the jackal-headed
>   Anubis to recognise a Lord's body
>   and weight the worth of those
>   for whom we pray
>   *et lux perpetua luceat eis.*'

The final paragraph is a re-statement of the theme, that all
man's ritual acts are fundamentally one, with a final adaptation
of the Pange Lingua of Aquinas, **recumbent at the garnished
supper** being an echo of 'In supremae noctis coenae / recumbens
cum fratribus', 'On the night of the last supper, seated with
his brothers'. **The Axile Tree:** the tree on which the world
revolves; 'Stat crux, dum volvitur orbis'.

D. had great difficulty with the ending of the poem, and was
not happy about 'recumbent at the garnished supper'. He
writes (23 February 1953, to D.M.C.), ' Garnished *must* stay,
that's a key word' (cf. by garnished *Baum* at the head of p.242).
As to 'recumbent' it had a chequered history. In one draft the
passage ran

> What did he do
>   board recumbent
> at the garnished supper, seated
> what did he do other
>   riding the Axile Tree.

243 But clearly I wanted both 'other' and 'yet other' as both the supper and Calvary are in different ways *other* from what the traditional rite demanded. Also I wanted the allusion to *Recumbens cum fratribus* in the Pange Lingua. At another stage of the MS I had a further line, since deleted, which read (I've forgotten exactly how) something about 'with his warband of twelve' – again an allusion to the Pange Lingua's turbae duodenae. Anyway, I could not work it. So it resulted in the text as printed'.

VMBRAM FVGAT VERITAS

BIBLIOGRAPHY

– only in the sense of a note concerning a few books (some of which have been referred to in the text under an abbreviated form) which may well add to the enjoyment and understanding of *The Anathemata*. Any number of other doors, easy enough to unlock, are indicated on pp. 36–7 of the Preface to the poem.

First, then, David Jones's other published writings: *In Parenthesis* (1937), *Epoch and Artist* (1959), *An Introduction to the Rime of the Ancient Mariner* (1972), *The Sleeping Lord* (1974), *The Narrows* (in *Agenda*, Spring, 1974), *The Kensington Mass* (1975). All references are to these first editions.

Apollodorus, with trans. by Sir J. G. Frazer (Loeb Classical Library), 2 vols., 1921.

Matthew Arnold, *On the Study of Celtic Literature* (1867), Everyman's Library ed., 1910: on which see *Epoch and Artist*, p. 240, where D. is not, I believe, quite fair to Arnold.

Donald Attwater (ed.), *The Catholic Encyclopaedic Dictionary*, 1931.

David Blamires, *David Jones*, Manchester and Toronto, Ontario, 1971.

Gaston Boissier, *Nouvelles Promenades Archéologiques*, 2 vols., Paris, 1899 (vol. 2 in particular).

British Regional Geology (H.M.S.O.): *North Wales*, 3rd ed., 1961; *The Welsh Borderland*, 4th ed., 1930, reprinted 1968.

John Burnet, *Early Greek Philosophy*, 4th ed., 1930, reprinted 1968.

Clement of Alexandria, *Protrepticus*, with trans. by G. W. Butterworth (Loeb Classical Library), 1919.

R. G. Collingwood and J. N. L. Myres, *Roman Britain and the English Settlements*, 2nd ed., 1937, reprinted 1971.

M. C. D'Arcy, S.J., *The Mass and the Redemption*, 1926.

Christopher Dawson, *The Age of the Gods*, 1928.

Christopher Dawson, *Progress and Religion*, 1929.

M. de la Taille, S.J., *Mysterium Fidei*, 2nd ed., Paris, 1924. (The first two parts of this were published in an English translation by Fr. Joseph Carroll, in 1941 and 1950. The third part has never been translated.)

M. de la Taille, S.J., *The Mystery of Faith and Human Opinion Contrasted and Defined*, 1930.

M. de la Taille, S.J., *The Mystery of Faith, an Outline*, 1930.

Myles Dillon and Norah Chadwick, *The Celtic Realms*, 1967.

Dom Gregory Dix, *The Shape of the Liturgy*, 1945.

W. Warde Fowler, *The Religious Experience of the Roman People*, 1911.

W. Warde Fowler, *Virgil's 'Gathering of the Clans'*, 1916.

W. Warde Fowler, *Aeneas at the Site of Rome*, 1917.

W. Warde Fowler, *The Death of Turnus*, 1919.

Sir J. G. Frazer, *The Golden Bough*, 12 vols., 1911–18. Abridged edition, 1922, latest reprint 1971.

T. R. Glover, *The Conflict of Religions in the Early Roman Empire*, 1909.

R. H. Hodgkin, *A History of the Anglo-Saxons*, 2 vols., 1935.

E. O. James, *Sacrifice and Sacrament*, 1962.

Robin Ironside, *David Jones* (Penguin Modern Painters series), 1949.

W. P. Ker, *The Dark Ages*, 1904, republished with foreword by B. Ifor Evans, 1955.

W. F. Jackson Knight, *Vergil, Epic and Anthropology*, 1967, which contains the earlier *Vergil's Troy*, *Cumaean Gates*, and *The Holy City of the East*.

J. E. Lloyd, *A History of Wales from the Earliest Times to the Edwardian Conquest*, 2 vols., 1912.

John Masefield, *Badon Parchments*, 1947.

F. W. H. Myers, 'Virgil' in *Essays Classical*, 1883.

Hugo Rahner, S.J., *Greek Myths and Christian Mystery*, 1963, reprinted (New York) 1971.

Alwyn Rees and Brinley Rees, *Celtic Heritage*, 1961.

H. J. Rose, *Handbook of Greek Mythology*, 6th ed., 1958.

Seyffert's *Dictionary of Classical Antiquities* (ed. Nettleship and Sandys), 2nd ed., 1891.

Oswald Spengler, *The Decline of the West*, trans. C. F. Atkinson, 2 vols. in 1, 1932, reprinted 1971.

H. Stuart Jones, *A Companion to Roman History*, 1912.

Sir Frank Stenton, *Anglo-Saxon England*, 3rd ed., 1971.

John Stow, *The Survey of London*, (1598), Everyman's Library, 1912, latest reprint 1970.

E. G. R. Taylor, *The Haven-finding Art*, 1956.

Graham Webster, *The Roman Imperial Army of the First and Second Centuries A.D.*, 1974.

Jessie L. Weston, *From Ritual to Romance*, 1920.

Word and Image IV (*David Jones*), National Book League, 1972.

I have quoted at some length from Maurice de la Taille, Professor E. O. James and Sir Edmund Whittaker (*Space and Spirit*), and for permission to do so I am grateful to their publishers, Messrs Sheed & Ward, Thames & Hudson, and Thomas Nelson & Sons Ltd.